Judicial Transparency in China

Yiming Wang · He Tian

Judicial Transparency in China

Theory and Realization Path

中国社会科学出版社
CHINA SOCIAL SCIENCES PRESS

Springer

Yiming Wang
Institute of Law
Chinese Academy of Social Sciences
Beijing, China

He Tian
Institute of Law
Chinese Academy of Social Sciences
Beijing, China

Translated by
Fang Wang
Beijing, China

ISBN 978-981-19-7821-0 ISBN 978-981-19-7822-7 (eBook)
https://doi.org/10.1007/978-981-19-7822-7

Jointly published with China Social Sciences Press
The print edition is not for sale in China (Mainland). Customers from China (Mainland) please order the print book from: China Social Sciences Press.

This Springer imprint is published by the registered company Springer Nature Singapore Pte Ltd.
The registered company address is: 152 Beach Road, #21-01/04 Gateway East, Singapore 189721, Singapore

Foreword

Developing the Rule of Law by Furthering Openness
Promoting Jurisprudence by Interpreting Openness

Only when there is openness and transparency, can there be trustworthy justice and trust based on justice. Openness and transparency are the ultimate embodiment of the rule of law and an essential requirement of its practice. The socialist rule of law with Chinese characteristics and its practice is exceptionally open and transparent. In government management and judicial construction, openness is viewed as an essential means of meeting public demand and responding to public concerns. The significance of openness and transparency is that they can effectively regulate the exercise of power and make it more standardized and efficient. Accordingly, the public can understand the operation of power, enhance their trust in public authorities, and have clear expectations of their status and the realization of their rights and interests. In addition, openness and transparency help build the most efficient communication mechanism and realize the positive and orderly interaction between public authorities and the public.

In recent years, a research team led by the Department of Survey and Studies of National Situation of Rule of Law, Chinese Academy of Social Sciences Institute of Law has been concerned about China's law-based transparency construction. It has been actively involved in the relevant legislative work and the research on the national situation of the rule of law and third-party assessment of the rule of law index in respect of government transparency, judicial transparency, and prosecution transparency for many years. On the basis of empirical research, the team has objectively revealed what has been achieved and what remains to be improved in the rule of law construction. The team has also put forward a series of constructive countermeasures to promote openness and transparency of the rule of law. This book is one of the academic results of the research practice mentioned above.

Based on the judicial transparency assessment data for 2019 and 2020, this book summarizes and analyzes the achievements and shortcomings in the current judicial openness of the people's courts. Compared with the *China Judicial Transparency Index Report* released annually in the *Blue Book of Rule of Law: Annual Report on Rule of Law in China*, this book not only discloses more detailed assessment data and comprehensively analyzes the data, but also carries out an in-depth theoretical study of judicial openness by exploring many theoretical and practical issues including why judicial openness should be furthered, why judicial openness can be furthered in contemporary China, and how judicial openness can be furthered.

Exploiting interdisciplinary strengths and exploring the intrinsic relevance of history to the present is arguably the first feature of this book. Reading through this book, we can find that it not only describes the basis and situation of the current judicial openness, but also further analyzes the ideological and institutional sources of judicial openness. Especially the book reviews its development in history, including responding to doubts about whether judicial openness was provided and practiced in ancient China. Learning history enables us to know right from wrong. History tells us that judicial openness has been practiced in China since ancient times and that judicial openness is not unique to the west. It must be admitted that judicial openness in ancient China is fundamentally different from that in the present. An illustration of examples of judicial openness in ancient China is not aimed at rejecting outstanding fruits of judicial openness in the west, but at exploring the openness in Chinese judicial culture with a view to using the past for the present and carrying it forward in the socialist rule of law system with Chinese characteristics. Therefore, this book systematically reveals the fundamental differences between judicial openness in socialist China, judicial openness in ancient China, and judicial openness in western countries. That is a valuable part of the book's discussion of judicial openness.

The second feature of this book is the innovative research methodology and the organic integration of theory and practice. Theoretical discussion without practice is inconvincible, and practice without theoretical preparation and support may be shallow and unsustainable. The Institute of Law of the Chinese Academy of Social Sciences has always emphasized the links between theory and practice in legal research. That is also what the research team led by Researcher Tian He of the Institute of Law is persistently pursuing. The research methodology adopted in this book is to objectively observe the situation of judicial openness of the sample courts and visually reflect the condition and effects of judicial openness with various actual data and their correspondence by virtue of a complete and systematic assessment index system based on the theories of the rule of law construction and judicial openness. This innovative scientific method is different from traditional methods like historical analysis, documentary analysis, and questionnaire surveys. It is a new type of field research that expands the empirical research method by putting the researcher in the position of those who need judicial openness and the development of the rule of law (i.e., the general public) and investigating the operation of judicial openness. With the aid of such a scientific method, this book applies various theories of judicial openness to observe its actual operation. This book also tests and develops the theories of judicial openness and the rule of law construction while observing the operation of judicial openness.

The third feature of this book is that it focuses on the organic combination of a system and its effects. Whether a system is well designed, whether it is realistic, and whether it can solve practical problems requires repeated tests in practice. Therefore, in assessing the rule of law, we should first focus on its actual operation. This book is precisely an "in-person observation" of the operation of judicial openness, an essential system in the development of the rule of law. The results of the in-person observation are actual rather than mimetic, not only finding the highlights and effects of judicial openness but also, more crucially, finding where the system still lags and, even further, what flaws the system itself has. The book summarizes the problems comprehensively, rather than just praising the highlights; analyzes the causes systematically, rather than simply enumerating various phenomena; and constructively puts forward suggestions for its improvement, rather than stopping at disclosing the problems. That is the focus of the academic pursuit by the authors and their research team. By reading this book, one can understand the current situation of judicial openness in China through a set of data and discover the path to further judicial openness and the judicial system by analyzing various significant aspects. Moreover, one can think about the methodological improvement and academic innovation of legal research through judicial openness. We hope there will be more research results like this, which will help promote the rule of law and jointly improve legal research practically and innovatively.

Beijing, China
April 2021

Chen Su

Contents

Chapter 1
Justice: From Mystery to Openness

Judicial openness in contemporary China includes six aspects: open case filings, public trials, open enforcement, open hearings, publication of judgments, and open trial affairs. However, historically the origin of judicial openness, both in the history of the Chinese legal system and foreign legal systems, is mainly an open trial. According to current research findings, "public trial or open trial" is the result of the bourgeois struggle against feudalism; in the modern West, "public trial" first became the fundamental principle of litigation. This conclusion is biased due to the lack of an in-depth understanding of the judicial history of China. As the historical origin of judicial openness, public trials in the history of the Chinese legal system and foreign legal systems have been developing independently but have the same effect.

1 Judicial Openness in Ancient China

1.1 Movement of Enacting Statutes and Openness of Laws

The campaign to eliminate legal mysticism was launched in the early legal history of China. In the Spring and Autumn Period, the imperial tactic of "unpublished penal laws resulting in unpredictable power" was rendered backward by a statutory movement on a grand and spectacular scale. This movement was consequent upon the monopoly of the old slave-owning aristocracy on law and justice, which restricted the development of the emerging landlord class. Fundamentally, the publication of written laws equally shows that law is in nature a political instrument; however, regarding the development of the legal system, it has opened up a new era for maintaining social order with written and open laws.

Legal mysticism was the inevitable value orientation when the law was in the bud. According to the *Interpretation of The Shoo King (The Book of Historical*

Y. Wang and H. Tian, *Judicial Transparency in China*,
https://doi.org/10.1007/978-981-19-7822-7_1

Documents), "there are 3,000 penalties in the Xia Dynasty".[1] Nevertheless, the details of these penalties remain unknown for "the deceased emperors applied a system in which punishments varied with cases, instead of making penalties in advance for fear of the revolt of the masses…,"[2] and "a penalty will be set for a particular case, and there is no established law".[3] When law emerged, the masses had a vague understanding of it, could not distinguish it from other social norms, and were even ignorant of how to apply it, let alone necessary restrictions on its application. In the early times, the law could function upon the request of the ruling class due to its uncertainty and mystery. On the other hand, the ruled class suffered a lot from such uncertainty, and the fear that any action might be punished hung over everyone. Once the emerging class's pursuit of higher status undermined the political and economic interests of the old aristocracy, it would, of course, become the top priority to eliminate threats that such uncertainty might pose. Consequently, the vassal states began to publish their statutory laws. In 536 BC, Zi Chan, in charge of government affairs of Zheng, a state in the Spring and Autumn Period, ordered to cast the provisions of the criminal law on the cauldron, and in 513 BC, the provisions of the criminal law were cast on the cauldron in the Jin State. The movement of enacting statutes continued with objections going on. "When the masses find that there is a law, they will not be obedient. Suppose they intend to fight for power and profits and use the published criminal law as a weapon to achieve a fluke success; in that case, it is hard to govern the state."[4] Attacking Jin's "casting the provisions of the criminal law on the cauldron" from the perspective of the feudal ethical code, Confucius held, "I am afraid that the Jin State will perish due to the abandonment of hierarchy. Tang Shu, Jin's earliest ancestor, developed ideas of humbleness and nobleness to govern his people and manage aristocrats according to their levels. In this way, the higher officials could be held in high esteem by the civilians and therefore could have the ancestors' estate in good protection. 'Du', namely the hierarchy, makes a clear distinction between the noble and the humble. Jin Wengong, in charge of appointing officials, made a law when hunting and reviewing troops in Beilu, which contributed to his status as the chief of the vassals. Nowadays, the hierarchy respected by Tang Shu was repealed, and the criminal law provisions were cast on the cauldron. The civilians hence were exposed to those provisions cast thereon. How could they show respect to the noble? What estate to protect for the noble? Once the hierarchy was disrupted, how to govern the state? Besides, Zhao Xuanzi's penal decree made during his inspection of the troops in Yi seriously damaged the hierarchy and could not function as law."[5] In spite of such surging objections as "the state will be in ferment", the movement of enacting statutes could not be stopped, which was the

[1] Fu [1].

[2] *Zuozhuan (Commentary on the "Spring and Autumn Annals"), The 6th Year of the Duke Zhao Period.*

[3] Wang [2].

[4] *Zuozhuan (Commentary on the "Spring and Autumn Annals"): The 6th Year of the Duke Zhao Period.*

[5] Ibid.

inevitable result of the class struggle and that of the development of law as an objective thing. After all, the practice that "a penalty will be set for a particular case" was not in conformity with the principle of efficiency, which should have been improved after the extensive application of the law. On the contrary, statutes could provide people with enlightenment once published, and then a return to enigmatic and arbitrary justice was out of the question. Nevertheless, law is, in nature, the tool for the ruling class to govern the state. In the era of exploiting classes, any emerging ruling class's control of legal resources for its benefit was doomed to the old way of monopoly. The development of the law would be shrouded in its mystery repeatedly.

1.2 Public Trials in Ancient China

The promulgation of written laws marked the maturity of law, where the concept of "law" was separated from other norms and became self-contained and which was supposed to be the source of the concept of "justice" in a more strict sense. Accordingly, although there had been de facto judicial activities prior to the advent of statutory laws, the concept of "fa (law)" rather than "Bing", "Li", or "Xing" logically is thought to have originated after the promulgation of statutory laws. Its development is the same as that of "law". The publicity of law came after the advent of written laws. However, public trials have been existing in the history of China. The judicial process was open to the public to varying degrees, even in the early times when "the emperors convicted a person of a crime after discussing the severity of a particular case, instead of applying penal laws made in advance."

China's tradition of public trials can be found in ancient legends. When the cognitive abilities of ancient people were underdeveloped, judgment by divinities was prevalent. Endorsing the legitimacy of a divine judgment in most cases involved some degree of public participation, which demonstrated the benighted rationality supported by public approval. Legend has it that the earliest judge in China decided cases with the help of Haechi, "which is an imaginary goat with a single horn, born with the ability to know whether a person is guilty or not. Gao Yao, when deciding cases, would order Haechi to touch the suspect with its horn if it was difficult to determine whether he was guilty. Haechi would do so if he were guilty."[6] In a trial, the judge and both parties were present; the presence of "both parties" is also a litigation tradition that accompanies law and justice. According to *The Shoo King: The Marquis of Lü on Punishments*, "After the plaintiff and the defendant are present, the judge will hear the statements from both sides respectively and determine the facts. If convicted, the defendant will be sentenced."

To a certain extent, public trials were also embodied in joint trials and collective discussions held in the litigation in ancient China. In *Zhouli (The Rites of Zhou)*:

[6] Wang Chong (the Eastern Han Dynasty), *Lung Heng (Balanced Enquiries): Shiying.*

Qiuguan (The Ministry of Xing): Xiao Sikou (Vice Minister of Xing), "Three interrogations were conducted to ensure that trials were right on the beam: interrogations of ministers, officials, and the people." The scope of public trials gradually expanded with the development of trial procedures. "The method of three interrogations" became the origin of the system of joint trials and collective discussions in later generations. Joint trials, such as "trials in the Tang Dynasty by the minister of Dalisi, the minister of Xing,[7] and the minister of the Censorate in major and complicated cases" "trials in the Ming Dynasty by the minister of Xing, the minister of Dalisi, and the minister of the Censorate in major and complicated cases" "reexamination in the Ming Dynasty by the minister of Justice, the minister of Dalisi, the minister of the Censorate, the minister of Li,[8] the minister of Hu,[9] the minister of Li,[10] the minister of Bing,[11] the minister of Gong,[12] and the minister in charge of documents submitted by ministers to the emperor and the sealed appeals from ministers and civilians in major and complicated cases reported from local authorities" "trials in Summer" "trials in Autumn" and "trials after Frost's Descent", were a reflection of public trials to some extent.

The tradition of public trials in ancient China is not only recorded in historical materials but can be found in many remains. The "Ming Yuan Drum"[13] placed outside a yamen[14] is a sign that the government made the case public when a complaint was filed. In many places, the relic of ancient yamens confirms the common saying of "two rows of brick walls outside of a yamen's gate being in the shape of the Chinese character 'eight'". Some agencies were arranged in a yamen along with this shape, which meant it was open to the people for their convenience to make complaints and offer advice. In terms of the shape and structure of the yamen, it was flat, simple, broad, and modest. A compound with spacious halls and extensive gardens was not typical of an ancient government office. In most yamens, outside its hall was a board hanging with characters of "Qinmin Tang (Pro-people Hall)" on it, while in the hall was a painting of "sea and the rising sun", which showed openness and justice to

[7] The Ministry of Xing: in charge of the nation's justice and administration, and mainly functioning as today's Minister of Justice.

[8] The Ministry of Li: in charge of the selection, examination, appointment and removal, promotion, transformation of, and the granting of ranks of nobility to government officials.

[9] The Ministry of Hu: in charge of national household registration, land, currency, various taxes, and salaries of government officials.

[10] The Ministry of Li: in charge of important ceremonies, imperial examinations and reception of foreign guests of the imperial court, and mainly functioning as today's Minister of Education and Minister of Foreign Affairs.

[11] The Ministry of Bing: in charge of the nation's military officers and their training and weapons, and mainly functioning as today's Minister of National Defense.

[12] The Ministry of Gong: in charge of the nation's water conservancy projects and civil engineering.

[13] In the Western Jin Dynasty, the "Deng Wen Gu" (a big drum people would beat when they tried to redress an injustice) outside the Imperial Court was used for people to "Gao Yu Zhuang" (appeal to the emperor). Later, similar drums were also put outside the local Yamens (governments in feudal China) to assist people in complaining on the "Day of Fang Gao" (the day when a plaque was hung at the Yamen's entrace to inform that people could accuse someone before the emperor).

[14] Government in feudal China.

pacify the public. Most cases were handled in the entrance hall, where a public trial was conducted. Before hearing the case, drums beat, and a drum roll could be heard miles away. "Beating drums before a trial was intended to inform the public that a case was to be tried 'in public'".[15] During the trial, "local people were allowed to be the audience."[16] Folk records reveal cases of people watching the hearing, commenting on the words of the judge and the parties, and even taking part in the hearing all at once. The public had no access to the second hall, where the officials dealt with cases in confidence. Theoretically, hearing cases in the second hall was rarely seen. The original intention of setting up a yamen and the normality of public trials seen in the remains and historical records of the yamen reveal an ideal state that the people in ancient China expected and the pursuit of imaginary harmony. Justice in ancient China had another face. Due to the increasingly aggravating judicial corruption in the Ming Dynasty and the Qing Dynasty, the administration of justice slipped back into its old ways, secret and arbitrary. Therefore, there was sarcasm that "the yamen is open, but you cannot win the case without offering a bribe."

1.3 Dissimilation and Extension of Public Trials: Open Trials, Publication of Judgments, and Open Enforcement

An open trial literally means that a case is tried in public. However, the connotation suggested by this term goes beyond its literal meaning and reveals the notion of "execution in public". In *Water Margin*, "Out of the prison was the old woman with the last name Wang taken out and thereafter a sentence was pronounced in public. After a sign announcing the sentence was made, she was forced to make her cross on it. Then, she was pushed to climb onto a wooden donkey with four long nails and three lashings used to fasten her tightly. Sentenced by the governor of Dongping to death by dismembering the body, she was taken out to the long street surrounded by the crowd. Broken drums and gongs being played, the criminal was clubbed and compelled to proceed. Two sharp knives raised and a paper flower waved, the old woman was led to the center of Dongping and dismembered." In this paragraph, "a sentence being pronounced in public" means pronouncing the sentence to the public. "Being surrounded" means that the criminal was "surrounded" up to the street by the onlookers following the government servants who led the way because there was no need to have such an old female offender "surrounded" by the servants. "The criminal being paraded in front of the crowd" and "the old woman being led to the center of Dongping and dismembered" shows public executions in ancient China. The etiquette that "royal family members are not sentenced and executed in public" proves that most executions of ordinary people were public.[17] In Lu Xun's *Medicine*, the scene where the crowd watched the execution is proof that public executions continued into

[15] Xu [3]

[16] Qu [4].

[17] *Zhouli (The Rites of Zhou): Qiuguan (The Ministry of Xing): Xiao Sikou (Vice Minister of Xing).*

modern times. In addition to the death penalty, many other punishments were carried out in public. Humiliating punishments such as "cangue", "ink", and "piercing" implied public executions.

According to Zhouli: Qiuguan: Xiao Sikou, "Xiao Sikou decides cases by applying five punishments. In cases where a crime is committed, Xiao SiKou will decide it in a reasonable way, a judgment will be rendered in ten days, and a penalty will be imposed after the judgment is made known." "To make a judgment known" means pronouncing the judgment in public. In addition, "Zhang Bang" was a method of official information disclosure handed down from ancient China, acting as a communication channel between officials and the public. Judicial documents were also made public through "Zhang Bang". "Zhang Bang", in its forms of "Bang Shi" and "Men Shi", included the disclosure of judicial documents produced at every stage of the litigation and had various functions such as case filings, collection and demonstration of evidence, disclosure of property information related to the litigation, improvement of judicial efficiency, openness of judgments, and publicity and education.[18] Judges also had a dereliction of duty when making the judicial documents public, which was an irregular practice as a secret trial was.

2 Judicial Openness in the Ancient West

In ancient Greece and ancient Rome, trials there were highly open due to the active participation of the public. It can be said that the public's participation in the hearing made the trial naturally open.

There is a lack of first-hand records of the ancient Greek legal system. Information thereabout can only be found scattered in the writings of ancient Greek thinkers and politicians. "After studying the ancient Greek political system, Aristotle tried to put forward his ideal political system. He held that there should be three functions in a political society: deliberation, administration, and adjudication. In his opinion, the adjudication organ was not the independent judicial organ as we call it today, but the Assembly."[19] Because of the slave-holding democracy in ancient Greece, many significant cases were decided by the Assembly. Even in ordinary cases, a trial organization was composed of many people and had a turnover; a vote was taken to find the defendant guilty to demonstrate democracy. As legend has it, the jury consisted of 501 citizens in the trial of Socrates. "In ancient Greece, the organ for adjudication was separate from that for punishment. Hippodamus of Miletus recorded the way of the trial. When voting, the adjudicators cast pebbles into a clay pot to determine whether the defendant was guilty or innocent according to the number of pebbles in the pot."[20]

[18] Zhu et al. [5].

[19] Xu [6].

[20] Xu [6].

In the special judicial procedures of adjudicating significant cases, public participation and judicial openness were more prominent, such as the "ὀστρακισμός" of the polis of Athens. "ὀστρακισμός", or ostracism, was enacted in around 500 BC and was first practised in 487 BC. Generally credited to Cleisthenes, an Athenian reformer, this law provided that the Council of 500 (or *boule*) convened a special Assembly every Spring where the participants decided verbally whether the democracy had been threatened and whether they would vote on ostracism. If anyone did ruin the democracy, then a formal Assembly was convened. Any citizen could vote against a particular candidate by writing his name on a piece of pottery, an ostrakon. For the result of ostracism to be effective, a minimum of 6,000 votes had to be cast. Then the man was announced to be ostracised and had to leave Athens within a specified period and stay away for ten years. He remained owner of his property. The banished man may return after his sentence was served and regain his citizenship. Ostracism was the procedure as a measure to prevent tyrants from usurping power and had an important effect on the maintenance of the slave-holding democracy in Athens.[21]

By contrast, there is a more successful historical record of the legal system in ancient Rome. The Law of the Twelve Tables was the earliest written code in ancient Rome and the beginning of the "written law movement" in ancient Rome and even in the whole of Europe. Furthermore, Ancient Rome had a large group of jurists that Ancient Greece did not have, which made every aspect of the Ancient Roman legal system supported by specific theories and Ancient Roman law the historical source of European law. Regarding public trial, "Cicero judicially advocated public trial and the principle of letting the punishment fit the crime. He proposed that a judicial trial be presided over by the consul but supervised by the senate and the comitia. A trial is open to the public. 'The powerful are not allowed to do whatever they want, and the people are not offered the chance of pretense. When honest people have no way of knowing others' opinions, a ballot board can cover up malicious votes.'"[22] Rousseau wrote civilians' participation in trials into his *The Social Contract*, "the most incredible fact of all is that, in the midst of all these abuses, the vast people, thanks to its ancient regulations, never ceased to elect magistrates, to pass laws, to judge cases, and to carry through business both public and private, almost as easily as the senate itself could have done."[23]

"In late Rome, absolutism gradually strengthened, and secret trials were prevalent in judicial practice."[24] By the Middle Ages in Europe, trials were conducted in two ways: religious and secular, both of which were secret. Mainly aimed to persecute the heresies, "the Inquisition" established by the Catholic Church encouraged whistleblowers, kept their information confidential, conducted a trial in secret, and extorted confessions by torture. Secret judicial acts of the Inquisition were the manifestation of excessive power and tyranny of the church and produced the spiritual oppression

---

[21] Lu and Xu [7].

[22] Liu [8].

[23] Rousseau [9].

[24] Depei [10].

of terror and intimidation. Trials by secular lords also moved from the autocratic centralization of late Rome towards secrecy and arbitrariness. In the Medieval Era, trials were not open to the public, and it was even difficult for those involved to participate in the proceedings, let alone defend themselves. Hence, the "documents only" trial became popular.

3 All Roads Lead to Rome: Value Selection and Practice of Ancient Judicial Openness Centered on the Establishment of Judicial Authority

Before the advent of the Age of Exploration, the bud from judicial mystery to judicial openness appeared spontaneously in different countries. Such historical "coincidence", which is deemed universal and inevitable, represents the value of the historical origin of judicial openness. In fact, in both China and the West, judicial openness is rooted in the need to prove the legitimacy of judicial acts and establish judicial authority.

From the evolution of the guiding principles of the early Chinese legal system, we can see the process by which the rulers continued to "justify" their means of governance. After the founding of the Western Zhou Dynasty, the concept of the "mandate of Heaven" from the Shang Dynasty was still followed. "Heaven rewarded Wan Wang, making our small state of Zhou prosperous. Through divination, Wan Wang inherited the great destiny granted by Heaven."[25] However, under the dominance of the doctrine of destiny, there were still some changes. The Zhou Dynasty justified its regime seized from the Shang Dynasty: "Fate changes,"[26] and "Heaven is just and impartial, and only helps those of virtue."[27] The concept of "virtue" broke through the unchanging view of destiny, proved the legitimacy of the transfer of power, and demonstrated the legitimacy of the rule of li (etiquette) and law. The saying goes, "Virtue deserves destiny, and virtue shall be applied more than punishment."[28] Such a way of governance, ideologically invoking the "mandate of Heaven" and practically "combining etiquette and punishment", had much more certainty than the theocratic thinking of "Heaven punishing criminals" in the Shang Dynasty. It at least used "virtue" as a criterion easily identified and had a relatively definite division between "etiquette" and "punishment". That is to say, "If a person behaves beyond the etiquette, he will fall into the scope of punishment. Etiquette and punishment are interdependent."[29] This ideology, out of question, functioned more to establish

[25] *The Shoo King (The Book of Historical Documents): The Great Announcement.*

[26] *The She King (The Book of Ancient Poetry): The Greater Odes of the Kingdom: The Decade of Wan Wang.*

[27] *Zuozhuan (Commentary on the "Spring and Autumn Annals"): The 5th Year of the Duke Xi Period.*

[28] *The Shoo King (The Book of Historical Documents): The Announcement to Prince Khang.*

[29] *Book of the Later Han: Biography of Chen Chong.*

the authority of laws and judicial acts than the theocratic thinking, which advocated arbitrary punishment under the pretense of the mandate of Heaven.

Public trial or judicial openness, such as "deliberation in three steps", was nothing more than to prove the legitimacy of judicial acts through the public's conviction and establish the authority of laws among the general public through the accumulation of cases. In the Warring States period, the idea that laws and trials should be open to the public further developed. Mencius once expounded the theory of "listening to both sides to tell the difference between right and wrong", "if the persons close to you hold that the suspect deserves death, ignore that opinion. If all the people around the state hold that the suspect deserves death, make an investigation. Kill him if it finally proves that he deserves death."[30] The Legalist School has a far-reaching influence on future generations of laws and judicial openness. Han Fei-tzu defined the law as follows, "laws are written by government agencies and promulgated to the public."[31] Shang Yang's story of "a log set up before the gate" also exemplifies the authority of laws through publicity.

Generally speaking, from mysterious theocratic law to judicial openness, the development of Chinese and Western laws is very similar. The range of openness was constantly expanded to establish the authority of laws and justice.

4 Judicial Openness in Modern Times

The old political system tried to struggle from death by keeping justice secret and corrupted. Such secrecy and corruption did not save it from dying but accelerated its demise. For the emerging class, the best way to prove the legitimacy of their revolution was to oppose secret justice. They could take this opportunity to gain the consensus to give the old system a deadly strike. Feudal nobles used openness as the most potent weapon to take judicial power from aristocratic slave owners. However, after they took the throne, monopolization and secrecy were all over again. History repeated itself. The bourgeoisie was also in pursuit of judicial openness at first. It was just the same old story, which happened in cycles of history, in the disguise of the Enlightenment. The openness of law and justice had been brought up again during the fight against feudalism. European Enlightenment thinkers then developed modern jurisprudence with openness as its essential character.

Locke held that "whatever form the commonwealth is under, the ruling power ought to govern by declared and received laws, and nor by extemporary dictates and undetermined resolutions: for then mankind will be in a far worse condition than in the state of nature, if they shall have armed one, or a few men with the joint power of a multitude, to force them to obey at pleasure the exorbitant and unlimited decrees of their sudden thoughts or unrestrained, and till that moment unknown wills, without

[30] *The Works of Mencius: King Hui Liang (Part 2).*

[31] *Han Fei Zi: Criticisms of the Ancients, Series Three.*

having any measures set down which may guide and justify their actions."[32] Beccaria wrote in his book *An Essay on Crimes and Punishments* published in 1764, "All trials should be public, that opinion, which is the best, or perhaps the only cement of society, may curb the authority of the powerful, and the passions of the judge."[33] These statements laid a theoretical foundation for judicial openness in modern times. Hegel elaborated on why justice should be open after the law is made public, "The rights of the subjective consciousness include not only that of making the laws publicly known (see §215), but also the possibility of knowing how the law is actualized in particular cases, i.e., of knowing the course of the external proceedings, legal argument, and so forth—the publicity of the administration of justice; for the course of law is in itself an occurrence of universal validity; and although the particular content of the case may be of interest only to the parties themselves, its universal content (i.e., the right within it and the decision on this right) is of interest to everyone."[34] After gaining the triumph of the bourgeois revolution, western countries successively provided the public trial system. The 1791 Amendments to the United States Constitution, also known as the Bill of Rights, is the world's first document to define the "public trial principle". Article VI of the Bill of Rights says, "In all criminal prosecutions, the accused shall enjoy the right to a speedy and public trial, by an impartial jury of the State and district wherein the crime shall have been committed, which district shall have been previously ascertained by law."[35] Thus, it was set as one of the basic principles of the modern litigation system in the form of a constitution.

The establishment of the public trial system was closely related to the rise of bourgeois democracy and human rights. With the development of the rule of law theory, in modern times, the legitimacy of the law as a rule of social governance no longer needed to be repeatedly proven. The gradual establishment of a democratic political system generally left unquestioned the credibility and authority of laws passed by the majority. Therefore, the focus was shifted to the legitimacy of applying laws, and higher requirements were raised for judicial openness. Beccaria said in *An Essay on Crimes and Punishments*, "Among a people hardly yet emerging from barbarity, they should be most severe, as strong impressions are required; but in proportion as the minds of men become softened by their intercourse in society, the severity of punishments should be diminished, if it be intended, that the necessary relation between the object and the sensation should be maintained."[36] Modern legal theories advocate that the judicial process should simultaneously have substantive justice and procedural justice. The legal motto is repeatedly quoted today: "Justice must not only be done, but must be seen to be done." Article 10 of the Universal Declaration of Human Rights adopted on December 10, 1948, reads, "Everyone is entitled in full equality to a fair and public hearing by an independent and impartial tribunal, in the determination of his rights and obligations and of any criminal charge

---

[32] Locke [11].

[33] Beccaria [12], p. 2.

[34] Hegel [13].

[35] Edited by Xie and Fang [14].

[36] Beccaria [12], p. 44.

against him." Thus, the public trial was defined as an express procedural human right. Similar provisions can be found in the 1966 International Covenant on Civil and Political Rights.

The guiding philosophy of China's modern public trial system changed under the influence of western learning. The public trial practice as a historical fact, without any doubt, is our tradition. In the late feudal society, autocracy assumed the extremes of judicial corruption, secrecy, and arbitrariness. However, we shall not deny that China's ancient public trial system lasted for thousands of years.

Shen Jiaben, the late Qing scholar-bureaucrat, who was in charge of law amendment, pointed out that the public trial is "the first priority for a constitutional government". "Open the court and allow the public to sit in so that everyone can witness the trial, justice and fairness can prove themselves, and government officials can be prevented from malpractices and corruption."[37] According to Article 13 of the Draft Act on the Criminal and Civil Proceeding Law of the Qing Dynasty enacted in the charge of Shen Jiaben, "all court trials shall be open to non-parties to a case and shall not be conducted in confidence, with exceptions regarding decency or special cases."[38] The Trial Regulations of Courts enacted in 1907 provided that "all prosecutions, initiated by prosecutors or investigating magistrates, will be assigned to judges by this court's commissioner. All cases shall be tried in public." "During the trial, the judge will try this incidental crime publicly if any incidental crime is found, and a preliminary hearing is not needed."[39] Article 55 of the Court Establishment Act provided that "all arguments shall be held and all judgments shall be pronounced in an open court."[40] Article 58 provided that "When there is any cause to stop opening the trial to the public, the court shall announce its decision and reasons to the audience and then order them to retire. However, the judgment still shall be pronounced in public."[41] These regulations failed to save the decadent Qing Dynasty from a downfall, although they had absorbed a lot of western legislative experience. After the founding of the Republic of China, the judicial openness theory advocated by western learning began to play its part.

Subject to Article 50 of the Provisional Constitution of the Republic of China, "All court trials shall be made public. If the openness of any trial is believed to jeopardize the harmony and order of society, it shall be held secretly."[42] The Provisional Constitution established the modern public trial principle in the form of the constitution. Hereafter, due to the unstable political power of the Republic of China, there came out several constitutions and constitutional documents. In terms of the public trial principle, some regulations kept consistent with the Provisional Constitution, while some took a backward step. In judicial practice, a conservative and inconsistent attitude appeared.

---

[37] Li [15].

[38] *Laws and Regulations of the Qing Dynasty* [16], p. 1911.

[39] Huai [17].

[40] *Laws and Regulations of the Qing Dynasty* [16], pp. 1824–1825.

[41] *Laws and Regulations of the Qing Dynasty* [16], pp. 1824–1825.

[42] Lai [18].

During the era of the Republic of China, the *Judicial Bulletin* became an important way to make public the judicial process and broaden its scope. "The *Judicial Bulletin* is a journal on justice published officially in the Republic of China".[43] "The *Judicial Bulletin* published its first issue in October 1912 and ceased publication in March 1948. For over 30 years, the *Bulletin* published more than 1,000 issues with records of various legislative and judicial conditions… The founders started the journal adhering to the spirit that 'Words carry out our minds. Reading one's writings is reading his thoughts. Words can reach the farthest place that is unreachable for one's mind and can be eternal', and with the aim that 'we make previous legal facts public to improve the judicial system'."[44] The *Bulletin*'s contents were plentiful. "According to Article 3 of the '*Brief of the Judicial Bulletin*' published in its first issue, the *Bulletin* contains figures, orders, regulations, official documents, judgments, reports, translations, selected comments, and miscellanies."[45] After that, changes to its style continued. The *Bulletin* also published the contents not having much relation to justice, and the contents relating to justice were enriching. Besides the national *Bulletin*, provincial governments also published their bulletins. Local governments had similar journals playing the part of judicial openness, such as "*Judicial Daily*", founded by Guangdong Province.

In addition, the modern legal profession system established in the period of the Republic of China also had a profound impact on judicial openness. "The legislation on lawyers in the period of the Republic of China has certain significance to the modern rule of law, mostly promoting judicial opennessThe original intention of the legislation was only to follow the lawyer defense system of western countries and learn the so-called western democracy. At the same time, it broke our several thousand years of closed legal traditions and provided legal protection for 'Songshi[46]' previously unrecognized. Lawyers' participation in litigation may promptly correct judges' improper judicial conduct, protect legitimate rights and interests of the parties, and improve judges' trial efficiency. A lawyer as the connection between the interested parties and the judge, can help reach a consensus between the parties, and between the parties and the judge."[47]

In this period, the judicial openness system once again experienced a historic regression when Kuomintang's "one-party autocracy" came to an end. The provision in the Provisional Constitution for secret trials of offenders "jeopardizing the harmony and order of society" was conservatively designed. Under the Nanjing National Government, such secret trials were used to suppress the communists. Similar provisions can also be found in the Regulations on Trials by Special Criminal Courts and the Interim Rules on Assessors in Anti-Revolution Cases. The Interpretation on the Organic Law of Courts explained, "The defense of a political criminal

[43] Zhao [19].

[44] Zhao [19].

[45] Zhao [20].

[46] In ancient China, Songshi was a person who gave advice to and wrote complaints for those in trouble.

[47] Chen [20].

is the most alarmist, making the audience have a strong desire to break the regime. That is why we shall keep the trials of political criminals in confidence."[48] Kuomintang wished to use secret trials to prevent the spread of communism and maintain its dying governance. Such a dark judiciary aroused more resistance and accelerated its demise. The historical cycle of judicial openness and secrecy repeated itself in modern China.

References

1. Fu Sheng, "The Interpretation of The Shoo King (Volume 2)" with Notes by Zheng Xuan, edited and proofread by Chen Shouqi. *The Commercial Press*, 1937, p. 109.
2. Wang Yinzhi, "The Basic Series on the History of Chinese Classics (Volume 6): Jing Yi Shu Wen (Part 2)", edited by Zhu Weizheng. Shanghai Bookstore Publishing House, 2012, p. 18.
3. Xu Zhongming, *The Story of Bao Zheng: from the Perspective of Investigating Chinese Legal Culture,* China University of Political Science and Law Press, 2022, p. 429
4. Qu Tongzu, *Local government in China under the Ch'ing*, translated by Fan Zhongxin and Yan Feng, Law Press China, 2003, p. 193.
5. Zhu, Wenhui, Bangshi, Dushi, & Menshi: "Judicial Information Disclosure in the Song Dynasty Based on a Collection of Judgments and Legal Documents in the Song Dynasty", *Zhejiang Academic Journal(05),* 2015.
6. Xu Aiguo, *Intelligence History of Western Criminal Law,* China Democracy and Legal System Publishing House, 2016, p. 19.
7. Lu Xin, Xu Shihong, *The Canon of Chinese and Foreign Legal Culture: Comparative Chronicles of Chinese and Foreign Law,* China University of Political Science and Law Press, 1994, p. 39
8. Liu Li, *An Overview of Chinese and Western Legal Culture from the Perspective of a Shared Future for Legal Professions,* Sichuan University Press, 2018, pp. 28–29.
9. Rousseau, *The Social Contract*, edited and translated by Shi Xinzhou, Beijing Press, 2012, p. 162
10. Han Depei (Editor-in-chief), *The Theory and Practice of Human Rights,* Wuhan University Press, 1995, p. 785.
11. Locke, *Two Treatises of Government (Book II)*, translated by Qu Junong and Ye Qifang, The Commercial Press, 2017, p. 87.
12. Beccaria, *An Essay On Crimes and Punishments*, translated by Huang Feng, Encyclopedia of China Publishing House, 1993, p. 2.
13. Hegel, *Elements of the Philosophy of Right*, translated by Fan Yang and Zhang Qitai. The Commercial Press, 2017, p. 264.
14. Edited by Xie Cai, Fang Xiao, *Organizational Setup and Functions of Foreign Governments.* Economic Press China, 1986, p. 187.
15. Li Guilian, *Biography of Shen Jiaben.* Peking University Press, 2000, p. 290.
16. *Laws and Regulations of the Qing Dynasty:Law (Volume 4),* Kaozheng Press, 1972, p. 1911.
17. Huai Xiaofeng (Editor-in-chief), *The History of Legal System Reform in the Late Qing Dynasty (Volume I).* China University of Political Science and Law Press, 2010, p. 459.
18. Lai Junnan, *Constitutional Road and China's Destiny: Selections of Chinese Modern Constitutional Documents (1840–1949) (Part 1),* Central Compilation & Translation Press, 2017, p. 359.
19. Zhao Xiaogeng, *A Brief Account of "Judicial Bulletin" in the Republic of China,* Journal of Shanxi University (Philosophy and Social Sciences Edition)(5), 2012.

[48] Zheng [21].

20. Chen Huali, The Legislation on Lawyers and Its Promotion on Judicial Openness in the Republic of China, *Social Sciences Review* (11), 2016.
21. Zheng Baohua, *Interpretations of the Organic Law of Courts*. Shanghai Legal Compilation & Translation Press, 1937, p. 249.

Chapter 2
Development of Contemporary China's Judicial Openness System

1 Tradition of People-Centered Judicial Openness

At its founding, the Communist Party of China (CPC) shouldered the historical mission of liberating the people. In the long-term struggle, guided by the Mass Line of "doing everything for the people, by the people, from the people, and to the people", the CPC led the people in continuously achieving new victories. "Wholeheartedly serving the people" is the Party's fundamental tenet and the purpose of all the Party's work. The regime established by the people under the leadership of the Party carried out "the people's democratic dictatorship". That is real democracy and different from bourgeois democracy in nature. Therefore, only under the leadership of the CPC could judicial openness throw off the "law of history" that judicial acts were conducted from in secret to in public and then back to in secret.

During the democratic revolution, the revolutionary governments in the base areas led by the CPC were committed to the principle of people-centered judicial openness and its practice. The Provisional Regulations of the Adjudication Department of the Soviet Republic of China on Organization and Adjudication provided in Article 16, "Trials must be open to the public; if there is some connection in a particular case, it can be tried in confidence, and the judgment shall be pronounced in public."[1] Documents like the Instructions of the High Court of the Shaanxi-Gansu-Ningxia Border Region on County Judicial Work, the Provisional Regulations on Organization and Adjudication, the Provisional Judicial System of the Taiyue Base Area, and the Interim Measures on the Assessor System of the Shanxi-Chahar-Hebei Border Region provided the public trial principle as well.

[1] Chunying [1].

Y. Wang and H. Tian, *Judicial Transparency in China*,
https://doi.org/10.1007/978-981-19-7822-7_2

2 Evolution of Judicial Openness After the Founding of the PRC

2.1 *From "Justice by the People" to "Justice for the People" After the Founding of the PRC*

Comrade Mao Zedong pointed out, "our regime is the people's democracy. Governments and departments of state power at all levels should be people-oriented. The word "people" should be added to their names, such as people's courts."[2] Comrade Dong Biwu's thinking on the rule of law helped a lot to the formation of the idea of justice by the people. On July 26, 1950, Dong Biwu put forward at the first National Conference on Justice that "the truth that the government does everything to serve the people should be adhered to and judicial work also serves the people".[3] On August 12, 1950, in his address to the Party's members and cadres participating in the Conference, Dong Biwu proposed the concept of "justice by the people" for the first time. He stated that "the mass perspective, one fundamental viewpoint on justice by the people, requires us to maintain close ties with and serve the people, safeguard social order, and guarantee the people's legitimate rights and interests."[4] In 1954, Dong Biwu put forward in his report delivered at the Central Cadre School of Political Science and Law that "judicial staff members must take a committed stand on the people's interests, and apply the weapon of justice by the people wholeheartedly... Otherwise, that would result in a big mistake. Therefore, we must utilize this weapon for the people's interests heart and soul."[5] Afterwards, on many occasions, Dong Biwu referred to the concept of justice by the people, which made that take root among judicial personnel and implemented in judicial work. People's courts exercise power on behalf of the people and thus receive supervision by the people. After the founding of the PRC, the General Principles of the Organization of People's Tribunals promulgated in 1950 provided in Article 5, "People are allowed to sit in on a court trial. During the trial, the audience may make a statement with permission." Besides, Article 8 of the Provisional Regulations on the Organization of People's Courts of the People's Republic of China enacted in 1951 provided, "Cases shall be heard in public by the People's courts unless otherwise provided by law." The Constitution of the People's Republic of China enacted in 1954 provided in Article 76, "Except under circumstances as specified by law, cases shall be heard in public by the People's courts; the accused shall enjoy the right to have the assistance of counsel for his defence." Since then, this judicial principle has been part of the fundamental law of China. Later on, the Organic Law of the People's Courts of the People's Republic of China, the Criminal Procedure Law of the People's Republic of China,

---

[2] Edited by the General Office of the Standing Committee of the National People's Congress and the CCCPC Party Literature Research Office [2].

[3] Dong [3].

[4] Dong [3].

[5] Dong [3].

the Civil Procedure Law of the People's Republic of China, and the Administrative Procedure Law of the People's Republic of China, explicitly provide the public trial principle. The above laws together have established the basic framework of the judicial system of the PRC and laid a solid foundation for the sustainable development of judicial openness.

All state undertakings flourished in the new historical period. The building of the rule of law constantly reached new heights, and the ideology of judicial work developed from "justice by the people" into "justice for the people". Judicial openness stepped into a new historical stage as one of the main methods of "justice for the people" for the convenience of the people.

The Party's governing philosophy fundamentally guided judicial openness at the new stage with its constant development. According to the Report to the 18th CPC National Congress, "To ensure proper exercise of power, we should put power, Party and government operations, and personnel management under institutional checks and uphold people's right to stay informed about, participate in, express views on, and oversee Party and government operations." "We should improve the mechanism for community-level self-governance under the leadership of community-level Party organizations to make it full of vitality. We should broaden the scope and channels of such self-governance and enrich its content and forms, with the focus on expanding orderly participation, promoting transparency in information, improving deliberation and consultation on public affairs, and strengthening oversight of the exercise of power, to ensure that the people have greater and more tangible democratic rights." "We should make the exercise of power more open and standardized and increase the transparency of the Party and government affairs, judicial openness, and transparent operation of other fields. We should improve the inquiry, accountability, economic responsibility auditing, resignation, and dismissal systems. We should strengthen intra-Party, democratic and legal oversight as well as oversight through public opinions to ensure that the people oversee the exercise of power and that power is exercised in a transparent manner."

The Decision of the CPC Central Committee on Major Issues Pertaining to Comprehensively Promoting the Rule of Law adopted at the Fourth Plenary Session of the 18th CPC Central Committee proposed, "The Party should ensure public participation in the administration of justice." "The judicial administration system and the judicial operation mechanism should be improved, judicial acts be regulated, supervision over judicial acts be strengthened, and efforts be made to ensure that people enjoy equity and justice in each and every case." "We must ensure that the people's administration of justice is for the people's interests, rely on the people to promote the fair administration of justice, and safeguard the people's rights and interests through the impartial administration of justice." "We should build an open, dynamic, transparent, and convenient judicial mechanism. We should promote openness in court proceedings and procuratorial, police, and prison affairs. As per the law, we should promptly disclose the grounds for, procedures and outcomes of law enforcement and the administration of justice, and legal instruments in force to prevent manipulation. We should strengthen the interpretation and construction of legal instruments and establish a unified online system for the public access to legal instruments in force."

According to the Report to the 19th CPC National Congress in 2017, "We must strengthen checks on and oversight of the exercise of power, and ensure that power is exercised under public oversight, in broad daylight, and within the confines of systemic checks."

Judicial openness is also a significant part of judicial reform that has put forward specific requirements for promoting judicial justice through judicial openness.

The nature of the PRC and its form (of government) mean that judicial power could no longer be monopolized by the minority of the people. Judicial openness in the new era is in the context of the supervised exercise of power. It mainly functions to regulate the exercise of power, prevent corruption, and implement justice for the people.

2.2 *General Secretary Xi Jinping's Remarks on Promoting Judicial Openness*

Many times Xi Jinping emphasized that the administration of justice should be people-centered, and power should be exercised in broad daylight. When presiding over the fourth group study session of the Political Bureau of the CPC Central Committee on February 23, 2013, he stressed that "We should strengthen judicial openness, and respond to the people's concerns about and expectations of judicial justice and openness."[6]

On January 7, 2014, Xi Jinping stressed at the Central political and legal work meeting on justice, procuratorate, and public security that "transparency is the best prevention of corruption. If the administration of power is not open to the public or is selectively open to the public, credibility will be undermined. The more open law enforcement and the administration of justice are to the public, the more authoritative and credible the government will be. There are very few cases involving the interests of ordinary people that need to be kept secret. Therefore, law enforcement and the administration of justice should be open to the public unless otherwise required by law." "We should continue to promote justice through openness and ensure impartiality through transparency. We should take the initiative in making public law enforcement and the administration of law and inviting supervision to render manipulation and judicial corruption impossible."[7]

On September 21, 2014, at the central conference on the 65th anniversary of the founding of the Chinese People's Political Consultative Conference, Xi Jinping stated that "we should make the exercise of power more open and standardized, and increase the transparency of Party, government and judicial operations and official operations in other fields. We should ensure that the people oversee the exercise of power and that power is exercised in a transparent manner."[8]

---

[6] Xi [4].

[7] Xi [4].

[8] President Xi Jinping [5].

In his speech addressed at the second plenary meeting of the Fourth Plenary Session of the 18th CPC Central Committee, Xi Jinping stated, "we should adhere to the principle that judicial openness can promote justice and increase credibility. We need to establish an open, dynamic, transparent, and convenient judicial mechanism to render manipulation and judicial corruption impossible."[9]

When presiding over the twenty-first group study session of the Political Bureau of the CPC Central Committee on March 24, 2015, Xi Jinping stressed, "judges and procurators have the power to try cases, and supervision should be strengthened over their exercise of power. Supervision by law, social supervision, and public opinions should be put in place. Judges and procurators should "act fairly". The exercise of power should be kept within the confines of systemic checks so that the sunshine of equity and justice will warm the hearts of the people and the people can benefit from such reforms."[10]

The Supreme People's Court and the Supreme People's Procuratorate have been implementing the Party's policies and Xi Jinping Thought on the rule of law and gradually integrating judicial openness into every judicial activity by sticking to the principle of "openness being the principle while non-openness an exception".

General Secretary Xi Jinping's remarks on judicial openness have laid a theoretical foundation for the work regarding judicial openness in the new era. In particular, the idea of developing "openness" to "transparency" makes this theoretical foundation more appropriate for new historical circumstances so that judicial openness can move towards judicial transparency.

2.3 *Building of China's Judicial Openness System*

China's judicial openness is grounded in the Constitution and laws, and the CPC Central Committee has contributed a lot to it. Meanwhile, the Supreme People's Court has been paying close attention to judicial openness when it is devoted to promoting judicial reform according to the arrangements by the Central Government. In particular, the judicial openness system has been systematized, which can be found in various documents and regulations issued in recent years on judicial openness. Since 2013, other judicial documents and interpretations have had judicial openness as the main content in addition to those documents specifically regulating judicial openness. Judicial openness has been deemed as an effective means of regulating trial and enforcement powers, safeguarding the parties' right of action and the public's right to know, responding to the concerns of society, increasing the public's knowledge of the law, promoting their recognition of the rule of law, maintaining judicial justice, and increasing judicial credibility.

---

[9] Xi [6].

[10] Xi [4].

2.3.1 Judicial Openness Prescribed by the Constitution and Laws

The provisions on public trial in the Constitution enacted in 1954 are adopted in Article 130 of the Constitution in effect: "Except in special circumstances as specified by law, all cases in the people's courts shall be heard in public. The accused shall have the assistance of counsel for his defence."

The three major procedure laws restate and implement the provisions of the Constitution and regulate the disclosure of trial procedures to varying degrees. For example, the Criminal Procedure Law 1979 provided that a copy of an indictment of a people's procuratorate shall be served to the accused. The accused shall be informed of his right to entrust a counsel prior to a court hearing. The Criminal Procedure Law in effect, amended in 2018 and based on years of criminal justice practice, provides that a people's court of first instance shall hear cases in public. However, where a case is not tried in public for reasons involving state secrets or other matters, such reasons must be announced in court. Moreover, after a people's court has decided to try a case in court, it shall determine the collegial panel members and serve a copy of the indictment of the people's procuratorate upon the accused and his advocate no later than ten days before the court session is held. If a case is to be heard in public, the cause of action, the name of the accused, and the time and place of the court session shall be announced no later than three days before the court session is held.

The civil procedure system concerns the settlement of disputes between equal parties, which requires openness to be demonstrated more explicitly. The Civil Procedure Law 1982 provided that civil cases shall be tried in public, except for those that involve state secrets or personal privacy or are to be tried otherwise as provided by the law. The trial process information shall be disclosed to the parties involved and the public. For example, a copy of a written complaint shall be served on the defendant after docketing the case. The parties and other participants shall be notified three days prior to a hearing; if a case is to be tried in public, the parties' names, cause of action, and time and place of the hearing shall be announced. As the rule of law develops, further protection of the parties' rights in civil cases has become significant in improving the civil procedure system. The regulations on trial process disclosure are becoming more elaborate. According to the Civil Procedure Law 1991, a people's court shall promptly notify the party whose property is subject to preservation when it has frozen the property. If it has decided to accept, a people's court shall advise the parties orally, or in the notice of acceptance of the case and response to the action, of their procedural rights and obligations. The parties shall be notified of the composition of a collegial panel within three days after the collegial panel members have been determined. Upon pronouncement of a judgment, the parties shall be advised of the right to appeal, time limit for appeal and the court with which an appeal may be lodged. The Civil Procedure Law revised in 2012 further provided that the general public may have access to effective judgments and rulings, except for those involving state secrets, trade secrets, and personal privacy, which has become the direct legal basis for the publication of judgments on the Internet. Such provisions on judicial openness in civil procedures also apply in the trial of administrative cases.

2.4 *Judicial Openness Prescribed by the Supreme People's Court*

(1) Requirement for judicial openness in the process of judicial reform

In recent years, the Supreme People's Court, in order to implement the requirements of the CPC Central Committee and legal requirements and respond to the public's growing demand for judicial openness, has taken judicial openness as a crucial means to promote people's courts' judicial reform. The Five-year Reform Program for the People's Courts (Fa Fa [1999] No. 28), issued by the Supreme People's Court on October 20, 1999, put forth that people's courts should fully implement the public trial system and reform trial methods, and the judicial mechanism with independence, justice, openness, efficiency, integrity, and proper operation should be further improved. In terms of the disclosure of judgments, the Program pointed out: that the reform of judgments must be accelerated and the quality thereof improved; the focus of the reform is to strengthen the analysis and authentication of the disputed evidence in confrontation and the reasoning of the judgment; a judgment records not only the adjudication process but also the reasons for the decision so that the judgment can be the carrier showing judicial justice to the public, as well as vivid materials for educating the public on the law. Furthermore, as stated by the Program, a people's court of second instance should hear a case in public and pronounce the judgment in public except for those which may be heard in secret as per law.

Subject to the Second Five-year Reform Program for the People's Courts (2004–2008) (Fa Fa [2005] No. 18) issued by the Supreme People's Court in 2005, people's courts should further implement the public trial principle according to law, adopt new measures for judicial openness, determine the scope and ways of disclosing relevant procedures in the operation of cases, provide various channels for the public to understand the functions and activities of the courts, and improve the transparency of trial, enforcement, and other work of people's courts. Besides, regarding enforcement, it was proposed to strengthen the management of and supervision over enforcement through the disclosure of enforcement information so as to ensure the impartiality of enforcement. In addition, the Program called for the disclosure of judicial data, i.e., expanding the range of data to be disclosed and enhancing the analysis and utilization of statistics.

The Third Five-Year Reform Program for the People's Courts (Fa Fa [2009] No. 14), issued by the Supreme People's Court in 2009, laid stress on improving the working mechanism of justice for the people and proposed the enhancement and perfection of the system of public trials and enforcement, including carrying forward the reform of the disclosure system in respect of trial and enforcement, strengthening the reasoning of judgments, enhancing judicial transparency, and promoting judicial democratization. In addition, this Program put forward that people's courts should improve the system "walk right in and sit right down," standardize live broadcasting and rebroadcasting of trials, improve the public hearing system, and establish a system for releasing judgments online and a system for inquiring about enforcement information online. In terms of personnel administration, the Program also proposed a scientific selection and appointment mechanism and an effective mechanism for supervising and managing court officials, and the enhancement of the transparency and openness of personnel management.

The Fourth Five-year Reform Program for the People's Courts (2014–2018) (Fa Fa [2015] No. 3), issued by the Supreme People's Court in 2014, made more demands on furthering judicial openness from the following four aspects. First, people's courts should improve the public trial system and establish a court trial announcement system and an announcement and reservation system for visitors' seats. People's courts should synchronize audio and video recordings with the entire trial process and standardize the scope and procedures of live broadcasting of court hearings through images, texts, videos, and other means. Second, people's courts should perfect the trial information database to facilitate the parties' access to online information on case filings and the judicial process from the date of acceptance of a case. Third, people's courts should continue to give impetus to the website China Judgements Online and publish on this website those effective judgments that should be made public according to the law under the principle of "disclosure being the general rule and non-disclosure being an exception". Fourth, people's courts should consolidate all kinds of enforcement information to enable litigants to follow online the enforcement progress and achieve a workable connection between the enforcement information disclosure platform and various credit investigation platforms.

The Supreme People's Court issued the Opinions on Furthering the Comprehensive Reform Supporting the Judicial System of the People's Courts—the Fifth Five-year Reform Program of the People's Courts (2019–2023) (Fa Fa [2019] No. 8) (namely the "Fifth Five" Reform Program) in 2019, proposing that people's courts should further judicial openness through the continuous improvement of four disclosure platforms, i.e., judicial process information, court trials, judgments, and enforcement information, expansion of judicial openness, the establishment of sound ways of promoting judicial openness, and the unimpeded access to judicial information by the parties and their lawyers so as to build a judicial system, more open, dynamic, transparent and convenient for the public. It is worth mentioning that the "Fifth Five" Reform Program specifically proposed the promotion of judicial openness in the part of "improving the open, dynamic, transparent and convenient judicial system". According to the "Fifth Five" Reform Program, people's courts should improve the working mechanism for judicial openness by implementing the principle of voluntary, comprehensive, timely, and substantive disclosure and disclosure by law, adhering to the principle of "disclosure being the general rule and non-disclosure an exception", continuously expanding judicial openness, improving its forms, keeping open disclosure channels, and strengthening platform construction and technical guarantee. People's courts should further advance the standardization and informatization construction of information disclosure in terms of judgments, court trials, judicial process, enforcement, litigation service, judicial reform, and judicial administration affairs. People's courts should improve the judicial openness system by accurately dividing standards for disclosure to the parties and the public, respectively, studying and issuing relevant business guides, technical standards, and operating rules, and identifying the subject of responsibility. Building and integrating the "four platforms" for judicial openness should be advanced. The functions of the platforms should be upgraded to highlight the new features of the mobile Internet era and promote those from one-way disclosure to multi-directional interaction so that litigation activities will be more transparent and litigation results will be more predictable. Moreover, the "Fifth Five" Reform Program stated the disclosure of approval process information, judgments, court trials, and enforcement information with the core of refining disclosure standards, improving the disclosure system, strengthening information security, and promoting centralized and unified disclosure on platforms.

In addition to the above reform programs, the Supreme People's Court issued opinions on implementing the reform of the judicial accountability system many times to emphasize judicial openness. According to the Certain Opinions on Improving the Judicial Accountability System in the People's Courts promulgated by the Supreme People's Court in 2015, people's courts at all levels should develop an open, dynamic, transparent, and convenient judicial mechanism with the aid of information technologies, build up and improve three platforms for judicial process information disclosure, judgment disclosure, and enforcement information disclosure, and subject themselves to public supervision.

The Supreme People's Court issued the Opinions on Further Comprehensively Implementing the Judicial Accountability System, providing that the decision made by the judicial committee and the grounds should be made public in a written judgment except as otherwise provided by law. In order to enhance judges' awareness of responsibility, people's courts should rely on the informationalized platform to carry out a quality evaluation of all judges' judgments uploaded and the disclosure of their court trials. Moreover, the Opinions specifically proposed the further improvement in judicial openness as follows: people's courts should strictly implement the Provisions of the Supreme People's Court on the Publication of Judgments by the People's Courts on the Internet (Revised) to make the disclosure of judgments more informationized and normalized and guarantee the comprehensive, timely, and accurate disclosure of the judgments that should be made public; people's courts should actively promote the use of automatic correction and technical processing software for judgments to eliminate all kinds of low-level errors and quality defects, effectively reduce the workload of publishing judgments, and constantly improve the level of judgment disclosure. People's courts should implement the Provisions of the Supreme People's Court on the Disclosure of Trial Procedures by the People's Courts on the Internet by upgrading and improving relevant information platforms without delay and by taking the initiative in establishing links with the unified national platform China Judicial Process Information Online so as to implement all requirements for the disclosure of judicial process information; people's courts should actively adapt to the new requirements for public trials in the Internet era, give full play to the advantages of the unified platform China Court Trial Online, and continuously advance the people's courts' work of disclosing court trials.

According to the Implementation Opinions on Deepening the Comprehensive Reform Supporting the Judicial Accountability System issued by the Supreme People's Court in 2020, people's courts at all levels should actively use the four platforms for judicial openness, develop an open, dynamic, transparent, and convenient judicial mechanism, and expand the breadth and depth of judicial openness to consciously accept supervision.

(2) Regulations governing the improvement on judicial openness

① General provisions

The Supreme People's Court has issued many judicial documents on judicial openness. The *Several* Provisions of the Supreme People's Court on Strictly Implementing the Public Trial System, issued in 1999, further specified the requirements for public trials. The Several Provisions of the Supreme People's Court on Enforcement Disclosure by the People's Courts, issued in 2006, specifically stated the disclosure of enforcement information. According to the Several Opinions of the Supreme People's Court on Strengthening Public Trials by the People's Courts promulgated in 2007 (hereinafter referred to as the Several Opinions), people's courts at all levels should establish and publish a case-handling inquiry mechanism to make it easy for the parties and their attorneys to keep abreast of trial and enforcement information about the parties' litigation rights and obligations. Subject to the Several Opinions, Chinese citizens may sit in on the cases that should be tried in public according to law, provided they present a valid certificate. People's courts should make proper arrangements for their attendance. Therefore, it is a general principle to attend public hearings with valid certificates; it is an exception to issue passes and limit the number. Besides, according to the Several Opinions, in light of the situation within its jurisdiction, a high people's court should formulate specific measures to publish effective judgments through mediums such as publications, LANs, and the Internet, thus gradually increasing the openness of effective judgments. In December 2009, the Supreme People's Court issued the Six Provisions on Judicial Openness, more systematically stating that people's courts shall implement judicial openness in judicial work, including disclosing case filings, court trials, enforcement, hearings, documents, and trial affairs.

In light of new situations coming along with information technology development, to implement requirements of judicial reform for promoting judicial openness, on November 28, 2013, the Supreme People's Court issued the Several Opinions on Promoting the Construction of Three Platforms for Judicial Openness, requiring people's courts to advance the disclosure of judicial process information, judgments, and enforcement information. According to the Opinions, the construction of three platforms is a key strategic measure for people's courts to adapt to the information technology era and meet the people's new expectation of judicial openness. People's courts should fully realize the openness and transparency of the trial process, judgments, and enforcement information by constructing information platforms for communicating and interacting with the public. In this way, the three platforms can be windows to show modern civilization of the rule of law, means to protect litigation rights of the parties, and ways to fulfill the social responsibility of people's courts.

People's courts should comprehensively promote the construction of the three platforms for judicial openness to make the people experience equity and justice in every judicial case.

The Opinions of the Supreme People's Court on Further Making Judicial Work More Convenient for and Beneficial to the People issued in 2014 included measures for people's courts at all levels to provide the public with high-quality judicial service under the principle of justice for the people. A majority of the measures involved judicial openness. For instance, people's courts should strengthen the construction of the platforms for the disclosure of judicial process information and integrate all kinds of judicial process information to provide the parties with comprehensive, whole-process, and timely disclosure service; people's courts should improve the system of the audience to court trials, and for a case that should be heard in public, the competent court should make known as per law the case title, court date, courtroom number, attendance seats and other trial information to facilitate the public's attendance; people's courts should enhance the interpretation of and the reasoning behind judgments, and a people's court should respond seriously and comprehensively to the claims and opinions from the parties, specify reasons and legal authorities for its acceptance or rejection, and ensure that facts are entirely ascertained and laws are correctly applied; with the construction of a "Balance Project" as the carrier, people's courts should speed up the construction of the three platforms for disclosing judicial process information, judgments, and enforcement information to give full play to modern scientific and technological information means.

In order to further advance judicial openness systematically, the Supreme People's Court promulgated the Opinions of the Supreme People's Court on Furthering Judicial Openness (hereinafter referred to as the "Opinions") in 2018, specifying measures to promote judicial openness and render the open, dynamic, transparent, and convenient judicial mechanism more mature. The Opinions proposed the adherence to the five principles of voluntary disclosure, disclosure by law, timely disclosure, overall disclosure, and substantive disclosure, and also made specific requests for developing the content and scope of judicial openness, improving and standardizing judicial openness procedures, enhancing the construction and management of the platforms, and strengthening organizational guarantees. In terms of the contents of judicial openness, according to the Opinions, people's courts should further information disclosure in respect of general information about the court, trials and enforcement, litigation service, judicial reform, administrative affairs of the judiciary, international judicial exchanges and cooperation, team building, and other aspects. People's courts should establish and perfect a dynamic adjustment system for judicial openness, promote the normalization and standardization of judicial openness, and expand judicial openness in an all-around manner. The Opinions proposed that people's courts should improve the forms of judicial openness to provide the parties and attorneys with unimpeded channels to get access to judicial information. People's courts should specify the subjects responsible for judicial openness and better the process management mechanism for judicial openness to ensure standardized and orderly progress of judicial openness. With regard to strengthening the construction of the platforms, the Opinions put forward that people's courts should strengthen the work relating to white papers and the construction and management of the websites on government affairs, promote the four platforms for judicial openness, give full play to the role of modern information technology, enhance the platforms' function of serving the people and publicity, consolidate good interaction with news media, strengthen the construction of the courts' media and the publicity for the courts' news, consolidate and expand carriers for judicial carriers, and promote standardized management and function optimization. Besides, according to the Opinions, people's courts should implement the accountability system and improve assessment, supervision, demonstration, and guidance mechanisms. People's courts should strengthen professional training and research on judicial openness, improve the supervision system, and strengthen publicity and education on the rule of law to promote the effect of judicial openness with sound institutional guarantees.

② Provisions on the disclosure of judgments

Regarding the disclosure of judgments, due to the lack of a unified platform and standards for local courts to publish them on the Internet, the disclosure was not comprehensive, timely, accurate, or convenient for the public's inquiries. The Provisions of the Supreme People's Court on the Publication of Judgments on the Internet by the People's Courts (Fa Shi [2013] No. 26) determined to set up the China Judgements Online to disclose effective judgments rendered by people's courts at all levels. The Provisions published in 2013 was amended by the Supreme People's Court in 2016. The Provisions of the Supreme People's Court on the Publication of Judgments on the Internet by the People's Courts (Fa Shi [2016] No. 19) detailed the scope of the disclosure, specified the categories of judgments not to be made public, and emphasized the use of information means to assist the disclosure. The Guiding Opinions of the Supreme People's Court on Strengthening and Standardizing the Interpretation and Reasoning of Judgments (Fa Shi [2018] No. 10) issued in 2018 stated how to strengthen the interpretation and reasoning of judgments. A judgment is practically the carrier used to reveal to the parties and the public the relevant information on ascertainment of facts and application of laws and regulations in trying a case.

③ Provisions on the disclosure of judicial process information

In terms of the disclosure of judicial process information, the Provisions of the Supreme People's Court on the Disclosure of Judicial Process Information on the Internet by the People's Courts (Fa Shi [2018] No. 7) published in 2018 specified the contents and forms of the disclosure of judicial process information. Subject to the Provisions, the website China Judicial Process Information Online is the unified platform for disclosing judicial process information by people's courts. People's courts at all levels shall set up links to the website on their portals and judicial openness platforms. In addition, the Provisions specified how to disclose judicial process information to the parties concerned. In the process of promotion, according to the Opinions of the Supreme People's Court on the Establishment of One-stop Diversified Dispute Resolution Mechanisms and One-stop Litigation Service Centers issued in 2019, people's courts should strengthen the standardization of litigation services, make a list of service items with "completion at one time" as the goal, and formulate and make public standardized working procedures and service guides "on completion at one time". People's courts should promote universal and convenient litigation services through standardization by regulating service processes, improving service quality, and differentiating between powers and responsibilities to promote equal acceptance and handling of the same service item.

④ Provisions on the disclosure of trial information

In terms of the recording and live broadcasting of court trials, the Provisions of the Supreme People's Court on the Live Broadcasting and Rebroadcasting of Court Trials by the People's Courts put forward that people's courts may select to live broadcast and rebroadcast the court proceedings of those cases of high public concern, a profound impact on society, and significance for increasing public awareness of the law. In order to demonstrate the latest achievements of the judicial system reform, respond to the new requirements and expectations of the public, guarantee the rights of litigation, regulate trial activities, further judicial openness, improve the efficiency of court hearings, and promote judicial justice, the Supreme People's Court published in 2017 the Several Provisions on Audio and Video Recording of Court Trials. The amended Provisions attached importance to the diversified demands for judicial openness in the Internet era, requiring audio–video recording throughout the trial process to construct transparent courts and resort to litigation service platforms to make it convenient to consult audio–video recordings.

⑤ Provisions on the disclosure of enforcement information

Regarding enforcement information disclosure, under the Several Provisions of the Supreme People's Court on Enforcement Disclosure by the People's Courts issued in 2006, people's courts shall disclose all information related to the enforcement of a case through notice, public announcement, the court's network, news media, and other means, except the information that is prohibited from being disclosed by law such as information on national secrets and trade secrets. The following information shall be made public: the standard for putting a case on record and the procedures for initiating enforcement, the standard for charging enforcement expenses, and fundamental conditions and procedures for the deduction, deferment, or exemption of such expenses, and all the legal documents and relevant materials formed in the enforcement process that are not confidential. The parties and other participants in the proceedings shall be informed of the following information: relevant information on putting the case on record, rights and obligations in the enforcement process and possible risks, the undertaker of the case, members of the collegial panel and their contact information, the property status of the person against whom the enforcement is sought found out in the investigation conducted by the court and the property status declared by the said person, enforcement measures adopted by the court such as sealing up, seizure, freeze and transfer, and compulsory measures adopted by the court such as detention, fine, and summoning by force. Besides, as for the termination of enforcement, the people's court shall produce a ruling paper and serve it upon both parties concerned, which shall bear sufficient reasons for such termination and expressly invoke applicable laws.

The Several Opinions on the Disclosure of the Enforcement Process of People's Courts issued by the Supreme People's Court in 2014 proposed that people's courts should follow the principle of "disclosure as a general rule and non-disclosure as an exception" in deciding whether to disclose enforcement process information. People's courts should disclose all enforcement procedures and information related hereto, which should and may be made public according to the law. In order to provide all-around, diversified, and real-time enforcement disclosure services to the parties and the public and promote transparent enforcement, a people's court should make public the entire handling process in an enforcement case, all stages, all procedures, and all judgments.

The Supreme People's Court planned to "basically solve the difficulties" within two to three years. It issued the Work Program on Implementing "the Basic Resolution of Difficulties in Enforcement Within Two to Three Years" in 2016. In order to further standardize the behaviors in the enforcement process and enhance the credibility of the enforcement work, the Program suggested making every effort to build a website, "China Enforcement Information Online", and disclose without delay to the public the enforcement process, the list of dishonest judgment debtors, and enforcement judgments. Only in this way can the parties' and the public's rights to know and oversee enforcement cases and enforcement work be guaranteed so that enforcement power will be exercised in public. With regard to non-standard handling of cases in which enforcement is terminated and adverse public criticism, the Provisions of the Supreme People's Court on Strictly Regulating the Termination of Enforcement Procedures (Trial) issued in 2016 stated that before ruling on the termination of the enforcement, a people's court shall inform the party applying for enforcement of enforcement details, property investigation measures, the property of the other party against whom the enforcement is sought, the grounds for and legal consequences of this termination, and other information, and solicit his opinions on such termination. According to law, a written ruling on the termination of enforcement procedures must be disclosed on the Internet.

The Opinions on Strengthening Comprehensive Governance to Solve Difficulties in Enforcement at the Source issued in 2019 by the Commission for Law-based Governance of the CPC Central Committee reiterated the proposal to "reinforce enforcement disclosure and promote transparent enforcement".

To effectively solve difficulties in enforcement, the Supreme People's Court issued the Opinions on Furthering the Reform in Enforcement and Improving the Long-term Mechanism for Solving Difficulties in Enforcement—the People's Courts' Work Program on Enforcement (2019–2023) in 2019. It emphasized the disclosure of enforcement information and the improvement of the open, dynamic, transparent, and convenient enforcement system. Firstly, people's courts should improve the mechanism for making public enforcement information. Specifically, people's courts should implement the principle of voluntary, lawful, comprehensive, timely, and substantial disclosure and adhere to the rule of "disclosure as a principle and non-disclosure as an exception". Courts should expand disclosure, improve its forms, establish unimpeded disclosure channels, and strengthen platform building and technical support. Courts should advance the normalization, standardization, and informatization of enforcement disclosure and accurately define the criteria for disclosing enforcement information to the parties and the public; courts should specify the subjects accountable for enforcement disclosure. Secondly, people's courts should expand enforcement disclosure and promote unified disclosure on the same platform of enforcement process information, judgment debtors, the list of dishonest judgment debtors, online judicial auctions, compulsory measures, property investigation, disposal measures, and the like. Thirdly, a people's court should build an intensive enforcement disclosure platform to develop the enforcement information disclosure website into an enforcement disclosure platform and keep connecting the platform and the management system for enforcement cases, the system for punishing dishonest judgment debtors, the system for restricting consumption, the inquiry and appraisal system, the online auction platform, and the system for ending the enforcement process. In this way, courts will provide better "one-stop" enforcement information disclosure services for the parties and the public. In addition, courts should make enforcement disclosure websites more workable to enhance exchange and interaction between the parties and competent judges, improve the functions of clue providing and reward announcement, and motivate all sectors of society to participate in, support, and supervise enforcement. Finally, people's courts should innovate the means of disclosing enforcement information. Subject to the Program, by the end of 2019, the courts where conditions allow will have used SMS, WeChat, litigation service hotlines, mobile APPs, and the like to notify the parties of the key dates regarding the enforcement process to meet the needs of the public to understand the enforcement work through multiple channels. Furthermore, courts should accelerate the establishment of a shared mechanism for fast-tracking information with relevant departments to send the process nodes and other enforcement information to litigants' mobiles.

The Several Provisions of the Supreme People's Court on Issuing the Information on the List of Dishonest Judgment Debtors issued in 2013 provided that people's courts at all levels shall enter the information on the list of dishonest judgment debtors into the database of the Supreme People's Court on the list of dishonest judgment debtors and publish these lists through this database in a unified manner. Besides, in light of actual conditions, people's courts may publish lists of dishonest judgments debtors through newspapers, radio, television, the Internet, bulletin boards of courts, and other means. Furthermore, regularly courts may publish through press conferences or other means to the public the information on implementing the list system for dishonest judgment debtors by these courts and courts within their respective jurisdictions. Under the *Opinions of the General Office of the CPC Central Committee and the General Office of the State Council on Accelerating the Advancement of the Development of a Credit Supervision, Warning and Punishment System for Dishonest Judgment Debtors* issued in 2016, people's courts should update the information on lists of dishonest judgment debtors timely and accurately and disclose such information for the public's free inquiries through the disclosure and inquiry platform of information on national courts' lists of dishonest judgment debtors, relevant websites, mobile applications, outdoor media, and other forms. Given joint discipline, a people's court may send the information recorded in the list to whoever is the employer of the dishonest judgment debtor so that the said employer can *ipso jure* use it in consideration of its work. For anyone subject to enforcement, if it is not suitable according to law to disclose information on his dishonesty, a people's court should notify his employer of it. The employer will decide how to treat him by laws and regulations.

⑥ Provisions on disclosure in other aspects

In terms of implementing the judicial accountability system reform, in order to implement the Provisions on Records of the Intervention in Case Handling by Staff Members of Judicial Organs and Investigations into Their Accountability issued by the Commission for Political and Legal Affairs of the CPC Central Committee, the Supreme People's Court promulgated the Measures for the people's courts' Implementation of "the Provisions on Records of the Intervention in Case Handling by Staff Members of Judicial Organs and Investigations into Their Accountability" in 2015. Under the Measures, the supervisory department of a people's court may, with the approval of the key leaders hereof, circulate within the people's court the investigations by the court and courts within its jurisdiction into the intervention in case handling by staff members of the said courts in violation of the Provisions and disclose such investigations to the public when necessary. Following the Opinions on Promoting the Reform of the Registration System for Filing Cases by the People's Courts, people's courts should make public case filing procedures, regulate the conduct in case filings, and strengthen the supervision over the case filing process. In order to carry out the overall arrangements of the CPC Central Committee for furthering the comprehensive supporting reform of the judicial system and improve the working mechanism of judicial committees of people's courts, the Supreme People's Court issued the Opinions on Improving and Perfecting the Working Mechanism of Judicial Committees of People's Courts in 2019, putting forward that the decision of a judicial committee after deliberation and the reasons should be disclosed in the written judgment, except as otherwise prescribed by law.

To formulate judicial interpretations more scientifically, the Supreme People's Court issued the Opinions of the Supreme People's Court on Improving the Working Mechanism for Unifying the Application of Law in 2020, proposing that any judicial interpretation involving the immediate interests of the people or significant and complicated issues should be open to the public to solicit opinions.

In terms of strengthening the organization and management of the people's mediation, the Supreme People's Court issued the Provisions of on Specially-Invited Mediation by the People's Courts in 2016, proposing that a people's court shall establish a register of specially-invited mediation organizations and mediators for its specially-invited mediation work, provide at such places as the litigation service center the register, and publish it on the bulletin board, official website or any other platform of the court to facilitate inquiries by the parties.

As regards improving litigation services, according to the Guiding Opinions of the Supreme People's Court on Comprehensively Promoting the Construction of Litigation Service Centers in the People's Courts, people's courts should establish litigation service websites. People's courts should improve databases to support the service websites, such as the information disclosure database, the judicial process information database, and the database on electronic litigation files. People's courts should connect litigation service websites and the three platforms and promote resource sharing. People's courts should use SMS, WeChat, Weibo, mobile APPs, or other communication service systems to voluntarily notify the parties, their agents, and attorneys of the key nodes regarding the trial process or send relevant information upon their application. People's courts should send to the public whatever should be disclosed by law.

In terms of strengthening the work of people's tribunals, the Several Opinions of the Supreme People's Court on Further Strengthening the Work of the People's Tribunals Under New Conditions issued in 2015 proposed that people's tribunals should fully disclose tribunal personnel information, management systems, codes of conduct, and litigation guides, and timely disclose case information, judicial grounds, litigation procedures, and judgments in accordance with the law to guarantee the parties' right to information and eliminate manipulation; in the process of advancing the construction of the "three platforms", people's tribunals should attach importance to the characteristics of their work; people's tribunals should actively take advantage of their taking root at the grassroots level and simplify the procedures for attending hearings to meet the public's needs without disrupting judicial security; people's tribunals should carry out activities with judicial openness as the theme and invite representatives from all walks of life to attend court hearings and visit how the tribunals work; people's tribunals should further give play to the unique function of circuit trials in judicial openness and publicity for the rule of law and enhance public recognition of the tribunals' work.

As far as judicial identification was concerned, the Supreme People's Court issued the Regulations on the Management of Entrusting External Judicial Identification by the People's Courts in 2002. It provided that the judicial identification institution of a people's court shall make a list of social identification institutions and specialists and randomly select and appoint experts to conduct judicial identification subject to professional and technical requirements of identification objects. The Regulations also stated that the identification specialists approved in the panel of judicial identification specialists of a people's court shall be announced in *People's Court Daily*.

As regards providing support and guarantee for Shenzhen to develop into a pilot demonstration zone of socialism with Chinese characteristics, the Opinions of the Supreme People's Court on Providing Support and Guarantee for Shenzhen to Build Itself into a Pilot Demonstration Zone of Socialism with Chinese Characteristics provided that people's courts should accelerate the construction of online judicial openness platforms to build a more open, dynamic, transparent, and convenient judicial system, and establish a registration and disclosure system for bankruptcy information.

To strengthen the trial of enterprise bankruptcy cases, the Supreme People's Court issued the *Provisions on the Information Disclosure Regarding Enterprise Bankruptcy Cases (Trial)* in 2016, specifying what information in enterprise bankruptcy cases shall be disclosed by people's courts and bankruptcy administrators. People's courts shall make public the following information: information about stages of the judicial process, announcements issued by people's courts during bankruptcy proceedings, legal instruments regarding bankruptcy proceedings prepared by people's courts, and other information which people's courts deem should be disclosed. Furthermore, the Supreme People's Court has set up the "National Enterprise Bankruptcy Information Disclosure Platform" to disclose information on bankruptcy cases in a centralized manner.

To solve the problem of commutation and parole cases not being handled in a standardized manner and with deep social concern over the past period, the Supreme People's Court issued the Provisions on Several Issues Concerning the Specific Application of Law in Handling Cases Relating to Commutation and Parole in 2012. According to the Provisions, people's courts shall release information on all hearings of commutation and parole cases at the public areas where the sentence is being served; where conditions permit, the release shall be made to the public for social supervision. Information to be released shall include but not be limited to: the name of the convict, the crime and sentence determined in the original judgment, previous commutation, the enforcement organ's suggestions and grounds for commutation and parole, the release period, and feedback channels. According to the Provisions of the Supreme People's Court on Trial Procedures for Commutation and Parole Cases issued in 2014, when handling a commutation or parole case, the people's court shall make public within five days after the case is filed the written proposal submitted by the enforcement organ for a commutation of the sentence or parole and other documents. The information to be released includes the profile of the criminal, the crime and sentence determined in the original judgment, the previous commutation of the sentence, and the enforcement organ's suggestions and grounds. The release period and feedback ways shall be made public, and the term is five days. In addition, a written ruling on commutation or parole shall be made public through the Internet according to law. The Supreme People's Court has established a national information platform for commutation, parole, and temporarily serving a sentence outside an incarceration facility to release information in a centralized manner on the above cases handled by courts across the country.

To regulate the appearance of the persons in charge of administrative agencies in court to respond to lawsuits, under the Provisions of the Supreme People's Court on Several Issues Concerning the Appearance of the Persons in Charge of Administrative Agencies in Court to Respond to Lawsuits issued in 2020, people's courts may make public in an appropriate form the appearance of the persons in charge of administrative agencies in court to respond to lawsuits.

Regarding judicial protection of intellectual property rights, under the Opinions of the Supreme People's Court on Comprehensively Strengthening Judicial Protection of Intellectual Property issued in 2020, people's courts should avail themselves of the four platforms for judicial process information disclosure, trial activities disclosure, judgment disclosure, and enforcement information disclosure to guarantee the parties' and the public's right to know and participate and their right of supervision to the maximum extent.

In terms of judicial relief, the *Provisions on the Procedures for the Handling of State Judicial Relief Cases by the People's Courts (Trial)* issued in 2019 provided that a people's court shall provide notes on the application for national judicial relief, application forms, and other documents through the case-filing window (litigation service center), the Internet and other channels.

Regarding public interest litigation cases, according to the Measures for the Implementation of the Pilot Program of Trial by People's Courts of Public Interest Litigation Cases Initiated by People's Procuratorates issued in 2016, the people's court should try in public according to law a public interest litigation case instituted by the people's procuratorate; the people's court may invite deputies to the people's congress, members of the CPPCC, and other persons to observe court proceedings and meet the needs of the public and media to know what is going on in a court trial through live broadcasting, recorded broadcasting, and other ways; the judgment should be published on the Internet in accordance with relevant regulations.

In terms of strengthening the protection of property rights, according to the Opinions of the Supreme People's Court on Fully Maximizing the Functions of Trials and Effectively Strengthening the Judicial Protection of Property Rights promulgated in 2016, we should reinforce the publicity of the rule of law, promote a favorable social atmosphere for protecting property rights, and publicize guidelines, policies, laws, and regulations of the Party and the state on equal protection of economic property rights under various forms of ownership through online judgments, live broadcasting of court trials, and other judicial openness channels to make the concept of equal, comprehensive, and lawful protection deeply rooted among the people, and to create a fair, impartial, transparent, and stable environment for the rule of law.

In terms of the equal protection of the non-public sector of the economy, the Opinions of the Supreme People's Court on Lawfully and Equally Protecting the Non-Public Economy and Advancing the Sound Development of the Non-Public Economy issued in 2015 emphasized the necessity of strengthening judicial openness and continuously improving the level of informatization services. Specifically, we should accelerate the informatization construction of people's courts and comprehensively improve judicial openness. We should bring into play the carriers such as the website China Judicial Process Information Online to disclose, according to law, all trial and enforcement activities to the public, including non-public economic entities. We should use the data platform for dishonest judgment debtors to carry out credit construction in conjunction with relevant departments and social organizations. On a best efforts basis, we should promote online judgments and strengthen the argumentation of the reasons for ascertaining facts and applying the law in judgments to increase the predictability by subjects of various types of ownership of their business operations and legal consequences. We should publicize the laws and regulations regarding the non-public sector of the economy and raise non-public enterprises' sense of law through public trials, interpretation of laws by case analysis, the release of important news and typical cases, and other forms.

To fight against false litigation, according to the Guiding Opinions of the Supreme People's Court on Preventing and Punishing False Litigation published in 2016, people's courts should exercise more efforts to conduct public trials and increase the transparency of case hearings. Where there is anyone who may have an interest in the disposition of a case, the court may use its discretion to tell him to attend the litigation to avoid any damage to his civil rights and interests and prevent false litigation. In addition, people's courts should deter false litigation activities by publishing model cases regarding false litigation and other means.

Regarding the people's courts' participation in implementing the rural revitalization strategy, under the Opinions of the Supreme People's Court on Providing Judicial Services and Guarantees for the Implementation of the Rural Revitalization Strategy issued in 2018, judicial openness was taken as one of the crucial means to publicize laws and protect legitimate rights and interests of the parties involved in cases related to agriculture, rural areas, and farmers. As provided in the Opinions, people's courts should adhere to live broadcasting of court trials and online judgments for the convenience of rural people to watch court trials and consult documents, which will help realize the visible and impartial administration of justice.

In regard to strengthening judicial protection of ecological civilization and a green economy, the Opinions of the Supreme People's Court on Fully Strengthening Environmental Resource Trial Work to Provide Great Judicial Safeguards for Promoting Eco-civilization Construction issued in 2014 proposed that people's courts should increase public participation and judicial openness in cases involving environmental resources, hold a positive attitude in responding to the public's willingness to participate in environmental resource protection, and fully carry out the participation of the people's assessors in such cases. People's courts should consciously accept the supervision of the public, promote the establishment of the website of China Environmental Resource Judgments Online, and timely upload the judgments thereon in effect. For cases bearing significant influences, people's courts may invite deputies to the people's congresses, members of the CPPCC, and other persons to observe court proceedings to make environmental resource trials more open and credible. People's courts may make full use of traditional media and new media such as WeChat, Weibo, and other news applications to publicize the laws and regulations in respect of environmental resource protection and raise public awareness thereof through public trials, interpretation of laws by case analysis, the release of important news and typical cases regarding environmental resources, and other means. According to the Opinions of the Supreme People's Court on Giving Full Play to Judicial Functions to Provide Judicial Services and Safeguards for Promoting Eco-civilization construction and a Green Economy released in 2016, people's courts should increase judicial openness and publicity and guide the public to participate in environmental governance in an orderly manner; people's courts should guarantee the public's right to know and right of supervision through the trial of administrative cases related to information disclosure, increase their enthusiasm for environmental protection, and implement the principle of public participation; people's courts should invite deputies to the people's congresses, members of the CPPCC, the public, and news media to observe the trial of complicated cases and increase the online disclosure of judgments; people's courts should make full use of new media and self-media to release crucial judicial information timely and regularly publish white papers on environmental resource trials.

In terms of safeguarding opening up, the Several Opinions of the Supreme People's Court on Providing Judicial Services and Safeguards for the Construction of the "Belt and Road" by People's Courts issued in 2015 proposed that people's courts should further the reform, improve openness, and constantly expand international influence and credibility of foreign-related cases. People's courts should improve judicial openness, give full play to the role of foreign-related justice as an international window, and constantly satisfy the right to know of both Chinese and foreign parties. Moreover, according to the Several Opinions, with openness, transparency, convenience, efficiency, sharing, and connectivity as the principles, people's courts should strengthen the top-level design of judicial safeguard informatization for the "Belt and Road". People's courts should adhere to innovation-driven development, promote the in-depth integration of information technologies with trial services, judicial openness, and justice for the convenience of the people, and build themselves into online, transparent, and intelligent courts conforming to the characteristics of the information age.

Regarding state compensation for miscarriages of justice in criminal cases, according to the Opinions of the Supreme People's Court on Further Strengthening the Work on State Compensation for Miscarriages of Justice in Criminal Cases issued in 2015, people's courts should adhere to the principle of openness and impartiality, handle cases under the law, standardize the work process, improve judicial openness, and consciously accept supervision. In addition, in consideration of the characteristics of state compensation cases, courts should introduce new means of judicial openness, expand it, and consciously accept the supervision of people's congresses, CPPCC committees, procuratorial organs, and all sectors of society.

Regarding protecting lawyers' rights and interests, under the Provisions on Legally and Effectively Protecting Lawyers' Rights in Litigation issued by the Supreme People's Court in 2015, people's courts shall continue improving the construction of the three platforms to provide lawyers with convenience to obtain litigation information timely. Furthermore, people's courts shall notify lawyers of important matters such as litigation procedures, protection of litigation rights, mediation and reconciliation, judgments, and progress.

The Several Opinions of the Supreme People's Court on Giving Full Play to Functions of Trials and Effectively Maintaining Public Security issued in 2015 proposed that people's courts should improve judicial openness and timely disclose relevant information to respond to public concerns about cases involving the masses. In addition, courts should use traditional media, WeChat, Weibo, news applications, and other new media to increase public awareness of the law and deter them from committing crimes by making public trials, interpreting laws by case analysis, publishing typical cases, and other means.

3 Informatization Construction of People's Courts and New Development of Judicial Openness

Since entering the twenty-first century, information technology has been developing rapidly, and informatization has been in the stage of popularization. Since the reform and opening up, China's informatization has experienced the process of exploration, integration, and innovation and has made remarkable achievements. At the 18th CPC National Congress, "informatization" was listed as one of the new "Four Modernizations" with Chinese characteristics, and "informatization to be dramatically improved by 2020" as a significant symbol of a moderately prosperous society in all respects. Guided by the Party and Government's policies, the informatization of Chinese courts has made considerable progress. During the "13th Five-Year Plan" period, the informatization thereof achieved remarkable fruits with its level at the forefront of the world, which provided strong scientific and technological support for the people's judicature.

Judicial openness and informatization have accompanied and promoted each other during the development of people's courts in recent years. The application of information technology in courts has expanded judicial openness. The constant demands from the public for judicial openness have also contributed to the promotion of courts' informatization.

The four disclosure platforms of Chinese courts are the brightest innovations among global judicial systems. With the advancement of judicial system reform and informatization, a series of online judicial disclosure platforms have been in operation, and judicial openness has made significant progress. Big data analysis and visual displays conducted on the judicial disclosure platforms have been constantly upgraded and improved. In 2020, with the help of judicial disclosure big data visualization techniques, the Information Center of the Supreme People's Court improved the slow retrieval speed caused by a large amount of index data on the website of China Judgements Online and the capacity to support concurrent users. The Center improved the anti-crawler mechanism of the website and increased the response speed of the public's request for judgments. The Center optimized the website's intelligent cloud platform for live audio and video broadcasting and recording to ensure smooth online display. The Center created a speech recognition algorithm model to shield the parties' privacy in a court hearing video and protect the privacy rights of the parties and related persons at the court hearing.

By the end of 2020, the website China Judicial Process Information Online had released more than 38,890 million cases to the public, with users' access over 407 million times. China Court Trial Online had had live broadcasts of court hearings more than 11.0494 million times. The total page views exceeded 31.904 billion times, making it the world's largest live broadcasting website on government affairs. The website China Judgements Online had published more than 100 million judgments in total, with page views exceeding 54.1 billion hits and users covering more than 210 countries and regions, making it the world's largest and the most high-profile public database of judgments. The website China Enforcement Information Online had been visited by over 330 million people.

The Supreme People's Court, in addition to the four disclosure platforms, has officially launched the National Enterprise Bankruptcy Information Disclosure Platform to promote the disclosure of enterprise bankruptcy information. By the end of 2020, the website had involved 8,246 bankruptcy administrators in charge of over 36,900 staff, issued 2,478 investor recruitment announcements, and convened 1,207 online creditor meetings, which had become an essential measure for people's courts to provide services for the supply-side structural reform.

References

1. Xin Chunying (Editor-in-chief), *Law Dictionary*, edited by the Editorial Board of the Law Dictionary, Institute of law of Chinese Academy of Social Sciences, Law Press China, 2003, p. 452.
2. Edited by the General Office of the Standing Committee of the National People's Congress and the CCCPC Party Literature Research Office, *The Important Literature on the System of the People's Congress (I)*, China Democracy and Legal System Publishing House, 2015, p. 5.
3. *Collected Writings of Dong Biwu on Law*, edited by the Editorial Board of the Collected Writings of Dong Biwu on Law, Law Press China, 2001, p. 43.
4. Xi Jinping Underlined at the Fourth Group Study Session of the Political Bureau of the CPC Central Committee: Coordinated Progress in Law-based Governance, Law-based Exercise of State Power, and Law-based Government Administration; Development of Rule of Law for the Country, the Government, and Society, 25th March, 2013, *People's Daily* (1st ed.).
5. President Xi Jinping Delivered Important Speech at the Central Conference on the 65th Anniversary of the Founding of the CPPCC and Underlined: Advancing Innovation in Theories, Institutions and Work of the CPPCC, Promoting Wide, Multifaceted and Institutionalized Socialist Consultative Democracy, 22nd September, 2014, *People's Daily* (1st ed.).
6. *Xi Jinping: the Governance of China (Volume II)*, Foreign Languages Press, 2017, p. 121.

Chapter 3
The Rationale Behind Judicial Transparency

1 Judicial Transparency and Judicial Openness

Judicial transparency refers to timely, comprehensive, accurate, and adequate disclosure of all trial activities of the court and information related thereto, except for matters involving state secrets, trade secrets, or personal privacy of the parties concerned and those that may affect normal trial proceedings. Judicial transparency means the disclosure of trial activities and related information to the parties concerned and other participants in the proceedings and the public. General Secretary Xi Jinping has creatively developed the concept of openness into transparency, which is significant guidance on judicial openness. Judicial transparency results from judicial openness, and the scope of judicial transparency is broader than that of judicial openness. First of all, judicial transparency emphasizes the openness of the whole process of judicial activities, including judicial proceedings and results. In other words, not only should the judicial process be open to the parties concerned and the public, but the results hereof, including judicial instruments, should be made public. Secondly, judicial transparency requires the disclosure of both judicial activities and all kinds of information related hereto. According to the modern rule of law principles, a public trial is the fundamental requirement of judicial activities. Except for matters involving state secrets, trade secrets, and personal privacy, trial activities and results (i.e., judgments) should be made public and subject to social supervision. However, judicial activities involved in so-called judicial openness or public trials are limited. In addition to trial activities, judicial organs should also make public all kinds of information related hereto. Promoting judicial transparency is aimed at the accessibility of information on various activities of judicial organs, including trial activities. It is stressed that a judicial organ should make public its activities to a maximum extent, not only judicial proceedings and results, but all kinds of information related to judicial activities, to achieve the utmost judicial transparency and eliminate judicial corruption. Finally, judicial transparency emphasizes the parties' access to all relevant information and other official activities of a judicial organ, such as the court's

Y. Wang and H. Tian, *Judicial Transparency in China*,
https://doi.org/10.1007/978-981-19-7822-7_3

data and its spending on official overseas visits, official vehicles, and official hospitality. Under judicial transparency, judicial activities and the justice achieved should be practical, timely, and perceivable.

2 Practical Significance of Judicial Transparency

Promoting judicial transparency is of great practical significance for furthering the reform of the judicial system and implementing the framework of promoting the rule of law.

2.1 *Effective Implementation of the Policy of Justice for the People*

From the perspective of delivering justice to people, judicial transparency is mainly reflected in facilitating the public's use of judicial resources, resolving social disputes, systematically publicizing the legal system and judicial system, and thus, enhancing the public's awareness of the law. A judicial organ's accurate, comprehensive, timely, and adequate disclosure of judicial information, especially information about its work, litigation guide, judicial process, and enforcement, helps the public understand the requirements for participating in judicial activities and their rights and litigation risks, and is conducive to their participation and the protection of their rights. A court's job is to ensure that citizens can find its address, get through to its telephone number, understand judicial documents, and know how to use the judicial process to protect their legitimate rights and interests. Otherwise, how can they effectively exercise their right of action? How can they file a lawsuit properly without being told about basic knowledge of litigation by the court? These are the fundamental requirements of justice for the people and where judicial transparency plays its role. Meanwhile, promoting judicial transparency is also crucial to the education campaign to increase the public's awareness of the law. The enhancement of judicial transparency helps the public receive vivid education on the legal system, learn about their rights and obligations, enhance their legal awareness, and improve their consciousness of abiding by the law and maintaining the legal system.

2.2 *Protection of the Public's Right to Know and Legitimate Rights and Interests of the Parties*

The right to know means the freedom to seek, receive and impart information and the right to be informed officially or unofficially. As a fundamental human right, the right to know was first enshrined in the Basic Law for the Federal Republic of Germany, put into effect in 1949. In accordance with Article 5 of the Basic Law, every person shall have the right to freely express and disseminate his opinions in speech, writing, and pictures and to inform himself without hindrance from generally accessible sources. The right to know can also be found in the constitutions of the Nordic countries. For example, the right of citizens to obtain official documents is specified in "On the Public Nature of Official Documents", Chapter 2 of the Freedom of the Press Act, one of the four fundamental laws that constitute the Constitution of Sweden.

Although many countries worldwide failed to specify this right in their constitutions, people generally believe that the basis for the existence of the right to know can be found in relevant provisions of the constitutions. From the perspective of popular sovereignty, citizens of a country shall be entitled to the right to know. In other words, popular sovereignty calls for a guarantee of the right to know. Modern countries recognize popular sovereignty and have created various systems to ensure citizens' effective participation in democratic decision-making. Citizens, who have their elected representatives govern the state, have the right to be fully informed of all matters relating to the administration of the state. If not, they will be unable to supervise the administrative activities of state organs and public servants or express their opinions on state affairs to affect the activities thereof, which will render the concept of popular sovereignty groundless. The right to know is a prerequisite for popular sovereignty. When citizens have adequate access to relevant information, they effectively participate in democratic politics.

Over an extended period, when it comes to the right to know, people always focus on obtaining and disseminating government information and then establishing and implementing the government information disclosure system. The government information disclosure system is essential to realizing and protecting the right to know. However, this system is generally applied to government organs. In other words, it is used to regulate how to disclose the information held by executive authorities. In effect, the objects of the right to know also include state organs, such as the legislative and judicial branches. Judicial transparency or judicial openness is undoubtedly a crucial mechanism to ensure the public's right to know about the activities of judicial organs. It is of great significance for it is about the public's right to know, the protection of which is to supervise judicial justice and maintain social justice.

To be more specific, promoting judicial transparency and ensuring the public's right to know about information related to judicial activities help the parties safeguard their legitimate rights and interests and enhance their acceptance of litigation results. Judicial transparency includes disclosing a judicial organ's work, litigation guide, judicial process, and enforcement so that the parties concerned can fully understand their right to sue, how to exercise it, and the legal risks they may face when exercising such a right. Moreover, it also helps them gain knowledge of the content and process of judicial activities and then correctly and timely exercise their rights and safeguard their legitimate rights and interests with lawful means. In addition, promoting judicial transparency is conducive to meeting the needs of other persons for information on judicial activities and facilitating their participation in and supervision over judicial activities. Judicial openness can fully protect the parties' and the public's right to know and ensure a people's court's independent exercise of judicial power by making public the details of a case and its trial proceedings.

With the rapid economic and social development and the continuous improvement of the public awareness of democracy and the rule of law, people have more requirements and expectations when it comes to judicial activities. The public demands fair judicial results and looks forward to the openness and transparency of the judicial process and the right to participate in and supervise judicial activities.

2.3 Prevention of Judicial Corruption and Realization of Judicial Justice

Justice must not only be done, but must also be seen to be done. The judiciary is the last line of defense for maintaining social justice. Upholding judicial justice and eradicating judicial corruption are essential to social stability and the credibility of public authorities. One of the most critical ways to eradicate judicial corruption is to promote judicial transparency and demonstrate judicial procedures and atmosphere to the parties concerned and even the public. Promoting transparency of the judicial process and results will make public the exercise of discretion by judges and various factors that have been taken into consideration so that the public can exercise the supervision right, and the judges will be urged to act cautiously. Judicial transparency will sharply increase the costs of judicial corruption and the risks of being discovered. Meanwhile, judicial organs and their personnel will be very cautious in their words and deeds to ensure that every activity is within the framework of the law and under the statutory procedures. Any judicial activity must be carried out in strict accordance with the law and based on facts. Any clue to judicial corruption, such as cases involving favors, personal relationships, and money, can be discovered by the public due to judicial transparency. Anyone who has abused judicial power will find no escape.

2.4 Enhancement of Judicial Credibility and Maintenance of Judicial Authority

Judicial credibility refers to the influence of integrity and impartiality established by judges in the long-term judicial activities through strict legal procedures and correct application of laws, which is the public's trust in and expectation of the judicial activities of courts. Maintaining judicial credibility and authority is the starting point and objective of the judicial activities of courts. Judicial credibility is the court's vitality, without which, the court will lose the legality of its existence, and the credibility and authority of the state will also directly be harmed. The only way to advance judicial credibility is to achieve judicial justice. Only by ensuring judicial justice can the parties concerned and the public be convinced that judicial organs handle cases according to the law through trustworthy due process. When recognized by the public, justice is credible and authoritative. It must be seen and felt. By providing the public with the judicial process and results in as much detail as possible, judicial transparency dispels the public's distrust of the judiciary, enhances judicial credibility, maintains judicial authority, and finally realizes judicial justice in a way that can be seen.

2.5 Improvement of Judicial Personnel's Competence and Judicial Proficiency

Judicial competence and judicial proficiency is the fundamental indicator to measure the ability of a judicial organ to handle cases and achieve judicial justice. With a high level of judicial proficiency, a judicial organ can accurately ascertain facts, correctly apply laws, and arrive at a proper conclusion conforming to legal provisions and objective facts. Over the years, Chinese judicial organs have been faced with questions about a low level of judicial proficiency. The Several Opinions of the Supreme People's Court on Enhancing Judicial Capacity and Improving Judicial Proficiency (Fa Fa [2005] No. 4) stated the low-level judicial performance as follows: the relatively low level of proper application of laws, immature dispute resolution skills, lack of a sound capacity for judging cases fairly, relatively weak stance on rendering impartial rulings, unfair adjudication and low efficiency in some cases that the people complain much about having yet to be solved, and repeatedly handling cases by a small number of judges based on their favor, personal relationships and money. Besides, low judicial proficiency can also be found in the judgments characterized by stereotyped writing. In some judgments, there is no reasoning or the reasoning is a mere formality; there are no inferences about fact-finding and law application; the judges have blindly copied the opinions of the parties concerned and the laws and regulations. Some judgments are full of wrongly written characters, ill-formed sentences, and confusing logic. Judicial transparency contributes to the improvement of judges' judicial proficiency. Take judicial process information disclosure as an example. Suppose the court is required to disclose the schedule of a court session, the judicial process, and a judgment. In that case, it will attach more importance to the legality of court proceedings, the sufficiency of the evidence, and the standardization of a written judgment. Judicial transparency renders judges' behaviors subject to the public's supervision, helps the judges be more cautious about the litigation participants' opinions, fact-finding, and law application, and effectively encourages them to promote judicial justice by drawing proper conclusions conforming to legal provisions and objective facts.

In conclusion, under judicial transparency, any judicial activity of a court will be subject to the supervision of the public, the parties concerned, and other participants in the judicial process anytime or anywhere whatsoever. Any conduct of a judicial organ and its judicial personnel and corresponding outcomes hereof are open to public comments. Any fact-finding and law application contrary to common sense may be questioned most severely and directly by the public. Therefore, judicial organs and their personnel must enhance their sense of responsibility and improve the level and quality of case handling. They must ensure to the maximum extent that any judicial activity has been conducted as per legal procedures, facts of the case, and legal provisions and that any decision can stand up to the public's scrutiny. In this way, the problem of judicial impartiality can be easily solved.

3 Judicial Openness in Controversy Firmly Moving Forward

Judicial openness is generally recognized. The legitimacy of judicial openness has been repeatedly proved in the course of its development and confirmed by fundamental legal documents of various countries and regions. In practice, conflicts arising from judicial openness are mainly about how far judicial openness should go and the competition and frictions between judicial openness and other pursuits of judicial value.

3.1 Scope of Judicial Openness

As the precursor to judicial openness, public trial refers to trying criminal cases in public in ancient and modern times. Cases under international covenants on human rights are also generally limited to criminal ones. The reason is easy to understand because criminal trials deal with fundamental human rights such as the right to property, liberty, politics, and even to life, which must be open to public supervision. In terms of domestic laws and judicial practice, both civil law countries and common law countries apply the public trial principle to civil proceedings.[1] This principle has branched out to administrative cases with the emergence of administrative proceedings. China's judicial openness under transparent judicial power is becoming more comprehensive and radical.

The expanding scope of judicial openness always triggers arguments about its extent and even boundaries. According to different objects, judicial openness can be divided into openness to the parties concerned and openness to the public. The legitimacy of judicial openness to the parties concerned is undisputed, so disclosure of judicial process information has received unanimous support. Judicial openness to the public has been challenged more. The value pursuit and theoretical basis of contemporary judicial openness reveal that the problems emerging in disclosing

[1] Bi et al. [1].

judicial activities to the public have nothing to do with right and wrong. In Hegel's opinion, "(But) a primary characteristic of a right is that the citizens should have confidence in it, and it is this aspect which requires that justice should be dispensed in public. The right of publicity is based on the fact that the end of the court is right, which as a universal should also come before the universal, and also on the fact that the citizens are thereby convinced that justice [Recht] is actually being done."[2] From the perspective of transparent power, there is no "invisible" corner in judicial activities hidden under popular sovereignty. We can solve specific problems such as judges' free evaluation of evidence and the right of privacy by changing means. They are not about the theoretical basis for judicial openness.

3.2 *Live Broadcasting of Court Hearings, Judges' Free Evaluation of Evidence, and Formation of a Judgment*

Hegel mentioned the reasons for judges' objection to judicial openness, "Straightforward common sense sees it as right and proper that the administration of justice should be public. A major obstacle to this has always been the high station of those with powers of jurisdiction, since they are reluctant to appear before the general public, seeing themselves as guardians of a right to which the laity should not have access."[3] Disclosure of court hearings is the concept closest to public trials supported by historical traditions. With the emergence of live broadcasting of court hearings, disputes over the disclosure of court hearings have returned to the public view.

The live broadcasting platform taking full advantage of information technology has changed the way of disclosing court hearings from the previous participation by a limited number of people in person to the remote disclosure to hundreds of millions of online users. There are many benefits delivered from such disclosure online. For instance, judges behave more properly; the parties concerned and other participants in proceedings are more cautious in their words and deeds; the judiciary's function of increasing the public's awareness of the law will be enhanced. However, at the same time, such an entirely new disclosure means may have an enormous impact on the mentality of judges.

The discomfort of working under the "spotlight" will last for some time. Breaking away from the old working mode will also take some time. However, judges' free evaluation of evidence will not be substantially influenced. The live broadcasting of court hearings does not constrain a judge from freely evaluating evidence. Nor does it restrict the parties' exercise of their right of defense. Most likely, it is the discomfort of working under supervision that has resulted in the possible wariness from judges and the parties concerned, rather than the high standard requirements brought by the live broadcasting. No means of disclosing court hearings conflicts with the right to protect the parties from "surprise attack of a judgment" and fully

---

[2] Hegel [2].

[3] Hegel [2].

express their opinions. The principle of judicial openness is precisely consistent with protecting the rights above. "Courts should not apply the law in secret but publicly state their views. If some viewpoints of law other than that held by the parties are considered in deciding a case, they should be given more opportunities to expound their views."[4]

The live broadcasting of court hearings does not go beyond case trial and judgment pronouncing. The deliberation of the collegial bench is still in confidence, and the process of fully expressing opinions and conducting discussions by the judges is duly protected. Such disclosure does not affect the formation of a judgment. Though both the judgment-making process and the disclosure of minority opinions are particularly worth discussing under the judicial accountability reform, they can be adequately addressed by strengthening the reasoning of judgments within the framework of judicial openness. On June 1, 2018, the Supreme People's Court issued the Guiding Opinions on Strengthening and Standardizing the Analysis and Reasoning in Judgments, which promoted the disclosure of the judgment-making process.

3.3 *Disclosure of Judgments and Potential Negative Effects*

In terms of judgment disclosure, some people still argue that risks and negative impacts will result from the publication of too many documents. For example, the publication of some judgments may trigger public sentiments. The second instance and retrial of a case may be affected by public opinions once the first instance judgment is published. Many judgments published on the website China Judgements Online are overwhelmed by hundreds of millions of documents. They will not attract attention or play the role of supervising the court and pushing it into higher quality case handling. Big data analysis of a sea of judgments may reveal sensitive economic and social development information. All the views above look very doubtful. So far, all public sentiments have been triggered by mistakes in the making of judgments such as spelling errors or problems in fact-finding and law application rather than such disclosure. The opinion that judgments may be overwhelmed by a large number of documents and fail to function is groundless. The people's courts should publish whatever needs disclosing. Public concern is another issue. It has been proved that any judgment of public concern will not be drowned out. The potential disclosure of sensitive information due to data analysis generally does not exist. Not all the disputes arising from economic and social development will enter court proceedings. Not all the cases entering such proceedings will be finally solved with a written judgment. Not all the judgments will be published on the website China Judgements Online. Therefore, although it is an extensive judgment database with written judgments of more than 100 million and a vast judicial database, there is still a long way to go before it becomes a comprehensive database capable of analyzing the core issues in economic and social development.

---

[4] Michael [3].

3.4 *Judicial Openness and Protection of Personal Information and Privacy*

The conflict between the right to know and the right of privacy is particularly pronounced in judicial openness. Despite the exceptions listed in the laws at different levels, it would seem that these provisions no longer meet the public's concern about personal information and privacy as their awareness of the rule of law increases.

The existing exceptions to judicial openness are generally vague, making it hard to balance the rights of all parties concerned. It is difficult to accurately determine the connotation and denotation of terms such as "personal privacy" and "trade secrets," which results in insufficient protection. Vague provisions such as "other situations that a people's court considers it inappropriate to publish on the Internet" create "save clauses" for the court's non-disclosure by law and regulations, which severely weakens judicial openness. In addition, the remedies for the infringement of personal information and privacy caused by judicial openness are not specified. Besides applying more precise legal terms and adding more remedy clauses, we can also adopt alternative schemes like removing some personal information.

In addition to the solutions mentioned above, a timely cognitive change in litigation can also help remove obstacles that hinder the development of judicial openness. For the parties in a civil action, litigation is just one of the formal ways of resolving disputes. Participation in court proceedings has nothing to do with morality, and hence society should not make negative comments about them. In conclusion, there is still room for acquainting citizens with basic knowledge of the law and cultivating their spirit of the rule of law.

Except for cases involving state secrets, personal privacy, and trade secrets, cases brought into litigation shall be heard in public and allowed to be observed. According to the existing regulations, live broadcasting and recording of court proceedings should also be permitted. Since court hearings can be made public, what else about the case cannot be made public? A judgment contains less information than a court hearing does. It is untenable to withhold information with excuses like personal privacy. In particular, it should be noted that even for a case not heard in public, the judgment must be pronounced in public. So why not publish the written judgment?

3.5 *Disputes Over Judicial Openness Caused by Court Informatization*

The argument that the application of judicial information technology may lead to so-called judicial "overexposure" identifies a wrong target. The theoretical foundation of justice itself determines the breadth and depth of judicial openness. Information technology only provides judicial openness with the means to transform ideas into reality but has never interfered with the determination of its boundaries. The limits of judicial openness have been defined in the context of judicial transparency. The informatization construction of Chinese courts is in a leading position, and the breadth and depth of China's judicial openness have also surpassed that of many countries. When various doubts arise, such as "why to disclose the information that has not been disclosed abroad," it is out of question that a confident response can be made about China's judicial openness, as we did in the informatization of Chinese courts. China's level of judicial openness is leading the world, and China has offered a Chinese approach to other countries.

The "actual problem" that needs solving in combination with judicial openness during informatization construction is information security. The development and application of big data allow fragmented information to be reorganized instantaneously. Personal privacy, economic and social trends, and the data relied on by the Party and governments in decision making may be improperly utilized through the information disclosed. It is crucial for intelligent court builders to figure out how to ensure information security and proper application of judicial information and seize the opportunity to use big judicial data to assist national governance.

Throughout history, judicial openness is always contrary to judicial traditions and fixed ideas but resolutely insistent on judicial justice. It has "reform" as its core spirit and is bound to be challenged ceaselessly but move forward steadfastly in the controversy.

References

1. Bi Yuqian, e.t. *On Judicial Publicity Under the Framework of Civil Proceedings*. China University of Political Science and Law Press, 2020, pp. 7–8.
2. Hegel, *Elements of the Philosophy of Right*, translated by Fan Yang and Zhang Qitai. The Commercial Press, 2017, pp. 264–265.
3. Edited by Michael Stirner, *Classics in the German Law of Civil Procedure*, translated by Zhao Xiuju. China University of Political Science and Law Press, 2005, p. 376.

Chapter 4
Methodologies for Researching Judicial Transparency

Since 2011, the Institute of Law of the Chinese Academy of Social Sciences has been assessing and researching the judicial openness of people's courts nationwide, an integral part of its research project on the rule of law index. In 2009, the Institute's research team on the rule of law started the assessment of government transparency, i.e., assessing the implementation of the government information disclosure system. The team developed an indicator system for the government transparency index assessment and established a set of assessment principles and methods. The core of the government transparency assessment lies in setting assessment indicators according to law and upholding objective assessment.[1] Since 2011, the assessment of the rule of law index has been extended to the judicial openness of people's courts. The index assessment has been conducted year after year with the Supreme People's Court, 31 high people's courts, and 49 intermediate people's courts in larger cities[2] as assessed objects.[3] The assessment mainly focuses on the core work of trial and enforcement, i.e., assessing the disclosure of trial affairs, case filings, court trials, judgments, and enforcement information.

Commissioned by the High People's Court of Zhejiang Province, the Institute's research team carried out the judicial transparency index assessment of the courts at all three levels within the province for three consecutive years from 2013 to 2015, which was an extension of the original judicial transparency index assessment. The original judicial transparency index assessment mainly relies on court portals to observe the judicial openness of relevant courts from the outside. Comparatively, the judicial transparency index assessment of Zhejiang courts was a combination of internal and external assessment with an academic institution, for the first time, closely observing the work of the courts from the inside. This assessment still covered

[1] The interpretations on the assessment principles and methods can be found in Lv and Tian [1].

[2] The 49 cities with local legislative power prior to the amendment to Legislation Law of the People's Republic of China.

[3] Previous annual assessment reports can be found in the *Blue Book of Rule of Law: Annual Report on Rule of Law in China* published by Social Sciences Academic Press (China) the following year.

Y. Wang and H. Tian, *Judicial Transparency in China*,
https://doi.org/10.1007/978-981-19-7822-7_4

the core activities of the courts, such as disclosure of case filings, court trials, judgments, and enforcement information. However, in addition to observing the portals of the assessed courts for information disclosure, the team members entered the case handling systems of Zhejiang courts. They retrieved a large number of case files and trial videos to retrace the disclosure of relevant information to the parties and society during the process of case handling, which was a milestone in the history of China's judicial system. Moreover, in addition to the judicial openness of the people's courts, the assessment involved the standardization of case handling.[4] Thereafter, the research team was commissioned to assess the courts in Beijing Municipality and Guangxi Zhuang Autonomous Region and the Primary People's Court of Yubei District of Chongqing Municipality.

Additionally, commissioned by the Supreme People's Court, from 2017 to 2018, the research team carried out a third-party assessment of the disclosure of judicial process information and judgments by some people's courts in the 31 provinces (autonomous regions and municipalities directly under the Central Government) and Xinjiang Production and Construction Corps. Regarding the disclosure of judicial process information, the team selected 128 courts to assess the disclosure of litigation guides and other information to the public and judicial process information to the parties involved. In terms of the disclosure of judgments, the team selected 160 courts to mainly assess within a given period the uploading rate of judgments, timely online announcement, disclosure of information items on the judgments not published online, and standardization of approval for the judgments not published online.

Since 2019, the judicial transparency index assessment has primarily been following the previous assessment items, and the assessment indicators have been improved and optimized in accordance with the latest judicial interpretations. The assessment consists of five first-level indicators, including the disclosure of trial affairs, trial information, enforcement information, judicial data, and information on judicial reform, covering 32 s-level indicators. The disclosure of trial affairs involves personnel information, roster information, office withdrawal, court documents, handling of the motions by deputies to people's congresses and the proposals by CPPCC members, and the construction of disclosure platforms. The disclosure of trial information involves litigation guides, judicial process information, court trials, judgments, information on significant cases, commutation cases, parole cases, bankruptcy cases, and judicial proposals. The disclosure of enforcement information involves case inquiry, information on punishing dishonest judgment debtors, enforcement exposure, cases whose enforcement proceedings are temporarily terminated, judicial auctions, and information on enforcement reporting. The disclosure of judicial data involves financial data, work reports, judicial business data, and judicial empirical analysis reports. The disclosure of information on judicial reform involves columns, judicial reform schemes, the progress of significant tasks, the quota system reform, case filings and registration, trial supervision mechanism reform, protection of lawyers' rights and interests, and records of intervention by those who are

[4] See Tian and Lv [2].

not parties to a case. The 2020 Assessment made a proper distinction between high people's courts and intermediate people's courts and between primary people's courts and specialized courts (see Table 1). The disclosure of litigation guides, observation of court trials, commutation cases, parole cases, bankruptcy cases, and information on punishing dishonest judgment debtors does not apply to the Supreme People's Court. For this reason, regarding the disclosure of various kinds of information in 2019, the following analysis is based on figures from the 93 courts, with the Supreme People's Court excluded. In addition, the weight value of some indicators in Table 1 is 0. They are used only for observation in the past two years of assessment.

The assessed objects were also adjusted. The following 94 courts were selected in the 2019 Assessment: (1) the Supreme People's Court; (2) high people's courts of all provinces, autonomous regions, and municipalities directly under the Central Government, and the Production and Construction Corps Branch of the High People's Court of Xinjiang Uygur Autonomous Region (32 courts altogether); (3) intermediate people's courts in larger cities (49 courts altogether); (4) three intellectual property courts in Beijing, Shanghai, and Guangzhou; (5) three internet courts in Beijing, Hangzhou, and Guangzhou; (6) the Primary People's Court of Guangdong Pilot Free Trade Zone (Nansha), the Primary People's Court of Qianhai Cooperation Zone of Shenzhen City, the Primary People's Court of Zhuhai Hengqin New Area, the Primary People's Court of Sichuan Pilot Free Trade Zone, and the Primary People's Court of Chongqing Pilot Free Trade Zone (5 courts altogether); and (7) Shanghai Financial Court. The Production and Construction Corps Branch of the High People's Court of Xinjiang Uygur Autonomous Region and 12 specialized courts were added to the 2019 Assessment for the first time.

Some primary people's courts have been included in the assessed objects since 2020 to strengthen judicial openness in primary people's courts. Assisted by the Adjudication Management Office of the Supreme People's Court, the project team obtained the number of cases accepted by the primary people's courts in 31 provinces (autonomous regions and municipalities directly under the Central Government) in 2019. The team selected four courts with more cases accepted in each of the 31 provinces (autonomous regions and municipalities directly under the Central Government). Also, there was at least one people's court of the county, one people's court of the city, and one people's court of the district among the four courts. Among the primary people's courts assessed in 2020, 25 of them are located in the top 100 counties of China or the top 100 districts of China. During the actual assessment process, the team found that most of the websites of the primary people's courts in Shanghai had been closed, such as the Primary People's Court of Jing'an District, the Primary People's Court of Minhang District, and the Primary People's Court of Hongkou District. Besides, the portals of the Primary People's Court of Xinshi District of Urumqi City and the Primary People's Court of Sayibak District of Urumqi City could not be reached. Consequently, the above courts were not considered in the final ranking but remained assessed objects. The Supreme People's Court has the main task of guiding lower courts on how to conduct judicial openness. It does not deal with a lot of specific businesses despite its established four disclosure platforms

Table 1 The indicator system for 2020 judicial transparency index assessment

First-level indicators	Second-level indicators (high and intermediate people's courts)		Third-level indicators (high and intermediate people's courts)	Second-level indicators (specialized courts and primary people's courts)		Third-level indicators (specialized courts and primary people's courts)	
Disclosure of information on trial affairs (20%)	Information on personnel	(40%)	Information on leaders (40%)	Information on personnel	(45%)	Information on leaders	(40%)
			Information on judges (35%)			Information on judges	(35%)
			Information on enforcement personnel (15%)			Information on enforcement personnel	(15%)
			Information on ancillary judicial personnel (10%)			Information on ancillary judicial personnel	(10%)
	Information on rosters	(20%)	Mediation roster (50%)	Information on rosters	(15%)	Mediation roster	(50%)
			Institution roster (50%)			Institution roster	(50%)
	Office withdrawal	(10%)	Office withdrawal roster (100%)	Office withdrawal	(0)	Office withdrawal roster	
	Disclosure of court documents (10%)			Disclosure of court documents (10%)			
	Results of handling the motions by deputies to people's congresses and the proposals by CPPCC members **(0)**		Columns	Results of handling the motions by deputies to people's congresses and the proposals by CPPCC members (0)		Columns	
			Results of handling the motions by deputies to people's congresses and the proposals by CPPCC members (abridged edition and full text)			Results of handling the motions by deputies to people's congresses and the proposals by CPPCC members (abridged edition and full text)	

(continued)

Table 1 (continued)

First-level indicators	Second-level indicators (high and intermediate people's courts)	Third-level indicators (high and intermediate people's courts)	Second-level indicators (specialized courts and primary people's courts)	Third-level indicators (specialized courts and primary people's courts)
	Construction of disclosure platforms (20%)	Portals (70%)	Construction of disclosure platforms (30%)	Portals (70%)
		Media platforms (30%)		Media platforms (30%)

First-level indicators	Second-level indicators (high and intermediate people's courts)	Third-level indicators (high and intermediate people's courts)		Second-level indicators (specialized courts and primary people's courts)	Third-level indicators (specialized courts and primary people's courts)	
Disclosure of trial information (30%)	Litigation guides (20%)	Convenience	(10%)	Litigation guides (30%)	Convenience	(10%)
		Integrity	(70%)		Integrity	(70%)
		Understandability	(20%)		Understandability	(20%)
	Disclosure of judicial process information (15%)	Configuration of links to China Judicial Process Information Online (50%)		Disclosure of judicial process information (20%)	Configuration of links to China Judicial Process Information Online (50%)	
		The entry to the platform for inquiring about the local court process (50%)			The entry to the platform for inquiring about the local court process (50%)	
	Disclosure of court trials (20%)	Observation of court trials (60%)		Disclosure of court trials (20%)	Observation of court trials (0)	
		Disclosure of court trials (40%)			Disclosure of court trials (100%)	
	Disclosure of judgments (20%)	Links to China judgements Online (40%)		Disclosure of judgments (20%)	Links to China judgements Online (100%)	
		Information disclosed on China judgements online by the court (0)			Information disclosed on China judgements online by the court (0)	
		Information items on judgments unpublished online (60%)			Information items on judgments unpublished online (0)	
	Disclosure of information on major cases (10%)	Information on major cases tried by the court	(100%)	Disclosure of information on major cases (10%)	Information on major cases tried by the court (100%)	

(continued)

Table 1 (continued)

First-level indicators	Second-level indicators (high and intermediate people's courts)	Third-level indicators (high and intermediate people's courts)		Second-level indicators (specialized courts and primary people's courts)	Third-level indicators (specialized courts and primary people's courts)
	Disclosure of information on commutation and parole cases (15%)	Publication of case filings	(25%)	Disclosure of information on commutation and parole cases (0)	Publication of case filings
		Announcement of court sessions	(25%)		Announcement of court sessions
		Disclosure of judgments	(25%)		Disclosure of judgments
		Disclosure of results	(25%)		Disclosure of results
	Disclosure of information on bankruptcy cases (0)	Declaration of bankruptcy		Disclosure of information on bankruptcy cases (0)	Declaration of bankruptcy
		Statistics of bankruptcy cases			Statistics of bankruptcy cases
	Disclosure of judicial proposals (0)	Columns		Disclosure of judicial proposals (0)	Columns
		Information on judicial proposals			Information on judicial proposals
		Contents of judicial proposals			Contents of judicial proposals

First-level indicators	Second-level indicators (high and intermediate people's courts)	Third-level indicators (high and intermediate people's courts)	Second-level indicators (specialized courts and primary people's courts)		Third-level indicators (specialized courts and primary people's courts)
Disclosure of enforcement information (20%)	Case inquiries (10%)	Links to the platform for inquiring about enforcement cases (100%)	Case inquiries (20%)		Links to the platform for inquiring about enforcement cases (100%)
	Disclosure of information on punishing dishonest judgment debtors (25%)	Fine (35%)	Disclosure of information on punishing dishonest judgment debtors	(0)	Fine
		Detention (35%)			Detention
		Restricted departure from the country (30%)			Restricted departure from the country

(continued)

Table 1 (continued)

First-level indicators	Second-level indicators (high and intermediate people's courts)	Third-level indicators (high and intermediate people's courts)	Second-level indicators (specialized courts and primary people's courts)		Third-level indicators (specialized courts and primary people's courts)
		Combating the crime of refusing to pay the judgment made by a people's court (0)			Combating the crime of refusing to pay the judgment made by a people's court
	Enforcement exposure (25%)	Dishonest judgment debtors (100%)	Enforcement exposure	(80%)	Dishonest judgment debtors (100%)
		Dishonest acts by special dishonest judgment debtors (0)			Dishonest acts by special dishonest judgment debtors (0)
	Disclosure of information on cases with the ongoing enforcement proceedings terminated (25%)	Lists of cases with the ongoing enforcement proceedings terminated (40%)	Cases with the ongoing enforcement proceedings terminated	(0)	Lists of cases with the ongoing enforcement proceedings terminated
		Rulings on cases with the ongoing enforcement proceedings terminated (60%)			Rulings on cases with the ongoing enforcement proceedings terminated
	Judicial auctions (0)	Notice of auction	Judicial auctions	(0)	Notice of auction
		Links to auction websites			Links to auction websites
	Enforcement reporting (15%)	Reporting channels (40%)	Enforcement reporting	(0)	Reporting channels
		Reward-offering announcements (60%)			Reward-offering announcements

(continued)

and a lot of disclosed information. Therefore, only deemed an assessed object, the Supreme People's Court has never been considered in the ranking since 2020.

In the light of the above standard, the following courts were assessed in the 2020 Assessment: (1) high people's courts of all provinces, autonomous regions, and municipalities directly under the Central Government, and the Production and Construction Corps Branch of the High People's Court of Xinjiang Uygur Autonomous Region (32 courts altogether); (2) intermediate people's courts in larger cities (49 courts altogether); (3) three intellectual property courts in Beijing, Shanghai, and Guangzhou; (4) three internet courts in Beijing, Hangzhou, and

Table 1 (continued)

First-level indicators	Second-level indicators (high and intermediate people's courts)	Third-level indicators (high and intermediate people's courts)		Second-level indicators (specialized courts and primary people's courts)	Third-level indicators (specialized courts and primary people's courts)	
Disclosure of judicial data (15%)	Financial data (30%)	Budget and final accounting of the court	(60%)	Financial data (50%)	Budget and final accounting of the court (60%)	
		Spending on official overseas visits, official vehicles and official hospitality	(40%)		Spending on official overseas visits, official vehicles and official hospitality (40%)	
		Data on money and goods involved in the case (0)			Data on money and goods involved in the case	(0)
		Charge for and refund of litigation costs (0)			Charge for and refund of litigation costs	(0)
	Work reports (30%)	Work reports	(60%)	Work reports (50%)	Work reports (100%)	
		Judicial white papers	(40%)		Judicial white papers (0)	
	Judicial business data (20%)	Judicial statistics (60%)		Judicial business data (0)	Judicial statistics	
		Dynamic data on case filing and closing (40%)			Dynamic data on case filing and closing	
	Empirical judicial analysis reports (20%)	Judicial big data analysis reports (50%)		Empirical judicial analysis reports (0)	Judicial big data analysis reports	

(continued)

Guangzhou; (5) the Primary People's Court of Guangdong Pilot Free Trade Zone (Nansha), the Primary People's Court of Qianhai Cooperation Zone of Shenzhen City, the Primary People's Court of Zhuhai Hengqin New Area, the Primary People's Court of Sichuan Pilot Free Trade Zone, and the Primary People's Court of Chongqing Pilot Free Trade Zone (5 courts altogether); (6) Shanghai Financial Court; and (7) 124 primary people's courts (with 119 of them considered in the index ranking).

Table 1 (continued)

First-level indicators	Second-level indicators (high and intermediate people's courts)	Third-level indicators (high and intermediate people's courts)	Second-level indicators (specialized courts and primary people's courts)	Third-level indicators (specialized courts and primary people's courts)
		Judicial research analysis reports (50%)		Judicial research analysis reports
First-level indicators	Second-level indicators (high and intermediate people's courts)	Third-level indicators (high and intermediate people's courts)	Second-level indicators (specialized courts and primary people's courts)	Third-level indicators (specialized courts and primary people's courts)
Disclosure of information on judicial reform (15%)	Columns (10%)		Columns (40%)	
	Judicial reform plans (30%)	The overall plan for judicial reform (100%)	Judicial reform plans (0)	The overall plan for judicial reform
		Plans for recruiting judges into the prescribed proportion (0)		Plans for recruiting judges into the prescribed proportion
		Plans for removing judges from the prescribed proportion (0)		Plans for removing judges from the prescribed proportion
		Vocational protection plans (0)		Vocational protection plans
	Progress of major reform tasks (30%)	Progress of reform tasks (100%)	Progress of major reform tasks (50%)	Progress of reform tasks (100%)
	Judge quota reform (0)	Cases handled by judges recruited under the quota system	Judge quota reform (0)	Cases handled by judges recruited under the quota system
		Cases handled by presidents and chief justices		Cases handled by presidents and chief justices
	Case-filing registration (30%)	Systems for supporting case filing (50%)	Case-filing registration (10%)	Systems for supporting case filing (50%)

(continued)

Regarding assessment methods, the team collected the information on judicial openness mainly from the judicial transparency platforms of the assessed objects, including their portals, judicial transparency websites, litigation service websites, China Judicial Process Information Online, and their media platforms such as WeChat and Weibo. The data collection period for the 2019 Assessment was from October

Table 1 (continued)

First-level indicators	Second-level indicators (high and intermediate people's courts)	Third-level indicators (high and intermediate people's courts)	Second-level indicators (specialized courts and primary people's courts)	Third-level indicators (specialized courts and primary people's courts)
		Dynamic data on case filing (50%)		Dynamic data on case filing (50%)
	Reform of the novel trial supervision mechanism (0)	Lists of powers and responsibilities	Reform of the novel trial supervision mechanism (0)	Lists of powers and responsibilities
		Regulations for supporting powers of trial administration and supervision		Regulations for supporting powers of trial administration and supervision
	Protection of lawyers' rights and interests (0)	Implementation mechanisms	Protection of lawyers' rights and interests (0)	Implementation mechanisms
		Feedback channels		Feedback channels
	Records of intervention by non-parties (0)		Records of intervention by non-parties (0)	

8th to December 31st, 2019. Even in the mobile Internet era, portals are still the chief platforms for judicial openness. Therefore, the team collected all kinds of information preferentially from the portal, judicial transparency platform, and litigation service website of each assessed object; for the first time, the team compared the information on those platforms above with that on China Judicial Process Information Online. Given the increasing significance of media platforms such as WeChat and Weibo, the team assessed their settings for the first time in 2020.

The data collection period for the 2020 Assessment was from July 22nd to December 31st, 2020. The project team obtained the data on the judgments from all the 218 courts with the help of the Adjudication Management Office of the Supreme People's Court when assessing judgment disclosure, which included information on the judgments published online from January 1st to September 30th, 2020 (containing case number, case type, judgment number, and judgment type), information on the judgments unpublished online (containing case number, case type, judgment number, judgment type, and reasons for not being published online), the time of making the judgments, and the time when they were published online. According to the data obtained, the project team analyzed the rate of online disclosure of judgments, the management of the unpublished judgments, and the time when they were published online.

The assessment indicators remained unchanged in 2019 and 2020, and the objects were adjusted in 2020 with some primary people's courts added, and the Supreme People's Court removed. This book will analyze the progress and problems in current judicial openness, focusing on the results released in the 2019 and 2020 Assessments and comparing the assessment results with those released in previous years.

References

1. Lv, Y., & Tian, H. (2017). *Chinese Government Transparency (2009–2016)*. Social Sciences Academic Press (China), pp. 14–15.
2. Tian, H., & Lv, Y. (2017). *Judicial Openness: From Dimness to Transparency——A Third Party Assessment of Zhejiang Court Judicial Transparency*. China Social Sciences Press.

Chapter 5
The Overall Situation of China's Judicial Transparency

According to the 2019 Assessment of judicial transparency, the top courts on the list are the Intermediate People's Court of Guangzhou City, the Intermediate People's Court of Nanjing City, the Intermediate People's Court of Jilin City, the High People's Court of Jilin Province, the Intermediate People's Court of Changchun City, the Intermediate People's Court of Haikou City, the Intermediate People's Court of Ningbo City, the Intermediate People's Court of Chengdu City, the High People's Court of Shandong Province, and the High People's Court of Zhejiang Province. The top high people's courts include the High People's Court of Jilin Province, the High People's Court of Shandong Province, the High People's Court of Zhejiang Province, the High People's Court of Beijing Municipality, the High People's Court of Guangdong Province, the High People's Court of Guangxi Province, the High People's Court of Jiangsu Province, the High People's Court of Sichuan Province, the High People's Court of Shanghai Municipality, and the High People's Court of Hainan Province (see Table 1). The top intermediate people's courts include the Intermediate People's Court of Guangzhou City, the Intermediate People's Court of Nanjing City, the Intermediate People's Court of Jilin City, the Intermediate People's Court of Changchun City, the Intermediate People's Court of Haikou City, the Intermediate People's Court of Ningbo City, the Intermediate People's Court of Chengdu City, the Intermediate People's Court of Xuzhou City, the Intermediate People's Court of Shenzhen City, and the Intermediate People's Court of Zhuhai City (see Table 2). The top specialized courts are the Primary People's Court of Guangdong Pilot Free Trade Zone (Nansha), Guangzhou Internet Court, The Primary People's Court of Qianhai Cooperation Zone of Shenzhen City of Guangdong Province, the Primary People's Court of Zhuhai Hengqin New Area, and Shanghai Financial Court (see Table 3).

As revealed by the 2020 Assessment of judicial transparency, the top high people's courts include the High People's Court of Jilin Province, the High People's Court of Sichuan Province, the High People's Court of Guangdong Province, the High People's Court of Beijing Municipality, the High People's Court of Zhejiang Province, the High People's Court of Shandong Province, the High People's Court

Y. Wang and H. Tian, *Judicial Transparency in China*,
https://doi.org/10.1007/978-981-19-7822-7_5

Table 1 Results of 2019 judicial transparency index assessment (High People's Courts)

Ranking	Court	Total score	GDP ranking 2018	GDP 2018 (100 million yuan)[1]	A comparison between the GDP ranking and the judicial transparency index ranking[2]	Disclosure of trial affairs (points)	Disclosure of trial information (points)	Disclosure of enforcement information (points)	Disclosure of judicial data (points)	Disclosure of information on judicial reform (points)
1	The High People's Court of Jilin Province	80.9	24	15,074.62	23	73.24	82	77	90	85
2	The High People's Court of Shandong Province	72.16	3	76,469.67	1	88.4	7	36.5	89.5	85

(continued)

[1] The GDP data of all assessed high people's courts, intermediate people's courts, and primary people's courts are the latest figures in 2018 collected from the statistical communiqués on national economic and social development, published on the government websites of the districts where the courts are located.

[2] A "comparison between the GDP ranking and the judicial transparency index ranking" is the difference between the GDP ranking of the assessed object and its judicial transparency index ranking, which is the same as below.

Table 1 (continued)

Ranking	Court	Total score	GDP ranking 2018	GDP 2018 (100 million yuan)	A comparison between the GDP ranking and the judicial transparency index ranking	Disclosure of trial affairs (points)	Disclosure of trial information (points)	Disclosure of enforcement information (points)	Disclosure of judicial data (points)	Disclosure of information on judicial reform (points)
3	The High People's Court of Zhejiang Province	70.73	4	56,197.15	1	70.94	71.5	63.5	84.25	65
4	The High People's Court of Beijing Municipality	67.66	12	30,319.98	8	68.92	63.5	69.5	74.5	65
5	The High People's Court of Guangdong Province	66.89	1	97,277.77	−4	79.94	65.75	68.5	81.5	35
6	The High People's Court of Guangxi Zhuang Autonomous Region	63.69	18	20,352.51	12	66.66	73.1	55.5	80.5	35

(continued)

Table 1 (continued)

Ranking	Court	Total score	GDP ranking 2018	GDP 2018 (100 million yuan)	A comparison between the GDP ranking and the judicial transparency index ranking	Disclosure of trial affairs (points)	Disclosure of trial information (points)	Disclosure of enforcement information (points)	Disclosure of judicial data (points)	Disclosure of information on judicial reform (points)
7	The High People's Court of Jiangsu Province	60.37	2	92,595.4	−5	54.8	62.6	65	72.5	45
8	The High People's Court of Sichuan Province	60.29	6	40,678.13	−2	73.6	52.1	35.5	57.25	95
9	The High People's Court of Shanghai Municipality	59.88	11	32,679.87	2	75.24	54.7	52.5	69.5	50

(continued)

Table 1 (continued)

Ranking	Court	Total score	GDP ranking 2018	GDP 2018 (100 million yuan)	A comparison between the GDP ranking and the judicial transparency index ranking	Disclosure of trial affairs (points)	Disclosure of trial information (points)	Disclosure of enforcement information (points)	Disclosure of judicial data (points)	Disclosure of information on judicial reform (points)
10	The High People's Court of Hainan Province	59.69	29	4832.05	19	47.52	49.7	45.5	79.5	95
11	The High People's Court of Hebei Province	58.51	9	36,010.27	−2	62.34	72.4	65	50.5	25
12	The High People's Court of Liaoning Province	54.79	14	25,315.35	2	55.94	56.5	77	50	25
13	The High People's Court of Xinjiang Uygur Autonomous Region	50.26	26	12,199.08	13	43.4	47.8	47.5	53.25	65

(continued)

Table 1 (continued)

Ranking	Court	Total score	GDP ranking 2018	GDP 2018 (100 million yuan)	A comparison between the GDP ranking and the judicial transparency index ranking	Disclosure of trial affairs (points)	Disclosure of trial information (points)	Disclosure of enforcement information (points)	Disclosure of judicial data (points)	Disclosure of information on judicial reform (points)
14	The High People's Court of Tianjin Municipality	50.25	19	18,809.64	5	57.8	61.8	44.5	40	35
15	The High People's Court of Jiangxi Province	50.08	16	21,984.78	1	66.46	63.3	26	59	25
16	The High People's Court of Fujian Province	48.87	10	35,804.04	−6	52.04	51.9	16	76.25	55
17	The High People's Court of Heilongjiang Province	46.86	23	16,361.62	6	50.96	38.4	77	40	25

(continued)

Table 1 (continued)

Ranking	Court	Total score	GDP ranking 2018	GDP 2018 (100 million yuan)	A comparison between the GDP ranking and the judicial transparency index ranking	Disclosure of trial affairs (points)	Disclosure of trial information (points)	Disclosure of enforcement information (points)	Disclosure of judicial data (points)	Disclosure of information on judicial reform (points)
18	The High People's Court of Anhui Province	46.79	13	30,006.82	−5	71.66	48.2	52.5	40	10
19	The High People's Court of Yunnan Province	46.64	20	17,881.12	1	56.44	64.75	24.5	38.5	35
20	The High People's Court of Inner Mongolia Autonomous Region	46.02	21	17,289.22	1	53.46	46.6	58	40	25
21	The High People's Court of Henan Province	46.02	5	48,055.86	−16	45.4	54.8	24.5	69	35

(continued)

Table 1 (continued)

Ranking	Court	Total score	GDP ranking 2018	GDP 2018 (100 million yuan)	A comparison between the GDP ranking and the judicial transparency index ranking	Disclosure of trial affairs (points)	Disclosure of trial information (points)	Disclosure of enforcement information (points)	Disclosure of judicial data (points)	Disclosure of information on judicial reform (points)
22	The High People's Court of Hubei Province	45.79	7	39,366.55	−15	49.74	53.65	54.5	34	25
23	The High People's Court of Hunan Province	44.94	8	36,425.78	−15	69.96	49.7	20	55.25	25
24	The High People's Court of Chongqing Municipality	44.27	17	20,363.19	−7	69.16	54.3	37	20	25
25	The High People's Court of Guizhou Province	43.45	25	14,806.45	0	45.44	53.8	57	20.5	25

(continued)

Table 1 (continued)

Ranking	Court	Total score	GDP ranking 2018	GDP 2018 (100 million yuan)	A comparison between the GDP ranking and the judicial transparency index ranking	Disclosure of trial affairs (points)	Disclosure of trial information (points)	Disclosure of enforcement information (points)	Disclosure of judicial data (points)	Disclosure of information on judicial reform (points)
26	The High People's Court of Qinghai Province	41	31	2865.23	5	37.4	42.1	49.5	53.25	20
27	The High People's Court of Ningxia Hui Autonomous Region	40.11	30	3705.18	3	36.4	63.6	20	40	25
28	The High People's Court of Xizang Autonomous Region	40.08	32	1477.63	4	54.9	49	57	10	10

(continued)

Table 1 (continued)

Ranking	Court	Total score	GDP ranking 2018	GDP 2018 (100 million yuan)	A comparison between the GDP ranking and the judicial transparency index ranking	Disclosure of trial affairs (points)	Disclosure of trial information (points)	Disclosure of enforcement information (points)	Disclosure of judicial data (points)	Disclosure of information on judicial reform (points)
29	The High People's Court of Shaanxi Province	39.85	15	24,438.32	−14	38.4	49.65	26	60.5	20
30	The High People's Court of Gansu Province	32.61	28	4832.05	−2	56	27.2	10	40	35
31	The High People's Court of Shanxi Province	29.78	22	16,818.11	−9	28.2	37.3	16	40	25

(continued)

Table 1 (continued)

Ranking	Court	Total score	GDP ranking 2018	GDP 2018 (100 million yuan)	A comparison between the GDP ranking and the judicial transparency index ranking	Disclosure of trial affairs (points)	Disclosure of trial information (points)	Disclosure of enforcement information (points)	Disclosure of judicial data (points)	Disclosure of information on judicial reform (points)
32	The Production and Construction Corps Branch of the High People's Court of Xinjiang Uygur Autonomous Region	22.43	27	12,199.08	−5	21.2	34.3	24.5	10	10

Table 2 Results of 2019 judicial transparency index assessment (Intermediate People's Court)

Ranking	Court	Total score	GDP ranking 2018	GDP 2018 (100 million yuan)[3]	A comparison between the GDP ranking and the judicial transparency index ranking	Disclosure of trial affairs (points)	Disclosure of trial information (points)	Disclosure of enforcement information (points)	Disclosure of judicial data (points)	Disclosure of information on judicial reform (points)
1	The Intermediate People's Court of Guangzhou City of Guangdong Province	92.23	2	21,002.44	1	100	94.6	80.5	100	85
2	The Intermediate People's Court of Nanjing City of Jiangsu Province	85.11	7	13,009.17	5	86.5	79.6	85	79.5	100

(continued)

[3] The GDP data of all assessed high people's courts, intermediate people's courts, and primary people's courts are the latest figures in 2018 collected from the statistical communiqués on national economic and social development, published on the government websites of the districts where the courts are located.

Table 2 (continued)

Ranking	Court	Total score	GDP ranking 2018	GDP 2018 (100 million yuan)	A comparison between the GDP ranking and the judicial transparency index ranking	Disclosure of trial affairs (points)	Disclosure of trial information (points)	Disclosure of enforcement information (points)	Disclosure of judicial data (points)	Disclosure of information on judicial reform (points)
3	The Intermediate People's Court of Jilin City of Jilin Province	81.63	39	2210.24	36	86.04	77.15	75.5	89.5	85
4	The Intermediate People's Court of Changchun City of Jilin Province	76.02	22	5635.1	18	83.5	64.45	73	84.25	85
5	The Intermediate People's Court of Haikou City of Hainan Province	75.61	42	1535.55	37	59.7	79.4	63.5	81	100

(continued)

Table 2 (continued)

Ranking	Court	Total score	GDP ranking 2018	GDP 2018 (100 million yuan)	A comparison between the GDP ranking and the judicial transparency index ranking	Disclosure of trial affairs (points)	Disclosure of trial information (points)	Disclosure of enforcement information (points)	Disclosure of judicial data (points)	Disclosure of information on judicial reform (points)
6	The Intermediate People's Court of Ningbo City of Zhejiang Province	74.99	9	11,193.14	3	87.6	77.15	85	60.5	55
7	The Intermediate People's Court of Chengdu City of Sichuan Province	72.85	4	15,698.94	−3	82.4	69.6	64	66.25	85

(continued)

Table 2 (continued)

Ranking	Court	Total score	GDP ranking 2018	GDP 2018 (100 million yuan)	A comparison between the GDP ranking and the judicial transparency index ranking	Disclosure of trial affairs (points)	Disclosure of trial information (points)	Disclosure of enforcement information (points)	Disclosure of judicial data (points)	Disclosure of information on judicial reform (points)
8	The Intermediate People's Court of Xuzhou City of Jiangsu Province	69.72	18	6755.23	10	75.4	72.35	64	69.25	65
9	The Intermediate People's Court of Shenzhen City of Guangdong Province	68.51	1	25,266.08	−8	76.84	72.55	26	79.5	95

(continued)

Table 2 (continued)

Ranking	Court	Total score	GDP ranking 2018	GDP 2018 (100 million yuan)	A comparison between the GDP ranking and the judicial transparency index ranking	Disclosure of trial affairs (points)	Disclosure of trial information (points)	Disclosure of enforcement information (points)	Disclosure of judicial data (points)	Disclosure of information on judicial reform (points)
10	The Intermediate People's Court of Zhuhai City of Guangdong Province	62.33	33	3216.78	23	57.96	59.7	68.5	62.5	65
11	The Intermediate People's Court of Zibo City of Shandong Province	57.43	31	3573	20	80.6	56.6	20	70.5	65

(continued)

Table 2 (continued)

Ranking	Court	Total score	GDP ranking 2018	GDP 2018 (100 million yuan)	A comparison between the GDP ranking and the judicial transparency index ranking	Disclosure of trial affairs (points)	Disclosure of trial information (points)	Disclosure of enforcement information (points)	Disclosure of judicial data (points)	Disclosure of information on judicial reform (points)
12	The Intermediate People's Court of Shantou City of Guangdong Province	56.74	38	2503.08	26	83.06	61	45	50.5	35
13	The Intermediate People's Court of Taiyuan City of Shanxi Province	55.92	29	3884.48	16	60.16	61.8	55.5	40	55

(continued)

Table 2 (continued)

Ranking	Court	Total score	GDP ranking 2018	GDP 2018 (100 million yuan)	A comparison between the GDP ranking and the judicial transparency index ranking	Disclosure of trial affairs (points)	Disclosure of trial information (points)	Disclosure of enforcement information (points)	Disclosure of judicial data (points)	Disclosure of information on judicial reform (points)
14	The Intermediate People's Court of Hangzhou City of Zhejiang Province	55.22	6	14,306.72	−8	78.36	41.9	58	82.5	20
15	The Intermediate People's Court of Xiamen City of Fujian Province	54.25	23	5468.61	8	70.36	74.5	32.5	50.5	25

(continued)

Table 2 (continued)

Ranking	Court	Total score	GDP ranking 2018	GDP 2018 (100 million yuan)	A comparison between the GDP ranking and the judicial transparency index ranking	Disclosure of trial affairs (points)	Disclosure of trial information (points)	Disclosure of enforcement information (points)	Disclosure of judicial data (points)	Disclosure of information on judicial reform (points)
16	The Intermediate People's Court of Guiyang City of Guizhou Province	52.7	30	3724.97	14	64.7	48.9	60	67.25	20
17	The Intermediate People's Court of Jinan City of Shandong Province	52.33	16	7745.8	−1	69.4	67.4	34.5	50.5	25

(continued)

Table 2 (continued)

Ranking	Court	Total score	GDP ranking 2018	GDP 2018 (100 million yuan)	A comparison between the GDP ranking and the judicial transparency index ranking	Disclosure of trial affairs (points)	Disclosure of trial information (points)	Disclosure of enforcement information (points)	Disclosure of judicial data (points)	Disclosure of information on judicial reform (points)
18	The Intermediate People's Court of Shenyang City of Liaoning Province	48.91	20	6101.92	2	57.04	52.25	45	60.5	25
19	The Intermediate People's Court of Tangshan City of Hebei Province	48.68	17	6955	−2	62.3	49.9	57.5	40	25

(continued)

Table 2 (continued)

Ranking	Court	Total score	GDP ranking 2018	GDP 2018 (100 million yuan)	A comparison between the GDP ranking and the judicial transparency index ranking	Disclosure of trial affairs (points)	Disclosure of trial information (points)	Disclosure of enforcement information (points)	Disclosure of judicial data (points)	Disclosure of information on judicial reform (points)
20	The Intermediate People's Court of Huainan City of Anhui Province	48.44	45	1197.1	25	60.7	55.5	49.5	40	25
21	The Intermediate People's Court of Urumqi City of Xinjiang Uygur Autonomous Region	48.18	34	3099.77	13	57.7	45.5	22.5	58.25	65

(continued)

Table 2 (continued)

Ranking	Court	Total score	GDP ranking 2018	GDP 2018 (100 million yuan)	A comparison between the GDP ranking and the judicial transparency index ranking	Disclosure of trial affairs (points)	Disclosure of trial information (points)	Disclosure of enforcement information (points)	Disclosure of judicial data (points)	Disclosure of information on judicial reform (points)
22	The Intermediate People's Court of Lanzhou City of Gansu Province	47.43	36	2660.19	14	66.76	51.6	55.5	40	10
23	The Intermediate People's Court of Qiqihar City of Heilongjiang Province	46.66	46	1052.2	23	51.2	53.9	45	40	35

(continued)

Table 2 (continued)

Ranking	Court	Total score	GDP ranking 2018	GDP 2018 (100 million yuan)	A comparison between the GDP ranking and the judicial transparency index ranking	Disclosure of trial affairs (points)	Disclosure of trial information (points)	Disclosure of enforcement information (points)	Disclosure of judicial data (points)	Disclosure of information on judicial reform (points)
24	The Intermediate People's Court of Xining City of Qinghai Province	44.54	43	1286.41	19	46.4	42.9	58.5	46.25	25
25	The Intermediate People's Court of Qingdao City of Shandong Province	44.29	11	10,949.38	−14	37.7	37.2	61	54.25	35

(continued)

Table 2 (continued)

Ranking	Court	Total score	GDP ranking 2018	GDP 2018 (100 million yuan)	A comparison between the GDP ranking and the judicial transparency index ranking	Disclosure of trial affairs (points)	Disclosure of trial information (points)	Disclosure of enforcement information (points)	Disclosure of judicial data (points)	Disclosure of information on judicial reform (points)
26	The Intermediate People's Court of Handan City of Hebei Province	43.94	32	3259.2	6	39.14	61.4	35	46.25	25
27	The Intermediate People's Court of Shijiazhuang City of Hebei Province	43.59	24	5375.1	−3	44.26	45.3	57	40	25

(continued)

Table 2 (continued)

Ranking	Court	Total score	GDP ranking 2018	GDP 2018 (100 million yuan)	A comparison between the GDP ranking and the judicial transparency index ranking	Disclosure of trial affairs (points)	Disclosure of trial information (points)	Disclosure of enforcement information (points)	Disclosure of judicial data (points)	Disclosure of information on judicial reform (points)
28	The Intermediate People's Court of Hefei City of Anhui Province	43.01	13	8605.1	−15	64	51.75	24.5	55.25	10
29	The Intermediate People's Court of Datong City of Shanxi Province	42.97	44	1231.2	15	62.4	33.8	30.5	40	55

(continued)

Table 2 (continued)

Ranking	Court	Total score	GDP ranking 2018	GDP 2018 (100 million yuan)	A comparison between the GDP ranking and the judicial transparency index ranking	Disclosure of trial affairs (points)	Disclosure of trial information (points)	Disclosure of enforcement information (points)	Disclosure of judicial data (points)	Disclosure of information on judicial reform (points)
30	The Intermediate People's Court of Dalian City of Liaoning Province	42.89	19	6500.9	−11	28.76	34.3	63	40	55
31	The Intermediate People's Court of Baotou City of Inner Mongolia Autonomous Region	41.92	35	2951.8	4	55.26	43.05	41	40	25

(continued)

Table 2 (continued)

Ranking	Court	Total score	GDP ranking 2018	GDP 2018 (100 million yuan)	A comparison between the GDP ranking and the judicial transparency index ranking	Disclosure of trial affairs (points)	Disclosure of trial information (points)	Disclosure of enforcement information (points)	Disclosure of judicial data (points)	Disclosure of information on judicial reform (points)
32	The Intermediate People's Court of Suzhou City of Jiangsu Province	41.79	3	18,263.48	−29	40.2	50	45	40	25
33	The Intermediate People's Court of Nanchang City of Jiangxi Province	41.12	25	5274.67	−8	37	58.1	10	55.25	40

(continued)

Table 2 (continued)

Ranking	Court	Total score	GDP ranking 2018	GDP 2018 (100 million yuan)	A comparison between the GDP ranking and the judicial transparency index ranking	Disclosure of trial affairs (points)	Disclosure of trial information (points)	Disclosure of enforcement information (points)	Disclosure of judicial data (points)	Disclosure of information on judicial reform (points)
34	The Intermediate People's Court of Hohhot City of Inner Mongolia Autonomous Region	39.78	37	2601.4	3	40	63.1	20	49	10
35	The Intermediate People's Court of Anshan City of Liaoning Province	36.92	41	1623.9	6	48.54	53.4	14.5	45.25	10

(continued)

Table 2 (continued)

Ranking	Court	Total score	GDP ranking 2018	GDP 2018 (100 million yuan)	A comparison between the GDP ranking and the judicial transparency index ranking	Disclosure of trial affairs (points)	Disclosure of trial information (points)	Disclosure of enforcement information (points)	Disclosure of judicial data (points)	Disclosure of information on judicial reform (points)
36	The Intermediate People's Court of Fuzhou City of Fujian Province	36.88	14	8516.09	−22	25.1	54.7	28.5	40	25
37	The Intermediate People's Court of Changsha City of Hunan Province	36.44	10	11,003.41	−27	43	48.8	51	10	10

(continued)

Table 2 (continued)

Ranking	Court	Total score	GDP ranking 2018	GDP 2018 (100 million yuan)	A comparison between the GDP ranking and the judicial transparency index ranking	Disclosure of trial affairs (points)	Disclosure of trial information (points)	Disclosure of enforcement information (points)	Disclosure of judicial data (points)	Disclosure of information on judicial reform (points)
38	The Intermediate People's Court of Benxi City of Liaoning Province	36.05	48	823.1	10	51.8	34.3	39.5	40	10
39	The Intermediate People's Court of Luoyang City of Henan Province	35.88	27	4613.5	−12	41.84	41.4	10	77.25	10

(continued)

Table 2 (continued)

Ranking	Court	Total score	GDP ranking 2018	GDP 2018 (100 million yuan)	A comparison between the GDP ranking and the judicial transparency index ranking	Disclosure of trial affairs (points)	Disclosure of trial information (points)	Disclosure of enforcement information (points)	Disclosure of judicial data (points)	Disclosure of information on judicial reform (points)
40	The Intermediate People's Court of Nanning City of Guangxi Zhuang Autonomous Region	35.74	28	4026.91	−12	34.2	39	35	58	10
41	The Intermediate People's Court of Zhengzhou City of Henan Province	35.39	12	10,670.1	−29	44.6	41.55	10	40	40

(continued)

Table 2 (continued)

Ranking	Court	Total score	GDP ranking 2018	GDP 2018 (100 million yuan)	A comparison between the GDP ranking and the judicial transparency index ranking	Disclosure of trial affairs (points)	Disclosure of trial information (points)	Disclosure of enforcement information (points)	Disclosure of judicial data (points)	Disclosure of information on judicial reform (points)
42	The Intermediate People's Court of Fushun City of Liaoning Province	34.49	47	1048.8	5	38.2	25.5	58.5	40	10
43	The Intermediate People's Court of Yinchuan City of Ningxia Hui Autonomous Region	33.52	40	1901.48	−3	15.8	53.7	22.5	40	25

(continued)

Table 2 (continued)

Ranking	Court	Total score	GDP ranking 2018	GDP 2018 (100 million yuan)	A comparison between the GDP ranking and the judicial transparency index ranking	Disclosure of trial affairs (points)	Disclosure of trial information (points)	Disclosure of enforcement information (points)	Disclosure of judicial data (points)	Disclosure of information on judicial reform (points)
44	The Intermediate People's Court of Lhasa City of Xizang Autonomous Region	33.07	49	540.78	5	45.24	32.9	14.5	50	25
45	The Intermediate People's Court of Wuxi City of Jiangsu Province	31.59	8	11,438.62	−37	41.2	22	35	40	25

(continued)

Table 2 (continued)

Ranking	Court	Total score	GDP ranking 2018	GDP 2018 (100 million yuan)	A comparison between the GDP ranking and the judicial transparency index ranking	Disclosure of trial affairs (points)	Disclosure of trial information (points)	Disclosure of enforcement information (points)	Disclosure of judicial data (points)	Disclosure of information on judicial reform (points)
46	The Intermediate People's Court of Xi'an City of Shaanxi Province	31.34	15	8499.41	−31	28.8	36.8	20	45.25	25
47	The Intermediate People's Court of Wuhan City of Hubei Province	31.18	5	14,928.72	−42	50	24.75	42.5	10	25
48	The Intermediate People's Court of Kunming City of Yunnan Province	30.54	21	6021	−27	54.26	32.3	35	10	10

(continued)

Table 2 (continued)

Ranking	Court	Total score	GDP ranking 2018	GDP 2018 (100 million yuan)	A comparison between the GDP ranking and the judicial transparency index ranking	Disclosure of trial affairs (points)	Disclosure of trial information (points)	Disclosure of enforcement information (points)	Disclosure of judicial data (points)	Disclosure of information on judicial reform (points)
49	The Intermediate People's Court of Harbin City of Heilongjiang Province	26.25	26	5010.1	−23	20.9	33.9	14.5	40	20

Table 3 Results of 2019 judicial transparency index assessment (Specialized Courts)

Ranking	Court	Total score	Disclosure of trial affairs (points)	Disclosure of trial information (points)	Disclosure of enforcement information (points)	Disclosure of judicial data (points)	Disclosure of information on judicial reform (points)
1	The Primary People's Court of Guangdong Pilot Free Trade Zone (Nansha)	69.47	83.4	70	68	86.25	35
2	Guangzhou Internet Court	67.5	87.6	40.8	74.5	67.25	85
3	The Primary People's Court of Qianhai Cooperation Zone of Shenzhen City	54.43	43.26	58.1	51	71	50
4	The Primary People's Court of Zhuhai Hengqin New Area	47.57	62	51.9	35	59	25
5	Shanghai Financial Court	41.58	59.2	56.8	41	20	10
6	Beijing Internet Court	37.79	33	55.3	10	49	35
7	Guangzhou Intellectual Property Court	36.66	50.02	38.7	10	52	35
8	Shanghai Intellectual Property Court	36.05	45.66	41.9	20	59	10

(continued)

Table 3 (continued)

Ranking	Court	Total score	Disclosure of trial affairs (points)	Disclosure of trial information (points)	Disclosure of enforcement information (points)	Disclosure of judicial data (points)	Disclosure of information on judicial reform (points)
9	The Primary People's Court of Chongqing Pilot Free Trade Zone	34.07	38.5	40.4	45	10	25
10	Hangzhou Internet Court	30.69	50.44	38	16	20	20
11	The Primary People's Court of Sichuan Pilot free Trade Zone	27.15	58.4	34.9	10	10	10
12	Beijing Intellectual Property Court	26.36	53.56	20	10	41	10

of Shanghai Municipality, the High People's Court of Jiangsu Province, the High People's Court of Guangxi Province, and the High People's Court of Hainan Province (see Table 4). The top-ranked intermediate people's courts are the Intermediate People's Court of Guangzhou City, the Intermediate People's Court of Shenzhen City, the Intermediate People's Court of Jilin City, the Intermediate People's Court of Nanjing City, the Intermediate People's Court of Ningbo City, the Intermediate People's Court of Haikou City, the Intermediate People's Court of Chengdu City, the Intermediate People's Court of Changchun City, the Intermediate People's Court of Shantou City, and the Intermediate People's Court of Qingdao City (see Table 5). The top five specialized courts are the Primary People's Court of Guangdong Pilot Free Trade Zone (Nansha), Guangzhou Internet Court, The Primary People's Court of Qianhai Cooperation Zone of Shenzhen City of Guangdong Province, Beijing Internet Court, and the Primary People's Court of Zhuhai Hengqin New Area (see Table 6). The top primary people's courts are the Primary People's Court of Futian District of Shenzhen City, Guangdong Province, the Primary People's Court of Yanji City of Jilin Province, the Primary People's Court of Yuexiu District of Guangzhou City, Guangdong Province, the Primary People's Court of Qian Gorlos Mongolia Autonomous County of Jilin Province, the Primary People's Court of Wujiang

District of Suzhou City, Jiangsu Province, the Primary People's Court of Chengmai County of Hainan Province, the Primary People's Court of Shuyang County of Jiangsu Province, the Primary People's Court of Yuhang District of Hangzhou City, Zhejiang Province, the Primary People's Court of Chaohu City of Anhui Province and the Primary People's Court of Xuanwei City of Yunnan Province (see Table 7).

1 Steady Improvements in Judicial Openness

The 2019 and 2020 assessment results and the comparison with the assessment results over the years show that courts at all levels have improved steadily and made impressive achievements in judicial openness.

1.1 Openness is an Important Means of Furthering Judicial System Reform

In recent years, the Supreme People's Court has continued to take judicial openness as an essential means of furthering judicial reforms and promoting courts' work. In order to promote courts' work in relevant fields, the Supreme People's Court has emphasized the idea of improving judicial openness not only in comprehensive documents about judicial reform but also in various judicial documents regarding specialized domains. As proposed in *the Implementation Opinions on Deepening the Comprehensive Reform Supporting the Judicial Accountability System* in 2020, people's courts should actively use the four major platforms for judicial openness, construct an open, dynamic, transparent, and convenient judicial mechanism, and expand judicial openness to accept supervision voluntarily. Similarly, as stated in *the Provisions of the Supreme People's Court on Several Issues Concerning the Appearance of the Persons in Charge of Administrative Agencies in Court to Respond to Lawsuit*, a people's court may appropriately make public the appearance of the persons in charge of an administrative agency in court to respond to a lawsuit. In addition, according to the Opinions of the Supreme People's Court on Comprehensively Strengthening Judicial Protection of Intellectual Property, people's courts should rely on the four platforms to make trials public and protect the parties' and the public's right to know and participate and their right of supervision. All of these have made judicial openness increasingly significant and indispensable.

Table 4 Results of 2020 judicial transparency index assessment (High People's Courts)

Ranking	Court	GDP ranking	GDP 2019 (100 million yuan)[4]	A comparison between the GDP ranking and the judicial transparency index ranking[5]	Total score	Disclosure of trial affairs (points)	Disclosure of trial information (points)	Disclosure of enforcement information (points)	Disclosure of judicial data (points)	Disclosure of information on judicial reform (points)
1	The High People's Court of Jilin Province	27	11,726.8	26	71.53	77.44	71.8	70.5	51	85
2	The High People's Court of Sichuan Province	6	46,615.82	4	65.06	90	74.6	23.5	78.2	55
3	The High People's Court of Guangdong Province	1	107,671.07	−2	64.86	73.44	54.75	60	90	55

(continued)

4 The GDP data of all assessed high people's courts, intermediate people's courts, and primary people's courts are the latest figures in 2019 collected from the statistical communiqués on national economic and social development, published on the government websites of the districts where the courts are located.

5 The formula is: GDP ranking—judicial transparency index ranking.

Table 4 (continued)

Ranking	Court	GDP ranking	GDP 2019 (100 million yuan)	A comparison between the GDP ranking and the judicial transparency index ranking	Total score	Disclosure of trial affairs (points)	Disclosure of trial information (points)	Disclosure of enforcement information (points)	Disclosure of judicial data (points)	Disclosure of information on judicial reform (points)
4	The High People's Court of Beijing Municipality	12	35,371.3	8	61.81	67.52	55.85	65.5	68	55
5	The High People's Court of Zhejiang Province	4	62,352	−1	61.46	60.32	71.5	70	68	25
6	The High People's Court of Shandong Province	3	71,067.5	−3	61.19	88.4	59.6	34.4	70	55
7	The High People's Court of Shanghai Municipality	10	38,155.32	3	56.12	70.06	56.7	55	54	40

(continued)

Table 4 (continued)

Ranking	Court	GDP ranking	GDP 2019 (100 million yuan)	A comparison between the GDP ranking and the judicial transparency index ranking	Total score	Disclosure of trial affairs (points)	Disclosure of trial information (points)	Disclosure of enforcement information (points)	Disclosure of judicial data (points)	Disclosure of information on judicial reform (points)
8	The High People's Court of Jiangsu Province	2	99,631.52	−6	55.64	48.24	56.8	66	60	45
9	The High People's Court of Guangxi Zhuang Autonomous Region	19	21,237.14	10	52.10	53.86	67.1	25	68	40
10	The High People's Court of Hainan Province	29	5308.94	19	50.18	50.72	47.3	14.5	68	85

(continued)

Table 4 (continued)

Ranking	Court	GDP ranking	GDP 2019 (100 million yuan)	A comparison between the GDP ranking and the judicial transparency index ranking	Total score	Disclosure of trial affairs (points)	Disclosure of trial information (points)	Disclosure of enforcement information (points)	Disclosure of judicial data (points)	Disclosure of information on judicial reform (points)
11	The High People's Court of Hebei Province	13	35,104.5	2	50.04	56.5	53.3	57.5	60	15
12	The High People's Court of Jiangxi Province	16	24,757.5	4	49.61	44.4	64.2	20.5	40.8	75
13	The High People's Court of Hunan Province	9	39,752.12	−4	47.60	59.96	45.55	5	54.6	85
14	The High People's Court of Inner Mongolia Autonomous Region	20	17,212.5	6	44.24	54.92	73.35	0	30	45

(continued)

Table 4 (continued)

Ranking	Court	GDP ranking	GDP 2019 (100 million yuan)	A comparison between the GDP ranking and the judicial transparency index ranking	Total score	Disclosure of trial affairs (points)	Disclosure of trial information (points)	Disclosure of enforcement information (points)	Disclosure of judicial data (points)	Disclosure of information on judicial reform (points)
15	The High People's Court of Fujian Province	8	42,395	−7	44.15	44.44	56.6	5	70.2	45
16	The High People's Court of Gansu Province	28	8718.3	12	43.81	55.46	57.55	0	48	55
17	The High People's Court of Guizhou Province	22	16,769.34	5	43.54	43.44	52	25	80	15
18	The High People's Court of Yunnan Province	18	23,223.75	0	43.33	51.22	69.45	5	60	15

(continued)

Table 4 (continued)

Ranking	Court	GDP ranking	GDP 2019 (100 million yuan)	A comparison between the GDP ranking and the judicial transparency index ranking	Total score	Disclosure of trial affairs (points)	Disclosure of trial information (points)	Disclosure of enforcement information (points)	Disclosure of judicial data (points)	Disclosure of information on judicial reform (points)
19	The High People's Court of Anhui Province	11	37,114	−8	40.14	51	52.5	30	54.6	0
20	The High People's Court of Henan Province	5	54,259.2	−15	40.11	35.4	45.8	30	33.6	55
21	The High People's Court of Tianjin Municipality	23	14,104.28	2	39.07	45.6	49.75	31	33.8	25
22	The High People's Court of Chongqing Municipality	17	23,605.77	−5	37.62	52.96	64.25	5	30	15

(continued)

Table 4 (continued)

Ranking	Court	GDP ranking	GDP 2019 (100 million yuan)	A comparison between the GDP ranking and the judicial transparency index ranking	Total score	Disclosure of trial affairs (points)	Disclosure of trial information (points)	Disclosure of enforcement information (points)	Disclosure of judicial data (points)	Disclosure of information on judicial reform (points)
23	The High People's Court of Liaoning Province	15	24,909.5	−8	35.06	48.04	51.2	5	45.6	15
24	The High People's Court of Xizang Autonomous Region	32	1697.82	8	34.19	58.3	56.75	9.5	24	0
25	The High People's Court of Hubei Province	7	45,828.31	−18	34.15	45	49.9	5	46.2	15
26	The High People's Court of Heilongjiang Province	24	13,612.7	−2	33.37	53.36	34.15	28.5	30	15

(continued)

Table 4 (continued)

Ranking	Court	GDP ranking	GDP 2019 (100 million yuan)	A comparison between the GDP ranking and the judicial transparency index ranking	Total score	Disclosure of trial affairs (points)	Disclosure of trial information (points)	Disclosure of enforcement information (points)	Disclosure of judicial data (points)	Disclosure of information on judicial reform (points)
27	The High People's Court of Xinjiang Uygur Autonomous Region	25	13,597.11	−2	32.73	31.3	52.9	5	9	55
28	The High People's Court of Ningxia Hui Autonomous Region	30	3748.48	2	32.38	34.8	52.85	10	35.4	15
29	The High People's Court of Shaanxi Province	14	25,793.17	−15	31.84	40	39.85	6	46.2	25

(continued)

Table 4 (continued)

Ranking	Court	GDP ranking	GDP 2019 (100 million yuan)	A comparison between the GDP ranking and the judicial transparency index ranking	Total score	Disclosure of trial affairs (points)	Disclosure of trial information (points)	Disclosure of enforcement information (points)	Disclosure of judicial data (points)	Disclosure of information on judicial reform (points)
30	The High People's Court of Shanxi Province	21	17,026.68	−9	29.03	28.2	41.6	10	44.4	15
31	The High People's Court of Qinghai Province	31	2965.95	0	22.70	51.2	28.3	5	19.8	0
32	The Production and Construction Corps Branch of the High People's Court of Xinjiang Uygur Autonomous Region	26	13,597.11	−6	15.18	27.6	18.4	0	27.6	0

Table 5 Results of 2020 judicial transparency index assessment (Intermediate People's Courts)

Ranking	Court	GDP ranking	GDP (100 million yuan)	A comparison between the GDP ranking and the judicial transparency index ranking	Total score	Disclosure of trial affairs (points)	Disclosure of trial information (points)	Disclosure of enforcement information (points)	Disclosure of judicial data (points)	Disclosure of information on judicial reform (points)
1	The Intermediate People's Court of Guangzhou City of Guangdong Province	2	23,628.60	1	91.53	100.00	95.60	71.75	90.00	100.00
2	The Intermediate People's Court of Shenzhen City of Guangdong Province	1	26,297.09	−1	80.81	97.84	84.65	40.50	100.00	85.00
4	The Intermediate People's Court of Jilin City of Jilin Province	44	1316.60	41	80.51	89.04	80.35	54.25	100.00	85.00

(continued)

Table 5 (continued)

Ranking	Court	GDP ranking	GDP (100 million yuan)	A comparison between the GDP ranking and the judicial transparency index ranking	Total score	Disclosure of trial affairs (points)	Disclosure of trial information (points)	Disclosure of enforcement information (points)	Disclosure of judicial data (points)	Disclosure of information on judicial reform (points)
4	The Intermediate People's Court of Nanjing City of Jiangsu Province	7	14,030.15	3	79.87	98.00	81.90	60.00	88.00	70.00
5	The Intermediate People's Court of Ningbo City of Zhejiang Province	8	11,985.12	3	74.49	88.80	76.60	72.75	88.00	40.00
6	The Intermediate People's Court of Haikou City of Hainan Province	41	1671.93	35	74.01	89.70	70.40	60.00	68.00	85.00

(continued)

Table 5 (continued)

Ranking	Court	GDP ranking	GDP (100 million yuan)	A comparison between the GDP ranking and the judicial transparency index ranking	Total score	Disclosure of trial affairs (points)	Disclosure of trial information (points)	Disclosure of enforcement information (points)	Disclosure of judicial data (points)	Disclosure of information on judicial reform (points)
7	The Intermediate People's Court of Chengdu City of Sichuan Province	4	17,012.65	−3	71.55	90.00	74.80	51.00	54.40	85.00
8	The Intermediate People's Court of Changchun City of Jilin Province	23	5904.10	15	67.36	95.00	74.30	21.00	60.80	85.00
9	The Intermediate People's Court of Shantou City of Guangdong Province	38	2694.08	29	65.69	70.86	51.90	63.50	100.00	55.00

(continued)

Table 5 (continued)

Ranking	Court	GDP ranking	GDP (100 million yuan)	A comparison between the GDP ranking and the judicial transparency index ranking	Total score	Disclosure of trial affairs (points)	Disclosure of trial information (points)	Disclosure of enforcement information (points)	Disclosure of judicial data (points)	Disclosure of information on judicial reform (points)
10	The Intermediate People's Court of Qingdao City of Shandong Province	10	11,741.31	0	61.91	66.20	62.40	59.75	80.00	40.00
11	The Intermediate People's Court of Zibo City of Shandong Province	31	3642.40	20	61.17	73.80	57.85	30.50	68.00	85.00
12	The Intermediate People's Court of Xuzhou City of Jiangsu Province	17	7151.40	5	58.97	64.80	66.20	53.50	78.00	25.00

(continued)

Table 5 (continued)

Ranking	Court	GDP ranking	GDP (100 million yuan)	A comparison between the GDP ranking and the judicial transparency index ranking	Total score	Disclosure of trial affairs (points)	Disclosure of trial information (points)	Disclosure of enforcement information (points)	Disclosure of judicial data (points)	Disclosure of information on judicial reform (points)
13	The Intermediate People's Court of Hangzhou City of Zhejiang Province	6	15,373.05	−7	55.88	75.90	56.00	23.50	88.00	40.00
14	The Intermediate People's Court of Jinan City of Shandong Province	13	9443.40	−1	53.70	78.66	55.45	29.40	48.00	55.00
15	The Intermediate People's Court of Xiamen City of Fujian Province	22	5995.04	7	49.16	67.56	74.00	5.00	68.00	15.00

(continued)

Table 5 (continued)

Ranking	Court	GDP ranking	GDP (100 million yuan)	A comparison between the GDP ranking and the judicial transparency index ranking	Total score	Disclosure of trial affairs (points)	Disclosure of trial information (points)	Disclosure of enforcement information (points)	Disclosure of judicial data (points)	Disclosure of information on judicial reform (points)
16	The Intermediate People's Court of Datong City of Shanxi Province	43	1318.84	27	48.14	63.30	55.75	37.50	30.00	45.00
17	The Intermediate People's Court of Zhuhai City of Guangdong Province	34	3435.89	17	48.12	73.06	37.10	36.00	46.20	55.00
18	The Intermediate People's Court of Taiyuan City of Shanxi Province	30	4028.51	12	46.61	59.16	56.75	32.50	30.00	45.00

(continued)

Table 5 (continued)

Ranking	Court	GDP ranking	GDP (100 million yuan)	A comparison between the GDP ranking and the judicial transparency index ranking	Total score	Disclosure of trial affairs (points)	Disclosure of trial information (points)	Disclosure of enforcement information (points)	Disclosure of judicial data (points)	Disclosure of information on judicial reform (points)
19	The Intermediate People's Court of Nanchang City of Jiangxi Province	25	5596.18	6	41.40	50.64	53.10	11.00	42.60	45.00
20	The Intermediate People's Court of Shenyang City of Liaoning Province	21	6470.30	1	40.91	49.44	60.25	10.00	58.00	15.00

(continued)

Table 5 (continued)

Ranking	Court	GDP ranking	GDP (100 million yuan)	A comparison between the GDP ranking and the judicial transparency index ranking	Total score	Disclosure of trial affairs (points)	Disclosure of trial information (points)	Disclosure of enforcement information (points)	Disclosure of judicial data (points)	Disclosure of information on judicial reform (points)
21	The Intermediate People's Court of Lanzhou City of Gansu Province	35	2837.36	14	38.28	52.72	65.00	16.00	33.60	0.00
22	The Intermediate People's Court of Guiyang City of Guizhou Province	29	4039.60	7	38.21	51.70	30.40	44.40	40.80	25.00

(continued)

Table 5 (continued)

Ranking	Court	GDP ranking	GDP (100 million yuan)	A comparison between the GDP ranking and the judicial transparency index ranking	Total score	Disclosure of trial affairs (points)	Disclosure of trial information (points)	Disclosure of enforcement information (points)	Disclosure of judicial data (points)	Disclosure of information on judicial reform (points)
23	The Intermediate People's Court of Hefei City of Anhui Province	14	9409.40	−9	38.06	45.06	40.65	29.50	48.00	25.00
24	The Intermediate People's Court of Huainan City of Anhui Province	45	1296.20	21	38.00	60.56	42.50	22.50	42.60	15.00

(continued)

Table 5 (continued)

Ranking	Court	GDP ranking	GDP (100 million yuan)	A comparison between the GDP ranking and the judicial transparency index ranking	Total score	Disclosure of trial affairs (points)	Disclosure of trial information (points)	Disclosure of enforcement information (points)	Disclosure of judicial data (points)	Disclosure of information on judicial reform (points)
25	The Intermediate People's Court of Qiqihar City of Heilongjiang Province	46	1128.90	21	37.85	49.20	48.60	20.50	37.20	25.00
26	The Intermediate People's Court of Tangshan City of Hebei Province	19	6890.00	−7	37.19	31.70	50.20	27.50	53.60	15.00

(continued)

Table 5 (continued)

Ranking	Court	GDP ranking	GDP (100 million yuan)	A comparison between the GDP ranking and the judicial transparency index ranking	Total score	Disclosure of trial affairs (points)	Disclosure of trial information (points)	Disclosure of enforcement information (points)	Disclosure of judicial data (points)	Disclosure of information on judicial reform (points)
27	The Intermediate People's Court of Luoyang City of Henan Province	27	5034.90	0	36.83	24.80	45.80	11.00	46.20	60.00
28	The Intermediate People's Court of Hohhot City of Inner Mongolia Autonomous Region	36	2791.46	8	36.35	39.44	65.60	16.00	37.20	0.00

(continued)

Table 5 (continued)

Ranking	Court	GDP ranking	GDP (100 million yuan)	A comparison between the GDP ranking and the judicial transparency index ranking	Total score	Disclosure of trial affairs (points)	Disclosure of trial information (points)	Disclosure of enforcement information (points)	Disclosure of judicial data (points)	Disclosure of information on judicial reform (points)
29	The Intermediate People's Court of Wuxi City of Jiangsu Province	9	11,852.32	−20	35.19	30.00	43.85	35.00	45.20	15.00
30	The Intermediate People's Court of Xining City of Qinghai Province	42	1382.89	12	34.77	36.40	43.80	5.00	59.00	30.00

(continued)

Table 5 (continued)

Ranking	Court	GDP ranking	GDP (100 million yuan)	A comparison between the GDP ranking and the judicial transparency index ranking	Total score	Disclosure of trial affairs (points)	Disclosure of trial information (points)	Disclosure of enforcement information (points)	Disclosure of judicial data (points)	Disclosure of information on judicial reform (points)
31	The Intermediate People's Court of Baotou City of Inner Mongolia Autonomous Region	37	2714.47	6	33.52	57.36	51.00	0.00	30.00	15.00
32	The Intermediate People's Court of Yinchuan City of Ningxia Hui Autonomous Region	39	2021.27	7	32.91	7.00	52.25	45.40	30.00	15.00

(continued)

Table 5 (continued)

Ranking	Court	GDP ranking	GDP (100 million yuan)	A comparison between the GDP ranking and the judicial transparency index ranking	Total score	Disclosure of trial affairs (points)	Disclosure of trial information (points)	Disclosure of enforcement information (points)	Disclosure of judicial data (points)	Disclosure of information on judicial reform (points)
33	The Intermediate People's Court of Suzhou City of Jiangsu Province	3	19,235.80	−30	32.90	25.30	40.00	36.00	42.60	15.00
34	The Intermediate People's Court of Nanning City of Guangxi Zhuang Autonomous Region	28	4506.56	−6	32.88	45.12	35.60	5.00	66.20	15.00

(continued)

Table 5 (continued)

Ranking	Court	GDP ranking	GDP (100 million yuan)	A comparison between the GDP ranking and the judicial transparency index ranking	Total score	Disclosure of trial affairs (points)	Disclosure of trial information (points)	Disclosure of enforcement information (points)	Disclosure of judicial data (points)	Disclosure of information on judicial reform (points)
35	The Intermediate People's Court of Anshan City of Liaoning Province	40	1745.30	5	32.00	42.44	47.15	5.00	40.80	15.00
36	The Intermediate People's Court of Harbin City of Heilongjiang Province	26	5249.40	−10	30.09	24.10	48.60	12.50	54.60	0.00

(continued)

Table 5 (continued)

Ranking	Court	GDP ranking	GDP (100 million yuan)	A comparison between the GDP ranking and the judicial transparency index ranking	Total score	Disclosure of trial affairs (points)	Disclosure of trial information (points)	Disclosure of enforcement information (points)	Disclosure of judicial data (points)	Disclosure of information on judicial reform (points)
37	The Intermediate People's Court of Kunming City of Yunnan Province	20	6475.88	−17	29.83	51.96	40.30	30.00	9.00	0.00
38	The Intermediate People's Court of Zhengzhou City of Henan Province	11	11,589.70	−27	29.46	39.00	25.75	5.00	56.20	30.00

(continued)

Table 5 (continued)

Ranking	Court	GDP ranking	GDP (100 million yuan)	A comparison between the GDP ranking and the judicial transparency index ranking	Total score	Disclosure of trial affairs (points)	Disclosure of trial information (points)	Disclosure of enforcement information (points)	Disclosure of judicial data (points)	Disclosure of information on judicial reform (points)
39	The Intermediate People's Court of Handan City of Hebei Province	32	3486.00	−7	29.39	35.02	46.35	10.00	28.20	15.00
40	The Intermediate People's Court of Lhasa City of Xizang Autonomous Region	49	617.88	9	29.23	33.00	21.90	27.50	55.40	15.00

(continued)

Table 5 (continued)

Ranking	Court	GDP ranking	GDP (100 million yuan)	A comparison between the GDP ranking and the judicial transparency index ranking	Total score	Disclosure of trial affairs (points)	Disclosure of trial information (points)	Disclosure of enforcement information (points)	Disclosure of judicial data (points)	Disclosure of information on judicial reform (points)
41	The Intermediate People's Court of Shijiazhuang City of Hebei Province	24	5809.90	−17	27.95	44.86	31.10	14.50	30.00	15.00
42	The Intermediate People's Court of Changsha City of Hunan Province	12	11,574.22	−30	27.08	40.00	42.10	6.00	20.00	15.00

(continued)

Table 5 (continued)

Ranking	Court	GDP ranking	GDP (100 million yuan)	A comparison between the GDP ranking and the judicial transparency index ranking	Total score	Disclosure of trial affairs (points)	Disclosure of trial information (points)	Disclosure of enforcement information (points)	Disclosure of judicial data (points)	Disclosure of information on judicial reform (points)
43	The Intermediate People's Court of Wuhan City of Hubei Province	5	16,223.21	−38	27.04	40.00	26.95	30.00	18.00	15.00
44	The Intermediate People's Court of Fuzhou City of Fujian Province	15	9392.30	−29	26.73	27.20	48.45	0.00	30.00	15.00

(continued)

Table 5 (continued)

Ranking	Court	GDP ranking	GDP (100 million yuan)	A comparison between the GDP ranking and the judicial transparency index ranking	Total score	Disclosure of trial affairs (points)	Disclosure of trial information (points)	Disclosure of enforcement information (points)	Disclosure of judicial data (points)	Disclosure of information on judicial reform (points)
45	The Intermediate People's Court of Fushun City of Liaoning Province	47	847.10	2	25.23	35.20	36.00	5.00	42.60	0.00
46	The Intermediate People's Court of Xi'an City of Shaanxi Province	16	9321.19	−30	24.39	18.80	44.70	10.00	19.80	15.00

(continued)

Table 5 (continued)

Ranking	Court	GDP ranking	GDP (100 million yuan)	A comparison between the GDP ranking and the judicial transparency index ranking	Total score	Disclosure of trial affairs (points)	Disclosure of trial information (points)	Disclosure of enforcement information (points)	Disclosure of judicial data (points)	Disclosure of information on judicial reform (points)
47	The Intermediate People's Court of Urumqi City of Xinjiang Uygur Autonomous Region	33	3450.10	−14	24.11	38.46	36.75	17.50	12.60	0.00
48	The Intermediate People's Court of Dalian City of Liaoning Province	18	7001.70	−30	22.29	30.92	34.70	6.00	30.00	0.00

(continued)

Table 5 (continued)

Ranking	Court	GDP ranking	GDP (100 million yuan)	A comparison between the GDP ranking and the judicial transparency index ranking	Total score	Disclosure of trial affairs (points)	Disclosure of trial information (points)	Disclosure of enforcement information (points)	Disclosure of judicial data (points)	Disclosure of information on judicial reform (points)
49	The Intermediate People's Court of Benxi City of Liaoning Province	48	781.10	−1	22.05	41.80	22.30	5.00	40.00	0.00

Table 6 Results of 2020 judicial transparency index assessment (Specialized Courts)

Ranking	Court	Total score	Disclosure of trial affairs (points)	Disclosure of trial information (points)	Disclosure of enforcement information (points)	Disclosure of judicial data (points)	Disclosure of information on judicial reform (points)
1	The Primary People's Court of Guangdong Pilot Free Trade Zone (Nansha)	89.41	90.05	85.50	90.00	90.00	95.00
2	Guangzhou Internet Court	66.81	97.50	50.20	90.00	50.00	45.00
3	The Primary People's Court of Qianhai Cooperation Zone of Shenzhen City	64.26	56.80	87.00	74.00	35.00	45.00
4	Beijing Internet Court	53.15	45.77	56.50	64.00	50.00	45.00
5	The Primary People's Court of Zhuhai Hengqin New Area	51.72	83.16	82.80	10.00	50.00	5.00
6	Guangzhou Intellectual Property Court	45.16	68.91	57.10	0.00	50.00	45.00
7	Hangzhou Internet Court	39.41	55.05	68.00	10.00	0.00	40.00
8	Shanghai Financial Court	38.26	80.06	50.00	10.00	35.00	0.00

(continued)

Table 6 (continued)

Ranking	Court	Total score	Disclosure of trial affairs (points)	Disclosure of trial information (points)	Disclosure of enforcement information (points)	Disclosure of judicial data (points)	Disclosure of information on judicial reform (points)
9	Shanghai Intellectual Property Court	38.17	56.67	47.80	10.00	15.00	55.00
10	The Primary People's Court of Chongqing Pilot Free Trade Zone	36.25	51.25	55.00	10.00	50.00	0.00
11	Beijing Intellectual Property Court	35.47	54.86	45.00	10.00	60.00	0.00
12	The Primary People's Court of Sichuan Pilot free Trade Zone	31.09	59.03	50.10	10.00	15.00	0.00

1.2 *Information Involved in Judicial Openness is Expanding*

As judicial openness develops, courts have greatly expanded judicial openness in response to various documents issued by the Supreme People's Court. Compared with the trial affairs information and adjudication and enforcement information involved in the daily work of the court,, the information that courts used to pay little attention to has now been gradually included in judicial openness. For example, according to the 2019 Assessment, 40 courts have set up columns for judicial reforms, among which 38 courts are the originally assessed objects. Eighteen out of the 38 courts have uploaded overall plans for judicial reforms on their websites. The result revealed in the 2019 Assessment has outperformed that revealed in the 2018 Assessment. Seven courts have made public the judicial proposals issued in 2019, nine courts have disclosed the full texts concerning the results of handling the suggestions by deputies to people's congresses and the proposals by CPPCC members, and four courts have unveiled the abstracts of the above handling results. That demonstrates that driven by the documents such as the *Opinions of the Supreme People's Court on Further Deepening Judicial Openness*, the courts have disclosed more information

Table 7 Results of 2020 judicial transparency index assessment (Primary People's Courts)

Ranking	Province/Municipality/Autonomous Region	Court	GDP ranking	GDP (100 million yuan)	A comparison between the GDP ranking and the judicial transparency index ranking	Total score (points)	Disclosure of trial affairs (points)	Disclosure of trial information (points)	Disclosure of enforcement information (points)	Disclosure of judicial data (points)	Disclosure of information on judicial reform (points)	Whether it belongs to the top 100 counties, cities or districts	Top 100 ranking (districts, and cities and counties are ranked respectively)
1	Guangdong	The Primary People's Court of Futian District of Shenzhen City	6	4546.50	5	85. 73	76.02	80.10	90.00	100.00	90.00	No	
2	Jilin	The Primary People's Court of Yanji City	89	319.95	87	79.94	96.25	72.30	90.00	95.00	45.00	Yes	68
3	Guangdong	The Primary People's Court of Yuexiu District of Guangzhou City	10	3135.47	7	78.37	65.77	66.40	84.00	95.00	95.00	No	
4	Jilin	The Primary People's Court of Qian Gorlos Mongolia Autonomous County	107	141.67	103	69.40	96.25	78.00	10.00	70.00	95.00	No	

(continued)

Table 7 (continued)

Ranking	Province/Municipality/Autonomous Region	Court	GDP ranking	GDP (100 million yuan)	A comparison between the GDP ranking and the judicial transparency index ranking	Total score (points)	Disclosure of trial affairs (points)	Disclosure of trial information (points)	Disclosure of enforcement information (points)	Disclosure of judicial data (points)	Disclosure of information on judicial reform (points)	Whether it belongs to the top 100 counties, cities or districts	Top 100 ranking (districts, and cities and counties are ranked respectively)
5	Jiangsu	The Primary People's Court of Wujiang District of Suzhou City	17	1958.16	12	68.28	64.56	87.90	100.00	55.00	5.00	Yes	8
6	Hainan	The Primary People's Court of Chengmai County	87	330.18	81	68.23	61.48	75.60	80.00	70.00	45.00	No	
7	Jiangsu	The Primary People's Court of Shuyang County	49	950.17	42	67.57	56.21	78.60	100.00	85.00	0.00	Yes	61
8	Zhejiang	The Primary People's Court of Yuhang District of Hangzhou City	11	2824.02	3	66.29	70.75	57.80	90.00	72.00	40.00	Yes	7
9	Anhui	The Primary People's Court of Chaohu City	73	475.00	64	64.88	47.28	72.90	74.00	75.00	50.00	No	

(continued)

Table 7 (continued)

Ranking	Province/Municipality/Autonomous Region	Court	GDP ranking	GDP (100 million yuan)	A comparison between the GDP ranking and the judicial transparency index ranking	Total score (points)	Disclosure of trial affairs (points)	Disclosure of trial information (points)	Disclosure of enforcement information (points)	Disclosure of judicial data (points)	Disclosure of information on judicial reform (points)	Whether it belongs to the top 100 counties, cities or districts	Top 100 ranking (districts, and cities and counties are ranked respectively)
10	Yunnan	The Primary People's Court of Xuanwei City	84	360.22	74	63.55	76.46	78.70	82.00	55.00	0.00	No	
11	Guangxi	The Primary People's Court of Binyang County	95	271.96	84	62.65	92.30	70.80	72.00	57.00	0.00	No	
12	Henan	The Primary People's Court of Jinshui District of Zhengzhou City	21	1752.48	9	61.60	57.32	61.30	80.00	50.00	55.00	No	
13	Zhejiang	The Primary People's Court of Yiwu City	23	1421.14	10	61.02	69.00	64.90	90.00	25.00	40.00	Yes	13
14	Jilin	The Primary People's Court of Chaoyang District of Changchun City	63	600.00	49	59.08	96.25	78.60	10.00	50.00	45.00	No	

(continued)

Table 7 (continued)

Ranking	Province/Municipality/Autonomous Region	Court	GDP ranking	GDP (100 million yuan)	A comparison between the GDP ranking and the judicial transparency index ranking	Total score (points)	Disclosure of trial affairs (points)	Disclosure of trial information (points)	Disclosure of enforcement information (points)	Disclosure of judicial data (points)	Disclosure of information on judicial reform (points)	Whether it belongs to the top 100 counties, cities or districts	Top 100 ranking (districts, and cities and counties are ranked respectively)
15	Hebei	The Primary People's Court of Chang'an District of Shijiazhuang City	64	598.90	49	58.58	74.42	46.50	100.00	15.00	50.00	No	
16	Guizhou	The Primary People's Court of Xishui County	102	186.75	86	57.04	46.54	48.60	72.00	75.00	50.00	No	
17	Guangxi	The Primary People's Court of Guiping City	86	342.90	69	56.81	69.87	66.30	72.00	57.00	0.00	No	
18	Guangxi	The Primary People's Court of Xixiangtang District of Nanning City	54	789.12	36	56.50	90.05	47.80	72.00	65.00	0.00	No	

(continued)

Table 7 (continued)

Ranking	Province/Municipality/Autonomous Region	Court	GDP ranking	GDP (100 million yuan)	A comparison between the GDP ranking and the judicial transparency index ranking	Total score (points)	Disclosure of trial affairs (points)	Disclosure of trial information (points)	Disclosure of enforcement information (points)	Disclosure of judicial data (points)	Disclosure of information on judicial reform (points)	Whether it belongs to the top 100 counties, cities or districts	Top 100 ranking (districts, and cities and counties are ranked respectively)
19	Anhui	The Primary People's Court of Yaohai District of Hefei City	47	956.60	28	56.11	68.53	67.00	74.00	0.00	50.00	Yes	90
20	Ningxia	The Primary People's Court of Helan County	109	138.95	89	56.03	13.20	70.80	82.00	100.00	5.00	No	
21	Sichuan	The Primary People's Court of Qingyang District of Chengdu City	33	1283.94	12	55.61	51.25	53.70	90.00	25.00	50.00	No	
22	Zhejiang	The Primary People's Court of Zhuji City	29	1312.36	7	55.56	71.05	44.50	80.00	40.00	40.00	Yes	14
23	Fujian	The Primary People's Court of Jinjiang City	12	2546.18	−11	53.47	78.60	30.00	80.00	85.00	0.00	Yes	8

(continued)

Table 7 (continued)

Ranking	Province/Municipality/Autonomous Region	Court	GDP ranking	GDP (100 million yuan)	A comparison between the GDP ranking and the judicial transparency index ranking	Total score (points)	Disclosure of trial affairs (points)	Disclosure of trial information (points)	Disclosure of enforcement information (points)	Disclosure of judicial data (points)	Disclosure of information on judicial reform (points)	Whether it belongs to the top 100 counties, cities or districts	Top 100 ranking (districts, and cities and counties are ranked respectively)
24	Hunan	The Primary People's Court of Yuelu District of Changsha City	32	1288.20	8	53.10	63.62	78.60	84.00	0.00	0.00	Yes	62
25	Anhui	The Primary People's Court of Baohe District of Hefei City	27	1333.46	2	52.91	59.23	80.20	10.00	50.00	50.00	Yes	41
26	Guangxi	The Primary People's Court of Qingxiu District of Nanning City	37	1158.98	11	52.81	68.34	57.80	64.00	60.00	0.00	Yes	74
27	Ningxia	The Primary People's Court of Xingqing District of Yinchuan City	67	531.58	40	52.58	37.93	70.80	10.00	90.00	55.00	No	

(continued)

Table 7 (continued)

Ranking	Province/Municipality/Autonomous Region	Court	GDP ranking	GDP (100 million yuan)	A comparison between the GDP ranking and the judicial transparency index ranking	Total score (points)	Disclosure of trial affairs (points)	Disclosure of trial information (points)	Disclosure of enforcement information (points)	Disclosure of judicial data (points)	Disclosure of information on judicial reform (points)	Whether it belongs to the top 100 counties, cities or districts	Top 100 ranking (districts, and cities and counties are ranked respectively)
28	Jilin	The Primary People's Court of Ningjiang District of Songyuan City	No specific data published on the website	No specific data published on the website	–	52.53	95.00	72.60	10.00	20.00	45.00	No	
29	Tianjin	The Primary People's Court of Nankai District of Tianjin Municipality	66	544.22	37	52.50	69.04	72.30	10.00	100.00	0.00	No	
30	Anhui	The Primary People's Court of Taihe County	75	454.40	45	52.11	84.37	65.80	10.00	40.00	50.00	No	
31	Sichuan	The Primary People's Court of Chengdu High–Tech Industrial Development Zone	15	2285.56	−16	52.03	50.00	60.10	90.00	40.00	0.00	No	

(continued)

Table 7 (continued)

Ranking	Province/Municipality/Autonomous Region	Court	GDP ranking	GDP (100 million yuan)	A comparison between the GDP ranking and the judicial transparency index ranking	Total score (points)	Disclosure of trial affairs (points)	Disclosure of trial information (points)	Disclosure of enforcement information (points)	Disclosure of judicial data (points)	Disclosure of information on judicial reform (points)	Whether it belongs to the top 100 counties, cities or districts	Top 100 ranking (districts, and cities and counties are ranked respectively)
32	Jiangsu	The Primary People's Court of Kunshan City	7	4045.06	−25	51.80	30.00	73.50	100.00	20.00	5.00	Yes	1
33	Fujian	The Primary People's Court of Hui'an County	28	1318.11	−5	51.25	83.65	47.40	64.00	50.00	0.00	Yes	35
34	Yunnan	The Primary People's Court of Xishan District of Kunming City	50	859.05	16	50.24	42.28	77.10	82.00	15.00	0.00	No	
35	Guangdong	The Primary People's Court of Huidong County	61	626.30	26	50.17	40.08	58.00	0.00	70.00	95.00	No	

(continued)

Table 7 (continued)

Ranking	Province/Municipality/Autonomous Region	Court	GDP ranking	GDP (100 million yuan)	A comparison between the GDP ranking and the judicial transparency index ranking	Total score (points)	Disclosure of trial affairs (points)	Disclosure of trial information (points)	Disclosure of enforcement information (points)	Disclosure of judicial data (points)	Disclosure of information on judicial reform (points)	Whether it belongs to the top 100 counties, cities or districts	Top 100 ranking (districts, and cities and counties are ranked respectively)
36	Beijing	The Primary People's Court of Xicheng District of Beijing Municipality	5	5007.30	−31	49.84	65.64	65.70	10.00	50.00	50.00	No	
37	Yunnan	The Primary People's Court of Wuhua District of Kunming City	36	1195.65	−1	49.76	30.00	78.70	82.00	20.00	5.00	No	
38	Shandong	The Primary People's Court of Huangdao District of Qingdao City	9	3554.44	−29	49.41	52.50	42.20	90.00	55.00	0.00	No	
39	Hainan	The Primary People's Court of Meilan District of Haikou City	78	426.80	39	49.39	10.50	44.30	80.00	80.00	40.00	No	

(continued)

Table 7 (continued)

Ranking	Province/Municipality/Autonomous Region	Court	GDP ranking	GDP (100 million yuan)	A comparison between the GDP ranking and the judicial transparency index ranking	Total score (points)	Disclosure of trial affairs (points)	Disclosure of trial information (points)	Disclosure of enforcement information (points)	Disclosure of judicial data (points)	Disclosure of information on judicial reform (points)	Whether it belongs to the top 100 counties, cities or districts	Top 100 ranking (districts, and cities and counties are ranked respectively)
40	Tianjin	The Primary People's Court of Binhai New Area of Tianjin Municipality	2	8760.15	−38	48.73	69.03	66.40	0.00	100.00	0.00	No	
41	Jiangsu	The Primary People's Court of Jiangyin City	8	4001.12	−33	48.71	27.30	76.50	64.00	45.00	5.00	Yes	2
42	Jiangxi	The Primary People's Court of Xihu District of Nanchang City	62	614.56	20	48.51	42.42	66.60	74.00	30.00	5.00	No	
43	Hebei	The Primary People's Court of Sanhe City	70	504.80	27	48.47	63.75	61.40	10.00	12.00	90.00	No	

(continued)

Table 7 (continued)

Ranking	Province/Municipality/Autonomous Region	Court	GDP ranking	GDP (100 million yuan)	A comparison between the GDP ranking and the judicial transparency index ranking	Total score (points)	Disclosure of trial affairs (points)	Disclosure of trial information (points)	Disclosure of enforcement information (points)	Disclosure of judicial data (points)	Disclosure of information on judicial reform (points)	Whether it belongs to the top 100 counties, cities or districts	Top 100 ranking (districts, and cities and counties are ranked respectively)
44	Chongqing	The Primary People's Court of Jiangbei District of Chongqing Municipality	35	1240.07	−9	47.61	50.00	45.70	82.00	50.00	0.00	No	
45	Hainan	The Primary People's Court of Danzhou City	85	357.64	40	47.60	30.50	30.00	80.00	70.00	40.00	No	
46	Zhejiang	The Primary People's Court of Cangnan County	59	659.74	13	47.47	52.33	20.00	80.00	60.00	40.00	No	
47	Jiangxi	The Primary People's Court of Donghu District of Nanchang City	83	366.69	36	47.04	27.30	58.60	90.00	35.00	5.00	No	

(continued)

Table 7 (continued)

Ranking	Province/Municipality/Autonomous Region	Court	GDP ranking	GDP (100 million yuan)	A comparison between the GDP ranking and the judicial transparency index ranking	Total score (points)	Disclosure of trial affairs (points)	Disclosure of trial information (points)	Disclosure of enforcement information (points)	Disclosure of judicial data (points)	Disclosure of information on judicial reform (points)	Whether it belongs to the top 100 counties, cities or districts	Top 100 ranking (districts, and cities and counties are ranked respectively)
48	Qinghai	The Primary People's Court of Golmud City	No specific data published on the website	No specific data published on the website	–	46.91	52.50	47.20	10.00	45.00	90.00	No	
49	Gansu	The Primary People's Court of Longxi County	112	72.09	63	46.73	24.72	47.80	72.00	87.00	0.00	No	
50	Hunan	The Primary People's Court of Youxian County	No specific data published on the website	No specific data published on the website	–	46.24	38.37	61.90	100.00	0.00	0.00	No	
51	Shandong	The Primary People's Court of Lanshan District of Linyi City	39	1142.22	−12	46.00	83.80	50.80	10.00	80.00	0.00	Yes	39

(continued)

Table 7 (continued)

Ranking	Province/Municipality/Autonomous Region	Court	GDP ranking	GDP (100 million yuan)	A comparison between the GDP ranking and the judicial transparency index ranking	Total score (points)	Disclosure of trial affairs (points)	Disclosure of trial information (points)	Disclosure of enforcement information (points)	Disclosure of judicial data (points)	Disclosure of information on judicial reform (points)	Whether it belongs to the top 100 counties, cities or districts	Top 100 ranking (districts, and cities and counties are ranked respectively)
52	Beijing	The Primary People's Court of Fengtai District of Beijing Municipality	20	1829.60	−32	44.62	65.64	48.30	10.00	50.00	50.00	No	
53	Jiangxi	The Primary People's Court of Gao'an City	76	448.78	23	44.34	47.30	28.60	64.00	85.00	5.00	No	
54	Hebei	The Primary People's Court of Haigang District of Qinhuangdao City	71	500.66	17	44.12	74.42	65.80	10.00	0.00	50.00	No	
55	Shanxi	The Primary People's Court of Yanhu District of Yuncheng City	94	289.70	39	43.90	66.81	29.30	0.00	95.00	50.00	No	

(continued)

Table 7 (continued)

Ranking	Province/Municipality/Autonomous Region	Court	GDP ranking	GDP (100 million yuan)	A comparison between the GDP ranking and the judicial transparency index ranking	Total score (points)	Disclosure of trial affairs (points)	Disclosure of trial information (points)	Disclosure of enforcement information (points)	Disclosure of judicial data (points)	Disclosure of information on judicial reform (points)	Whether it belongs to the top 100 counties, cities or districts	Top 100 ranking (districts, and cities and counties are ranked respectively)
56	Ningxia	The Primary People's Court of Jinfeng District of Yinchuan City	93	290.38	37	43.88	13.20	70.80	10.00	65.00	55.00	No	
57	Ningxia	The Primary People's Court of Lingwu City	69	517.38	12	43.88	13.20	60.80	10.00	85.00	55.00	Yes	83
58	Gansu	The Primary People's Court of Ganzhou District of Zhangye City	101	193.95	43	43.34	64.75	42.30	72.00	22.00	0.00	No	
59	Yunnan	The Primary People's Court of Zhenxiong County	100	200.99	41	43.29	37.72	64.50	82.00	0.00	0.00	No	

(continued)

Table 7 (continued)

Ranking	Province/Municipality/Autonomous Region	Court	GDP ranking	GDP (100 million yuan)	A comparison between the GDP ranking and the judicial transparency index ranking	Total score (points)	Disclosure of trial affairs (points)	Disclosure of trial information (points)	Disclosure of enforcement information (points)	Disclosure of judicial data (points)	Disclosure of information on judicial reform (points)	Whether it belongs to the top 100 counties, cities or districts	Top 100 ranking (districts, and cities and counties are ranked respectively)
60	Chongqing	The Primary People's Court of Yubei District of Chongqing Municipality	19	1848.24	−41	43.25	13.20	55.70	82.00	50.00	0.00	No	
61	Gansu	The Primary People's Court of Chengguan District of Lanzhou City	42	1044.50	−19	42.61	24.27	45.70	64.00	75.00	0.00	No	
62	Guizhou	The Primary People's Court of Nanming District of Guiyang City	52	820.59	−10	42.21	47.30	46.50	64.00	40.00	0.00	Yes	84
63	Henan	The Primary People's Court of Huaxian County	82	372.60	19	41.88	57.32	51.40	0.00	50.00	50.00	No	

(continued)

Table 7 (continued)

Ranking	Province/Municipality/Autonomous Region	Court	GDP ranking	GDP (100 million yuan)	A comparison between the GDP ranking and the judicial transparency index ranking	Total score (points)	Disclosure of trial affairs (points)	Disclosure of trial information (points)	Disclosure of enforcement information (points)	Disclosure of judicial data (points)	Disclosure of information on judicial reform (points)	Whether it belongs to the top 100 counties, cities or districts	Top 100 ranking (districts, and cities and counties are ranked respectively)
64	Jiangxi	The Primary People's Court of Nanchang County	44	1027.80	−20	41.17	27.30	57.20	74.00	20.00	5.00	Yes	42
65	Tianjin	The Primary People's Court of Hexi District of Tianjin Municipality	58	702.82	−7	40.64	82.76	37.80	0.00	85.00	0.00	No	
66	Guizhou	The Primary People's Court of Yunyan District of Guiyang City	53	809.03	−13	40.58	27.30	44.40	64.00	60.00	0.00	Yes	95
67	Fujian	The Primary People's Court of Huli District of Xiamen City	31	1297.29	−36	39.97	42.77	56.40	20.00	20.00	50.00	No	
68	Guangdong	The Primary People's Court of Yingde City	88	326.83	20	39.83	30.00	58.60	10.00	95.00	0.00	No	

(continued)

Table 7 (continued)

Ranking	Province/Municipality/Autonomous Region	Court	GDP ranking	GDP (100 million yuan)	A comparison between the GDP ranking and the judicial transparency index ranking	Total score (points)	Disclosure of trial affairs (points)	Disclosure of trial information (points)	Disclosure of enforcement information (points)	Disclosure of judicial data (points)	Disclosure of information on judicial reform (points)	Whether it belongs to the top 100 counties, cities or districts	Top 100 ranking (districts, and cities and counties are ranked respectively)
69	Inner Mongolia	The Primary People's Court of Saihan District of Hohhot City	55	776.50	−14	39.01	58.55	53.50	0.00	75.00	0.00	Yes	58
70	Fujian	The Primary People's Court of Siming District of Xiamen City	18	1896.46	−52	38.42	44.22	26.60	72.00	43.00	5.00	No	
71	Henan	The Primary People's Court of Xinzheng City	57	720.32	−14	38.12	58.76	52.90	0.00	15.00	55.00	Yes	39
72	Heilongjiang	The Primary People's Court of Nangang District of Harbin City	41	1047.10	−31	37.87	47.15	59.80	0.00	20.00	50.00	Yes	55

(continued)

Table 7 (continued)

Ranking	Province/Municipality/Autonomous Region	Court	GDP ranking	GDP (100 million yuan)	A comparison between the GDP ranking and the judicial transparency index ranking	Total score (points)	Disclosure of trial affairs (points)	Disclosure of trial information (points)	Disclosure of enforcement information (points)	Disclosure of judicial data (points)	Disclosure of information on judicial reform (points)	Whether it belongs to the top 100 counties, cities or districts	Top 100 ranking (districts, and cities and counties are ranked respectively)
73	Hainan	The Primary People's Court of Longhua District of Haikou City	68	521.70	−5	37.10	30.50	0.00	80.00	60.00	40.00	No	
74	Beijing	The Primary People's Court of Chaoyang District of Beijing City	4	7108.00	−70	36.60	88.34	35.60	0.00	50.00	5.00	No	
75	Inner Mongolia	The Primary People's Court of Ar Horqin Banner of Inner Mongolia Autonomous Region	111	92.44	36	36.39	42.65	58.70	10.00	50.00	5.00	No	

(continued)

Table 7 (continued)

Ranking	Province/Municipality/Autonomous Region	Court	GDP ranking	GDP (100 million yuan)	A comparison between the GDP ranking and the judicial transparency index ranking	Total score (points)	Disclosure of trial affairs (points)	Disclosure of trial information (points)	Disclosure of enforcement information (points)	Disclosure of judicial data (points)	Disclosure of information on judicial reform (points)	Whether it belongs to the top 100 counties, cities or districts	Top 100 ranking (districts, and cities and counties are ranked respectively)
76	Hebei	The Primary People's Court of Weichang Manchu and Mongolia Autonomous County	No specific data published on the website	No specific data published on the website	–	36.31	65.81	70.50	10.00	0.00	0.00	No	
77	Shanxi	The Primary People's Court of Linyi County	108	140.10	31	36.28	70.84	48.70	0.00	50.00	0.00	No	
78	Shandong	The Primary People's Court of Jiaozhou City	38	1147.59	−40	36.27	20.43	35.10	82.00	35.00	0.00	No	
79	Henan	The Primary People's Court of Zhengzhou High-Tech Industrial Development Zone	72	496.24	−7	36.25	72.93	47.20	0.00	0.00	50.00	No	

(continued)

Table 7 (continued)

Ranking	Province/Municipality/Autonomous Region	Court	GDP ranking	GDP (100 million yuan)	A comparison between the GDP ranking and the judicial transparency index ranking	Total score (points)	Disclosure of trial affairs (points)	Disclosure of trial information (points)	Disclosure of enforcement information (points)	Disclosure of judicial data (points)	Disclosure of information on judicial reform (points)	Whether it belongs to the top 100 counties, cities or districts	Top 100 ranking (districts, and cities and counties are ranked respectively)
80	Qinghai	The Primary People's Court of Chengbei District of Xining City	No specific data published on the website	No specific data published on the website	–	35.50	86.16	25.90	0.00	70.00	0.00	No	
81	Chongqing	The Primary People's Court of Yunyang County of Chongqing Municipality	77	431.25	−4	34.25	44.40	52.90	10.00	50.00	0.00	No	
82	Beijing	The Primary People's Court of Haidian District of Beijing Municipality	3	7926.00	−79	33.21	61.50	17.20	0.00	50.00	55.00	No	

(continued)

Table 7 (continued)

Ranking	Province/Municipality/Autonomous Region	Court	GDP ranking	GDP (100 million yuan)	A comparison between the GDP ranking and the judicial transparency index ranking	Total score (points)	Disclosure of trial affairs (points)	Disclosure of trial information (points)	Disclosure of enforcement information (points)	Disclosure of judicial data (points)	Disclosure of information on judicial reform (points)	Whether it belongs to the top 100 counties, cities or districts	Top 100 ranking (districts, and cities and counties are ranked respectively)
83	Shaanxi	The Primary People's Court of Weiyang District of Xi'an City	34	1255.07	−49	32.67	47.30	45.70	10.00	50.00	0.00	No	
84	Liaoning	The Primary People's Court of Suizhong County	104	176.20	20	31.37	26.85	50.00	10.00	60.00	0.00	No	
85	Shandong	The Primary People's Court of Feixian County	80	390.70	−5	31.28	48.75	35.10	10.00	60.00	0.00	No	
86	Guizhou	The Primary People's Court of Xingyi City	74	465.38	−12	30.72	30.00	34.40	72.00	0.00	0.00	No	
87	Hubei	The Primary People's Court of Yangxin County	92	290.40	5	30.44	62.96	11.50	72.00	0.00	0.00	No	

(continued)

Table 7 (continued)

Ranking	Province/Municipality/Autonomous Region	Court	GDP ranking	GDP (100 million yuan)	A comparison between the GDP ranking and the judicial transparency index ranking	Total score (points)	Disclosure of trial affairs (points)	Disclosure of trial information (points)	Disclosure of enforcement information (points)	Disclosure of judicial data (points)	Disclosure of information on judicial reform (points)	Whether it belongs to the top 100 counties, cities or districts	Top 100 ranking (districts, and cities and counties are ranked respectively)
88	Sichuan	The Primary People's Court of Pixian County	60	631.89	−28	30.26	30.00	54.20	10.00	40.00	0.00	No	
89	Hunan	The Primary People's Court of Furong District of Changsha City	40	1126.32	−49	30.05	21.00	77.00	10.00	0.00	5.00	No	
90	Inner Mongolia	The Primary People's Court of Songshan District of Chifeng City	96	270.50	6	29.96	27.30	40.00	10.00	70.00	0.00	No	
91	Liaoning	The Primary People's Court of Heping District of Shenyang City	51	850.00	−40	29.68	35.02	55.60	0.00	40.00	0.00	No	

(continued)

Table 7 (continued)

Ranking	Province/Municipality/Autonomous Region	Court	GDP ranking	GDP (100 million yuan)	A comparison between the GDP ranking and the judicial transparency index ranking	Total score (points)	Disclosure of trial affairs (points)	Disclosure of trial information (points)	Disclosure of enforcement information (points)	Disclosure of judicial data (points)	Disclosure of information on judicial reform (points)	Whether it belongs to the top 100 counties, cities or districts	Top 100 ranking (districts, and cities and counties are ranked respectively)
92	Shanghai	The Primary People's Court of Pudong New Area of Shanghai Municipality	1	12,734.20	−91	28.73	46.30	64.90	0.00	0.00	0.00	No	
93	Heilongjiang	The Primary People's Court of Nehe City of Heilongjiang Province	110	116.63	17	28.66	46.85	26.80	0.00	75.00	0.00	No	
94	Shanxi	The Primary People's Court of Hejin City	99	250.60	5	28.23	26.85	38.70	0.00	75.00	0.00	No	
95	Chongqing	The Primary People's Court of Yuzhong District of Chongqing Municipality	30	1301.35	−65	26.76	58.82	25.00	0.00	50.00	0.00	No	

(continued)

Table 7 (continued)

Ranking	Province/Municipality/Autonomous Region	Court	GDP ranking	GDP (100 million yuan)	A comparison between the GDP ranking and the judicial transparency index ranking	Total score (points)	Disclosure of trial affairs (points)	Disclosure of trial information (points)	Disclosure of enforcement information (points)	Disclosure of judicial data (points)	Disclosure of information on judicial reform (points)	Whether it belongs to the top 100 counties, cities or districts	Top 100 ranking (districts, and cities and counties are ranked respectively)
96	Liaoning	The Primary People's Court of Shenhe District of Shenyang City	46	965.50	−50	26.25	58.82	48.30	0.00	0.00	0.00	No	
97	Gansu	The Primary People's Court of Yumen City	106	172.49	9	25.65	10.50	46.00	0.00	65.00	0.00	No	
98	Tianjin	The Primary People's Court of Wuqing District of Tianjin Municipality	48	950.73	−50	25.51	46.85	21.30	0.00	65.00	0.00	No	
99	Hunan	The Primary People's Court of Liuyang City	24	1408.85	−75	25.19	41.52	41.30	0.00	30.00	0.00	No	

(continued)

Table 7 (continued)

Ranking	Province/Municipality/Autonomous Region	Court	GDP ranking	GDP (100 million yuan)	A comparison between the GDP ranking and the judicial transparency index ranking	Total score (points)	Disclosure of trial affairs (points)	Disclosure of trial information (points)	Disclosure of enforcement information (points)	Disclosure of judicial data (points)	Disclosure of information on judicial reform (points)	Whether it belongs to the top 100 counties, cities or districts	Top 100 ranking (districts, and cities and counties are ranked respectively)
100	Shanxi	The Primary People's Court of Xiaodian District of Taiyuan City	45	1004.33	−55	24.95	48.57	50.80	0.00	0.00	0.00	No	
101	Qinghai	The Primary People's Court of Chengdong District of Xining City	No specific data published on the website	No specific data published on the website	–	24.77	51.85	23.00	0.00	50.00	0.00	No	
102	Heilongjiang	The Primary People's Court of Binxian County	105	175.80	3	24.22	47.30	24.20	0.00	50.00	0.00	No	
103	Xinjiang	The Primary People's Court of Changji City	79	402.04	−24	23.63	66.87	10.70	0.00	47.00	0.00	No	

(continued)

Table 7 (continued)

Ranking	Province/Municipality/Autonomous Region	Court	GDP ranking	GDP (100 million yuan)	A comparison between the GDP ranking and the judicial transparency index ranking	Total score (points)	Disclosure of trial affairs (points)	Disclosure of trial information (points)	Disclosure of enforcement information (points)	Disclosure of judicial data (points)	Disclosure of information on judicial reform (points)	Whether it belongs to the top 100 counties, cities or districts	Top 100 ranking (districts, and cities and counties are ranked respectively)
104	Xizang	The Primary People's Court of Chengguan District of Lhasa City	91	298.47	−13	23.18	24.15	33.00	10.00	43.00	0.00	No	
105	Xinjiang	The Primary People's Court of Kuqa City	97	268.08	−8	22.44	77.70	23.00	0.00	0.00	0.00	No	
106	Shaanxi	The Primary People's Court of Yanta District of Xi'an City	16	2271.01	−90	21.76	47.30	33.50	0.00	15.00	0.00	No	
107	Heilongjiang	The Primary People's Court of Shidaoli District of Harbin City	56	755.91	−51	21.25	33.20	48.70	0.00	0.00	0.00	No	

(continued)

Table 7 (continued)

Ranking	Province/Municipality/Autonomous Region	Court	GDP ranking	GDP (100 million yuan)	A comparison between the GDP ranking and the judicial transparency index ranking	Total score (points)	Disclosure of trial affairs (points)	Disclosure of trial information (points)	Disclosure of enforcement information (points)	Disclosure of judicial data (points)	Disclosure of information on judicial reform (points)	Whether it belongs to the top 100 counties, cities or districts	Top 100 ranking (districts, and cities and counties are ranked respectively)
108	Xizang	The Primary People's Court of Doilungdêqên County of Lhasa City	113	29.20	5	20.74	35.67	38.70	10.00	0.00	0.00	No	
109	Qinghai	The Primary People's Court of Huangzhong County	No specific data published on the website	No specific data published on the website	–	20.36	48.10	10.80	0.00	50.00	0.00	No	
110	Shaanxi	The Primary People's Court of Shenmu City	25	1362.88	−85	20.12	62.96	25.10	0.00	0.00	0.00	Yes	54
111	Inner Mongolia	The Primary People's Court of Ulanhot City	103	176.50	−8	19.63	44.15	6.00	0.00	60.00	0.00	No	
112	Xizang	The Primary People's Court of Linzhou County	114	15.30	2	19.34	41.70	30.00	10.00	0.00	0.00	No	

(continued)

Table 7 (continued)

Ranking	Province/Municipality/Autonomous Region	Court	GDP ranking	GDP (100 million yuan)	A comparison between the GDP ranking and the judicial transparency index ranking	Total score (points)	Disclosure of trial affairs (points)	Disclosure of trial information (points)	Disclosure of enforcement information (points)	Disclosure of judicial data (points)	Disclosure of information on judicial reform (points)	Whether it belongs to the top 100 counties, cities or districts	Top 100 ranking (districts, and cities and counties are ranked respectively)
113	Sichuan	The Primary People's Court of Langzhong City	98	254.01	−15	18.25	50.00	21.50	0.00	12.00	0.00	No	
114	Shaanxi	The Primary People's Court of Dingbian County	90	317.62	−24	18.24	27.30	35.10	0.00	15.00	0.00	No	
115	Xizang	The Primary People's Court of Gar County	No specific data published on the website	No specific data published on the website	–	18.08	24.15	30.00	10.00	15.00	0.00	No	
116	Hubei	The Primary People's Court of Wuchang District of Wuhan City	22	1522.04	−94	16.48	44.15	23.00	0.00	0.00	5.00	No	
117	Hubei	The Primary People's Court of Enshi City	81	379.52	−36	14.56	42.96	19.90	0.00	0.00	0.00	No	

(continued)

Table 7 (continued)

Ranking	Province/Municipality/Autonomous Region	Court	GDP ranking	GDP (100 million yuan)	A comparison between the GDP ranking and the judicial transparency index ranking	Total score (points)	Disclosure of trial affairs (points)	Disclosure of trial information (points)	Disclosure of enforcement information (points)	Disclosure of judicial data (points)	Disclosure of information on judicial reform (points)	Whether it belongs to the top 100 counties, cities or districts	Top 100 ranking (districts, and cities and counties are ranked respectively)
118	Liaoning	The Primary People's Court of Haicheng City	65	590.00	−53	14.04	27.30	3.60	0.00	50.00	0.00	Yes	10
119	Hubei	The Primary People's Court of Jiang'an District of Wuhan City	26	1335.90	−93	12.07	26.40	9.30	20.00	0.00	0.00	No	
No website	Shanghai	The Primary People's Court of Hongkou District of Shanghai Municipality	43	1033.00	–	No website	No website	No website	No website	No website	No website	No	
No website	Shanghai	The Primary People's Court of Jing'an District of Shanghai Municipality	14	2298.70	–	No website	No website	No website	No website	No website	No website	No	

(continued)

Table 7 (continued)

Ranking	Province/Municipality/Autonomous Region	Court	GDP ranking	GDP (100 million yuan)	A comparison between the GDP ranking and the judicial transparency index ranking	Total score (points)	Disclosure of trial affairs (points)	Disclosure of trial information (points)	Disclosure of enforcement information (points)	Disclosure of judicial data (points)	Disclosure of information on judicial reform (points)	Whether it belongs to the top 100 counties, cities or districts	Top 100 ranking (districts, and cities and counties are ranked respectively)
No website	Shanghai	The Primary People's Court of Minhang District of Shanghai Municipality	13	2520.80	–	No website	No website	No website	No website	No website	No website	No	
No website	Xinjiang	The Primary People's Court of Sayibak District of Urumqi City	No specific data published on the website	No specific data published on the website	–	No website	No website	No website	No website	No website	No website	No	
No website	Xinjiang	The Primary People's Court of Xinshi District of Urumqi City	No specific data published on the website	No specific data published on the website	–	No website	No website	No website	No website	No website	No website	Yes	34

on judicial openness, which is the requirement for furthering judicial reforms and the outgrowth of the response to social concerns.

1.3 *Informatization Construction Has Expanded Judicial Openness*

The informatization construction launched by the people's courts has advanced judicial openness. Backed up by information technology, court practice is more transparent than ever, and constant expansion can be seen in judicial openness, which means fairness and justice have been realized in the way that we can see. At the same time, judicial openness enables people to participate more in court and thus has fostered an efficient social supervision mechanism in a timely response to social concerns. Judicial openness supported by information technology exposes judicial corruption, thus tremendously enhancing judicial credibility and maintaining the authority of people's courts. In 2020, relying on the big data visualization of judicial openness, the Supreme People's Court solved the problem of slow retrieval speed caused by the heavy index data of the website China Judgements Online and facilitated concurrent users' access to the website. The establishment and operation of the website China Court Trial Online indicate that the four disclosure platforms regarding the judicial process, court trials, judgments, and enforcement information have jointly built a solid foundation for judicial openness. By the end of December 2020, China Court Trial Online had given 11.0494 million live broadcasts of trials, and the cumulative number of visits to the four platforms had exceeded 31.904 billion. The Supreme People's Court upgraded the intelligent cloud platform for audio and video live broadcasting and recording to ensure smooth online broadcasting. Besides, the Supreme People's Court managed to develop a function based on speech recognition algorithms and models to shield the privacy of the persons in trial videos, fully safeguarding that of the parties and relevant personnel at the trial site.

1.4 *Judgment Disclosure Has Become the Highlight of Judicial Openness*

According to the Supreme People's Court, the total number of judgments on China Judgements Online had exceeded 100 million, and the website had had nearly 48 billion visits by 6 pm on August 30, 2020. Publication of judgments plays an increasingly constructive role in promoting the standardized operation of judicial power, increasing public knowledge of the law, and relying on judicial big data to serve economic and social development.

1.5 *Judicial Openness of Many District Courts Has Improved Steadily*

According to the judicial transparency index ranking in 2020, the top 15 courts among the 49 intermediate people's courts are mainly located in Guangdong, Jilin, Jiangsu, Zhejiang, and Shandong, and the top 20 primary people's courts are mainly located in Jilin, Guangxi, Guangdong, Jiangsu, Zhejiang, and Anhui. The high people's courts in the above provinces ranked top as well. The ranking of the Intermediate People's Court of Guangzhou City remained stable, so did the primary people's courts and specialized courts within its jurisdiction. That proves that many courts have scored remarkable achievements in promoting judicial openness.

1.6 *Judicial Openness of the Courts Nationwide Has Fluctuated Slightly.*

A comparison of the index rankings of the assessed 81 intermediate and high people's courts in 2019 shows that eight courts retained their rankings in the past two years: the High People's Court of Shanghai Municipality, the Intermediate People's Court of Guangzhou City, the Intermediate People's Court of Jilin City, the Intermediate People's Court of Haikou City, the Intermediate People's Court of Xiamen City, the Intermediate People's Court of Baotou City, the Intermediate People's Court of Xi'an City, and the Intermediate People's Court of Xinjiang Production and Construction Corps. All the above courts except the latter two have made progress in advancing judicial openness.

The rankings of 36 courts fluctuated between plus and minus five, accounting for 44.44%, and 55 courts between plus and minus ten, accounting for 67.90%. Thirty-six courts ranked higher in 2020, 22 of which ranked higher by less than ten places (including ten places), and 14 of which ranked higher by more than ten places (excluding ten places). That shows quite a lot of courts have made some or significant progress in judicial openness in the past year (see Table 8).

2 Remaining Problems in Judicial Openness

However, it must be noted that while some progress has been made, there are still many problems in judicial openness, which calls for concerns.

Table 8 Fluctuation of judicial transparency index ranking in 2019 and 2020

Court	Ranking 2020	Ranking 2019	Ranking change[6]
The Intermediate People's Court of Urumqi City of Xinjiang Uygur Autonomous Region	77	37	−40
The High People's Court of Xinjiang Uygur Autonomous Region	61	30	−31
The High People's Court of Liaoning Province	52	26	−26
The Intermediate People's Court of Dalian City of Liaoning Province	79	55	−24
The High People's Court of Hebei Province	25	21	−4
The Intermediate People's Court of Lanzhou City of Gansu Province	42	38	−4
The Intermediate People's Court of Fushun City of Liaoning Province	75	71	−4
The Intermediate People's Court of Nanjing City of Jiangsu Province	4	2	−2
The Intermediate People's Court of Suzhou City of Jiangsu Province	59	57	−2
The High People's Court of Ningxia Hui Autonomous Region	62	60	−2
The High People's Court of Shaanxi Province	64	62	−2
The High People's Court of Beijing Municipality	14	13	−1
The Intermediate People's Court of Guangzhou City of Guangdong Province	1	1	0
The Intermediate People's Court of Jilin City of Jilin Province	3	3	0
The Intermediate People's Court of Haikou City of Hainan Province	6	6	0
The High People's Court of Shanghai Municipality	19	19	0

(continued)

[6] The fluctuation of rankings is the difference between the ranking in 2020 and that in 2019. A negative number means that the ranking declined in 2020, a positive number means that the ranking rose in 2020, and 0 means no change in the ranking.

Table 8 (continued)

Court	Ranking 2020	Ranking 2019	Ranking change
The Intermediate People's Court of Xiamen City of Fujian Province	27	27	0
The Intermediate People's Court of Baotou City of Inner Mongolia Autonomous Region	56	56	0
The Intermediate People's Court of Xi'an City of Shaanxi Province	76	76	0
The Production and Construction Corps Branch of the High People's Court of Xinjiang Uygur Autonomous Region	81	81	0
The Intermediate People's Court of Chengdu City of Sichuan Province	7	8	1
The High People's Court of Fujian Province	33	34	1
The High People's Court of Anhui Province	39	40	1
The Intermediate People's Court of Anshan City of Liaoning Province	63	64	1
The Intermediate People's Court of Ningbo City of Zhejiang Province	5	7	2
The High People's Court of Guangdong Province	12	14	2
The High People's Court of Chongqing Municipality	47	49	2
The Intermediate People's Court of Zhengzhou City of Henan Province	67	70	3
The High People's Court of Henan Province	40	44	4
The Intermediate People's Court of Lhasa City of Xizang Autonomous Region	69	73	4
The Intermediate People's Court of Wuhan City of Hubei Province	73	77	4
The Intermediate People's Court of Zibo City of Shandong Province	17	22	5
The Intermediate People's Court of Hangzhou City of Zhejiang Province	20	25	5
The High People's Court of Jiangxi Province	26	32	6

(continued)

Table 8 (continued)

Court	Ranking 2020	Ranking 2019	Ranking change
The High People's Court of Yunnan Province	36	42	6
The High People's Court of Sichuan Province	11	18	7
The Intermediate People's Court of Jinan City of Shandong Province	22	29	7
The High People's Court of Xizang autonomous Region	54	61	7
The Intermediate People's Court of Hefei City of Anhui Province	44	53	9
The Intermediate People's Court of Nanning City of Guangxi Zhuang Autonomous Region	60	69	9
The High People's Court of Shanxi Province	70	79	9
The Intermediate People's Court of Shenzhen City of Guangdong Province	2	12	10
The High People's Court of Inner Mongolia Autonomous Region	32	43	11
The Intermediate People's Court of Kunming City of Yunnan Province	66	78	12
The Intermediate People's Court of Shantou City of Guangdong Province	10	23	13
The Intermediate People's Court of Hohhot City of Inner Mongolia Autonomous Region	50	63	13
The Intermediate People's Court of Yinchuan City of Ningxia Hui Autonomous Region	58	72	14
The Intermediate People's Court of Harbin City of Heilongjiang Province	65	80	15
The High People's Court of Hunan Province	30	46	16
The High People's Court of Guizhou Province	35	52	17
The Intermediate People's Court of Luoyang City of Henan Province	49	68	19
The Intermediate People's Court of Nanchang City of Jiangxi Province	37	58	21

The fluctuation of rankings is the difference between the ranking in 2020 and that in 2019. A negative number means that the ranking declined in 2020, a positive number means that the ranking rose in 2020, and 0 means no change in the ranking

2.1 Large Gap Between Courts and Between Sections

Judicial openness is a requirement from courts and is necessary for court trials and enforcement of judgments. Besides, laws and judicial interpretations have made explicit provisions for judicial openness. However, over the years, the judicial transparency index assessments reveal a wide gap between courts at all levels regarding the overall situation and sections (see Table 9).

In the 2011 Assessment, among the 69 assessed courts (including 26 high people's courts and 43 intermediate people's courts in larger cities; excluding the high people's courts and intermediate people's courts in ethnic autonomous regions), the highest score was 73.5 points, the lowest was 0, and the average was 42.1 points. Only nine courts scored more than 60 points, while the other 60 courts scored below the average. Among the high people's courts, the highest score was 73.5 points, the lowest was 2.5 points, and the average was 45.93 points. Thirty-eight courts scored more than 60 points. Among the intermediate people's courts, the highest score was 69.75 points, the lowest was 0, and the average was 42.6 points. Six courts scored more than 60 points.

In the 2012 Assessment, among the 69 assessed courts (including 26 high people's courts and 43 intermediate people's courts in larger cities; excluding the high people's courts and intermediate people's courts in ethnic autonomous regions), the highest score was 65.5 points, the lowest was 0, and the average was 30.05 points. Only three courts scored more than 60 points, while the other courts scored lower than the average. Among the high people's courts, the highest score was 65.5 points, the lowest was 0, and the average was 33.6 points. Three courts gained more than 60 points. Among the intermediate people's courts, the highest score was 59.25 points, the lowest was 0, and the average was 28.73 points. No court scored over 60 points.

In the 2013 Assessment, among the 80 assessed courts (including 31 high people's courts and 49 intermediate people's courts in larger cities), the highest score was 76.5 points, the lowest was 0, and the average was 41.89 points. Only 15 courts scored more than 60 points, while the other 65 courts did not reach the average. Among the high people's courts, the highest was 76.5 points, the lowest was 0, and the average score was 39.48 points. Five courts scored more than 60 points. Among the intermediate people's courts, the highest score was 75.5 points, the lowest was 0, and the average was 42.53 points. Ten courts got more than 60 points.

In the 2014 Assessment, among the 80 assessed courts (including 31 high people's courts and 49 intermediate people's courts in larger cities), the highest score was 89.02 points, the lowest score was 30.06 points, and the average score was 58.9 points. Only 38 courts gained more than 60 points, while the other courts failed to arrive at the average. Among the high people's courts, the highest score was 84.85 points, the lowest was 31.93 points, and the average was 59.6 points. Twenty courts scored more than 60 points. Among the intermediate people's courts, the highest score was 89.02, the lowest was 30.06, and the average was 55. Eighteen courts achieved more than 60 points.

Table 9 2011–2020 judicial transparency scores[7]

		The highest score	The lowest score	The average score	The number of courts with more than 60 points
2011 Year	69 courts[8]	73.5	0	42.1	9
	High people's courts	73.5	2.5	45.93	3
	Intermediate people's courts	69.75	0	42.6	6
2012 Year	69 courts	65.5	0	30.05	3
	High people's courts	65.5	9	33.60	3
	Intermediate people's courts	59.25	0	28.73	0
2013 Year	80 courts	76.5	0	41.89	15
	High people's courts	76.5	0	39.48	5
	Intermediate people's courts	75.5	0	42.53	10
2014 Year	80 courts	89.02	30.06	58.90	38
	High people's courts	84.85	31.93	59.60	20
	Intermediate people's courts	89.02	30.06	55.00	18
2015 Year	80 courts	82.33	36.1	56.52	29
	High people's courts	71.85	38.34	56.24	16
	Intermediate people's courts	82.33	36.1	54.71	13
2016 Year	80 courts	91.82	33.28	57.51	29
	High people's courts	82.95	33.28	56.74	12

(continued)

[7] Assessment results (2011–2018) can be found in Blue Book of Rule of Law: Annual Report on Rule of Law in China (2012–2019), published by Social Sciences Academic Press (China).

[8] The high people's courts of the Ethnic Autonomous Regions and the intermediate people's court within the jurisdiction are not included in the 2011 and 2012 assessments, so the number of assessed courts in the two years is 69.

Table 9 (continued)

		The highest score	The lowest score	The average score	The number of courts with more than 60 points
	Intermediate people's courts	91.82	35.38	57.82	17
2017 Year	80 courts	92.68	33.4	56.04	21
	High people's courts	81.08	38.4	58.12	9
	Intermediate people's courts	92.68	33.4	54.73	12
2018 Year	80 courts	91.7	34	56.49	24
	High people's courts	84.87	41.9	58.53	12
	Intermediate people's courts	91.7	34	55.20	12
2019Year	93 courts	92.23	22.43	48.90	20
	High people's courts	80.9	22.43	47.66	8
	Intermediate people's courts	92.23	26.25	49.19	10
	Specialized courts	69.47	26.36	50.76	2
2020Year	212 courts	91.53	12.07	43.18	33
	High people's courts	71.53	15.18	44.49	6
	Intermediate people's courts	91.53	22.05	44.11	11
	Specialized courts	89.41	31.09	49.10	3
	Primary people's courts	85.73	12.07	41.84	13

In the 2015 Assessment, among the 80 assessed courts (including 31 high people's courts and 49 intermediate people's courts in larger cities), the highest score was 82.33 points, the lowest score was 36.1 points, and the average score was 56.52 points. Only 29 courts gained over 60 points, while the other courts reached lower than the average. Among the high people's courts, the highest score was 71.85 points, the lowest was 38.34 points, and the average was 56.24 points. Sixteen courts gained over 60 points. Among the intermediate people's courts, the highest score was 82.33 points, the lowest was 36.1 points, and the average was 54.71 points. Thirteen courts scored more than 60 points.

In the 2016 Assessment, among the 80 assessed courts (including 31 high people's courts and 49 intermediate people's courts in larger cities), the highest score was

91.82 points, the lowest score was 33.28 points, and the average score was 57.51 points. Only 29 courts scored more than 60 points, while the other courts did not reach the average. Among the high people's courts, the highest score was 82.95 points, the lowest was 33.28 points, and the average was 56.74 points. Twelve courts got more than 60 points. Among the intermediate people's courts, the highest was 91.82 points, the lowest was 35.38 points, and the average score was 57.82 points. Seventeen courts scored over 60 points.

In the 2017 Assessment, among the 80 assessed courts (including 31 high people's courts and 49 intermediate people's courts in larger cities), the highest score was 92.86 points, the lowest score was 33.4 points, and the average score was 56.04 points. Only 21 courts gained more than 60 points, while the other courts reached lower than the average. Among the high people's courts, the highest score was 81.08 points, the lowest was 38.4 points, and the average was 58.12 points. Nine courts scored more than 60 points. Among the intermediate people's courts, the highest score was 92.68 points, the lowest was 33.4 points, and the average was 54.73 points. Twelve courts gained over 60 points.

In the 2018 Assessment, among the 80 assessed courts (including 31 high people's courts and 49 intermediate people's courts in larger cities), the highest score was 91.7 points, the lowest score was 34 points, and the average score was 56.49 points. Only 24 courts gained over 60 points, while the other courts reached below the average. Among the high people's courts, the highest score was 84.87 points, the lowest was 41.9 points, and the average score was 58.53 points. Twelve courts scored more than 60 points. Among the intermediate people's courts, the highest score was 91.7 points, the lowest was 34 points, and the average was 55.2 points. Twelve courts scored more than 60 points.

In the 2019 Assessment, among the 93 assessed courts, the highest score was 92.33 points, the lowest score was 22.43 points, and the average score was 48.9 points. Only 20 courts scored more than 60 points, while the other courts failed to reach the average. Among the high people's courts, the highest score was 80.9 points, the lowest was 22.43 points, and the average score was 47.66 points. Eight courts scored more than 60 points. Among the intermediate people's courts, the highest score was 92.23 points, the lowest was 26.25 points, and the average score was 49.19 points. Ten courts got more than 60 points. The highest score among the specialized courts was 69.47 points, the lowest score was 26.36 points, and the average score was 50.76 points. Two courts scored more than 60 points.

In the 2020 Assessment, the Intermediate People's Court of Guangzhou City gained the highest score of 91.53 points, and the lowest score was only 12.07 points. Among the assessed high people's courts, the highest score was 71.53 points, and the lowest was 15.18 points. The highest score among the assessed intermediate people's courts was 91.53 points, and the lowest was 22.05 points. The highest score among the assessed primary people's courts was 85.73 points, and the lowest was 12.07 points. The highest score among the assessed specialized courts was 89.41 points, and the lowest was 31.09 points. A comparison between the average score of the top 10% courts and that of the bottom 10% courts reveals that the average difference of 44.85 points, 57.83 points, 52.05 points, and 58.32 points among the high people's courts, the intermediate people's courts, the primary people's courts, and specialized courts, respectively. These data indicate a wide disparity in judicial openness between courts nationwide.

In addition to the gap between the total points, the score gap under each assessment indicator also remains large. Since the 2011 Assessment, the assessment indicators and weights have been adjusted constantly. Therefore, this book only briefly compares the 2019 Assessment with the 2020 Assessment. The target 93 courts are identical in these two assessments. The weighting system for the specialized courts adopts the 2019 standard. The assessment results reveal that the score gap between the courts is also significant in the assessed five sectors. Regarding disclosure of the information on trial affairs, the highest score in 2019 was 100 points, the lowest score was 15.80 points, and the average score was 56.28 points. Thirty-six courts scored more than 60 points. The highest score in 2020 remained 100 points, the lowest was 7 points, and the average was 55.19 points. Thirty courts gained more than 60 points. In terms of judicial process information disclosure, the highest score in 2019 was 94.60 points, the lowest was 20 points, and the average was 52.43 points. Twenty-tight courts scored more than 60 points. The highest score in 2020 was 95.60 points, the lowest was 18.40 points, and the average was 53.71 points. Twenty-six courts scored over 60 points. Regarding enforcement information disclosure, the highest score in 2019 was 85 points, the lowest was 10 points, and the average was 42.85 points. Twenty-two courts scored more than 60 points. The highest score in 2020 was 90 points, the lowest was 0, and the average was 26.79 points. Fourteen courts got more than 60 points. As regards judicial data disclosure, the highest score in 2019 was 100 points, the lowest was 10 points, and the average was 51.81 points. Thirty courts gained more than 60 points. The highest score in 2020 was also 100 points, the lowest was 0, and the average was 49.29 points. Twenty-eight courts scored more than 60 points. In regard to disclosure of judicial reform information, the highest score in 2019 was 100 points, the lowest was 10 points, and the average was 37.31 points. Nineteen courts gained over 60 points. The highest score in 2020 was also 100 points, the lowest was 0, and the average was 33.23 points. Fourteen courts achieved over 60 points (see Figs. 1 and 2).

A separate comparison of the scores of the primary people's courts newly assessed in 2020 reveals similar problems. According to the data, among the 119 primary people's courts (excluding five courts without websites), in terms of disclosure of the information on trial affairs, the highest score was 96.25 points, the lowest score was 10.50 points, and the average score was 51.25 points. Forty-two courts gained more than 60 points. Regarding judicial process information disclosure, the highest score was 87.90 points, the lowest was 0, and the average was 49.09 points. Thirty-nine courts scored over 60 points. In terms of enforcement information disclosure, the highest score was 100 points, the lowest was 0, and the average was 37.03 points. Fifty-one courts gained more than 60 points. In respect of judicial data disclosure, the highest score was 100 points, the lowest was 0, and the average score was 44.89 points. Forty-one courts got more than 60 points. Regarding disclosure of judicial reform information, the highest score was 95 points, the lowest was 0, and the average was 18.19 points. Six courts gained more than 60 points (see Fig. 3)

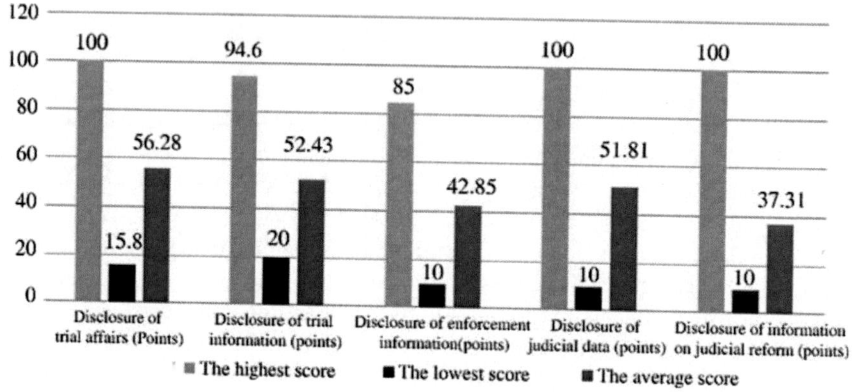

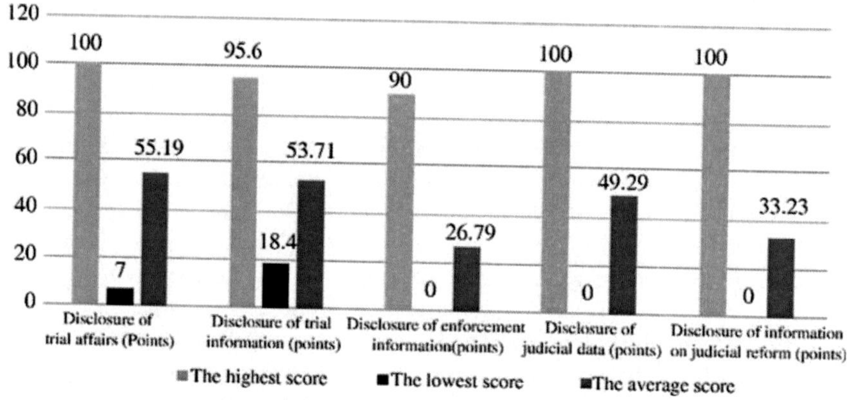

Fig. 2 A comparison of the scores in five sectors in 2020

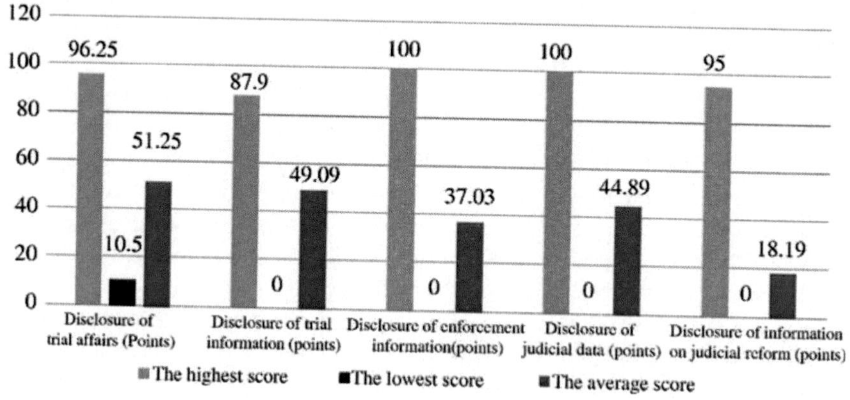

Fig. 3 A comparison of the scores in five sectors of the primary people's courts in 2020

The above data shows that in terms of the overall situation and specific sections, the implementation of judicial openness varies from court to court, and some are still relatively slow and lagging.

In addition, according to the above data, the horizontal comparison of the five assessed sections reveals the uneven development of judicial openness and the unsatisfactory situation in the disclosure of judicial reform information and enforcement information. The three groups of data show that disclosure of the information on trial affairs has overall sound momentum; disclosure of judicial reform information is generally unsatisfactory; disclosure of enforcement information still faces challenges. Though enforcement difficulties have been solved after two or three years of effort, the overall situation on enforcement information disclosure is far less impressive. That indicates a long journey before establishing a long-term mechanism for solving these difficulties. Regarding disclosure of judicial reform information, the situation is still unsatisfying even if we ignore the differences among the higher, intermediate, and other specialized courts in respect of their roles in judicial reforms.

2.2 *Relatively Slow Progress in Judicial Openness*

As the assessments show, the courts at all levels and of all kinds have made little progress in judicial openness. The data below show that the courts have performed poorly in the five major areas under the Level 1 indicators, with the original assessed objects' data almost unchanged. Subject to the strict standards, the results of the 2020 Assessment have turned out to be disappointing and are slightly worse than those of the 2019 Assessment, no matter on the whole or in each section. Vast amounts of information that should have been made public as required by relevant judicial interpretations and documents issued by the Supreme People's Court remain undisclosed. The courts at all levels have not actively disclosed the information that should have been accessible to the public as required by the *Opinions of the Supreme People's Court on Furthering Judicial Openness* (No. 20 [2018] of the Supreme People's Court). For example, the courts have moved slowly to disclose the research reports of judicial data and the results of handling the suggestions by deputies to people's congresses and the proposals by CPPCC members. Furthermore, the information about court personnel, litigation guides, enforcement, judicial data, and judicial reforms has been updated slowly, irregularly, or failed to be updated. Judicial openness has stagnated.

2.3 *Insufficient Judicial Openness in Primary people's Courts*

Among the four tiers of courts, primary people's courts have the heaviest caseload and the closest relationship with the public, which calls for higher-quality judicial service. In order to have the vast majority of disputes settled by primary courts, we must strengthen their standardized construction and improve their capacity for trial and enforcement to increase judicial credibility and authority. That requires a primary people's court to provide judicial openness service commensurate with its status and public demands. However, the 2020 Assessment reveals the relatively weak judicial openness of the primary people's courts. In 2020, among the 124 primary people's courts, five of them were not considered in the index ranking and data statistics due to their lack of websites then, namely the Primary People's Court of Jing'an District of Shanghai Municipality, the Primary People's Court of Hongkou District of Shanghai Municipality, the Primary People's Court of Minhang District of Shanghai Municipality, the Primary People's Court of Xinshi District of Urumqi City, and the Primary People's Court of Sayibak District of Urumqi City. The average score of the remaining 119 courts was 41.84 points. By comparison, the average score of the high people's courts was 44.49 points, that of the intermediate people's courts was 44.11 points, and that of the 12 specialized courts was 49.10 points. Despite the similar average scores among the four tiers of courts, the average score of the primary people's courts was lower than those of the intermediate people's courts and the high people's courts, respectively, even if the weight setting for assessing those primary people's courts in 2020 was not that rigorous.

In terms of distribution of the scores, 13 courts scored more than 60 points, accounting for 10.92%; 22 courts 50 to 60 points (excluding 60 points), accounting for 18.49%; 31 courts 40 to 50 points (excluding 50 points), accounting for 26.05%; 23 courts 30 to 40 points (excluding 40 points), accounting for 19.33%; 21 courts 20 to 30 points (excluding 30 points), accounting for 17.65%; nine courts below 20 points (excluding 20 points), accounting for 7.56%. Most of the courts scored below 60 points (see Fig. 4). Moreover, the following analysis of the data on most indicators shows that the primary people's courts have performed the least satisfyingly in judicial openness, which demonstrates that the courts still have a lot to do in moving forward with judicial openness.

2.4 *Judicial Openness in Some Courts Incommensurate with Local Development*

The rule of law guarantees the best business environment, and the judiciary is the last line of defense to safeguard social fairness and justice. High-quality trial and enforcement demonstrate the local courts' capacity for efficiently resolving disputes and protecting the parties' legitimate rights and interests and how local construction of the rule of law develops. As a crucial means to equally protect various subjects under the law, judicial transparency gives expression to the courts' ability to provide judicial service for society and how well-regulated the trial and enforcement powers can be to a great extent. For this reason, the degree of judicial openness is directly related to whether enterprises and people can have high expectations of protecting their legitimate rights and interests according to the law and is a crucial indicator of

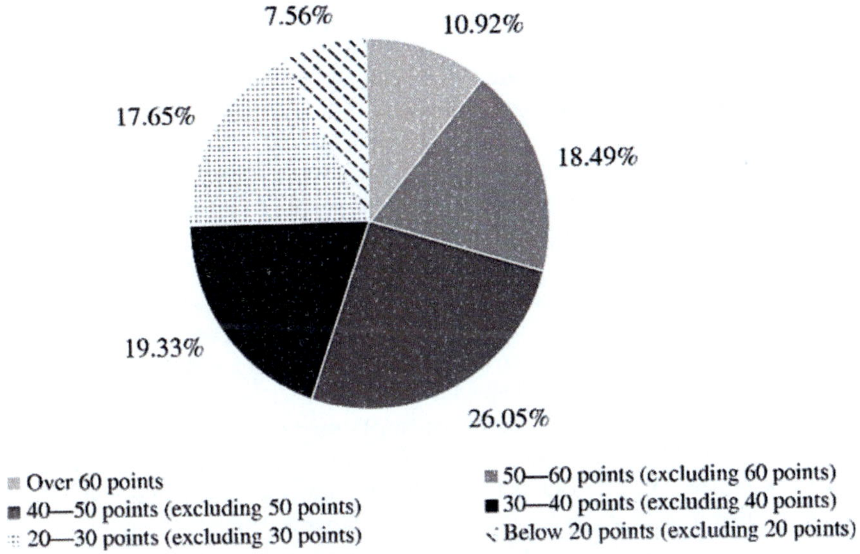

Fig. 4 Distribution of the primary people's courts' scores in the 2020 assessment

evaluating the local business environment. Without comprehensively implemented judicial openness, the standardized operation of judicial power and the highly efficient judicial service can not be guaranteed. However, according to the assessments, some courts' degree of judicial openness failed to conform to the local economic development. Taking the judicial openness in the high people's courts and intermediate people's courts as an example, the assessment results in some of the courts did not match the local economic development to a certain extent or obviously.

According to the 2019 results, ten high people's courts and 17 intermediate people's courts ranked in the judicial transparency index below the GDP rankings of the provinces where they were located in the previous year by five places. That is to say, their rankings in the judicial transparency index were remarkably lower, even though these provinces in which the above courts were located had higher GDP rankings. For instance, among the high people's courts, the High People's Court of Fujian Province, the High People's Court of Henan Province, the High People's Court of Hubei Province, the High People's Court of Hunan Province, the High People's Court of Shaanxi Province, and the High People's Court of Shanxi Province ranked in sequence 16th, 21st, 22nd, 23rd, 29th, and 31st while the provinces where they were located ranked in sequence 10th, 5th, 7th, 8th, 15th, and 22nd in terms of GDP in 2018 (see Table 1). That was especially true in the intermediate people's courts. Among the 49 intermediate people's courts in major cities, the following courts ranked in the judicial transparency index below the GDP rankings of those cities where the courts were located: the Intermediate People's Court of Qingdao City, the Intermediate People's Court of Hefei City, the Intermediate People's Court of Dalian City, the Intermediate People's Court of Suzhou City, the Intermediate

People's Court of Fuzhou City, the Intermediate People's Court of Changsha City, the Intermediate People's Court of Luoyang City, the Intermediate People's Court of Zhengzhou City, the Intermediate People's Court of Wuxi City, the Intermediate People's Court of Xi'an City, the Intermediate People's Court of Wuhan City, the Intermediate People's Court of Kunming City, and the Intermediate People's Court of Harbin City (see Table 2).

According to the 2020 Assessment, ten high people's courts, 17 intermediate people's courts, and 52 primary people's courts ranked below the GDP rankings of the cities in which these courts were located by five places in the previous year (13 courts not considered due to the lack of websites or the GDP data in the previous year) (see Tables 4, 5 and 7). Among the 24 primary people's courts located in the top 100 counties and districts nationwide, only six courts ranked in the top 20 in the judicial transparency index, namely the Primary People's Court of Yanji City of Jilin Province, the Primary People's Court of Wujiang District of Suzhou City, the Primary People's Court of Shuyang County of Jiangsu Province, the Primary People's Court of Yuhang District of Hangzhou City of Zhejiang Province, the Primary People's Court of Yiwu City of Zhejiang Province, the Primary People's Court of Yaohai District of Hefei City of Anhui Province. Ten courts ranked below the 50th (five courts without websites not included) (see Table 7).

To a certain degree, it indicates that a prosperous economy does not necessarily imply more progressive or better judicial openness. However, at least it shows that in terms of optimizing the business environment, the courts of some places have provided little support. Judicial openness in some courts has fallen far behind the local economy. Their participation in social governance and the upgrading of the business environment deserves further concern.

2.5 *Erratic Performance in Judicial Openness by Some Courts*

According to the 2019 and 2020 assessments, most courts have experienced a slight fluctuation in judicial openness. However, the comparisons between the 2019 index rankings of the original 81 intermediate and high people's courts and their 2020 index rankings reveal that a few courts have fluctuated significantly, which deserves attention. The rankings of 36 courts dropped in 2020 (see Table 8), out of which the rankings of 22 courts fell by less than ten places (including ten places), and the rankings of 14 courts slipped by more than ten places (excluding ten places). It is reasonable to infer that some courts declined in rankings due to their lack of attention to judicial openness or inadequate contribution.

2.6 *Further Efforts to Be Made for Judicial Openness by Specialized Courts*

The specialized courts assessed in 2019 and 2020 involved those specialized fields with higher professional standards, such as free trade zones, intellectual property, Internet, and finance. Their judicial level and judicial openness were supposed to be more standardized. However, the reality is quite the opposite. Firstly, the judicial openness of the courts located in the free trade zones failed to meet the expectations. In the 2019 Assessment, only one court scored more than 60 points, and the lowest score was 27.15 points. In 2020, only two of the five courts in the free trade zones gained over 60 points, and the lowest score was 31.09 points. Such results were not in line with the free trade zones' requests for transparency to improve judicial service and optimize the business environment. Secondly, the judicial openness of the internet courts was insufficient. Internet courts, emphasizing the support of Internet technology, enable the whole process of judicial cases to be handled online. Hence, internet courts should also have taken the lead in pressing ahead with judicial openness by relying on the Internet. On the contrary, the assessment results reveal the mediocre performance of the three internet courts. In particular, as regards the disclosure of the information on trial affairs, judicial process information, and other core businesses, these courts failed to exploit their advantages to the full, and some courts performed poorly in the disclosure of enforcement information and judicial data. At last, the intellectual property courts, on the whole, ranked poorly. In 2019 and 2020, all three intellectual property courts scored less than 60 points; the disclosure of trial information and enforcement information was unsatisfactory. The above suggests that specialized courts should play the strengths different from those of traditional courts and set an example in standardizing judicial openness and ensuring justice for the people.

2.7 *Problems to Be Solved Regarding Judgment Disclosure*

Unlike the previous assessments, which mainly observed the forms of judgment disclosure, the 2020 Assessment focused more on retrieving internal data to analyze and compare the proportion of judgments disclosed and the standardization of identifying the reasons for not publishing some judgments on the Internet. Since the operation of China Judgements Online, the most incredible progress has been made in judgment disclosure with the most remarkable achievements. The principle that disclosure is the rule and non-disclosure is the exception has enjoyed widespread support. By 6 pm on August 30, 2020, the total number of judgments on China Judgements Online had exceeded 100 million, with nearly 48 billion visits. However, an analysis of the data on the assessed courts shows that despite the increasing judgments uploaded to China Judgements Online, the proportion of those with the unpublished main body is that high. 22.28% of the selected judgments had information items disclosed, such as the case number and the reasons for not being published online, 51.22% of which were not published in full text for other reasons. The team found a higher proportion in some courts. Such proportion in many courts exceeded 90%. The percentage of the judgments whose full texts were not published online for involving state secrets or any other statutory cause was relatively low. To figure out whether it is due to the less comprehensive system for making judgments public online or less effective openness of relevant courts needs our further work.

2.8 *Weak Disclosure of the Information About Enforcement and Judicial Reforms*

The assessments prove the inadequate disclosure of enforcement information and judicial reform information. In the 2020 Assessment, the average scores in the five assessed sections of the 81 intermediate and high people's courts were 53.51 points, 52.59 points, 25.97 points, 50.42 points, and 33.52 points, respectively. Those of the primary people's courts were 51.25 points, 49.09 points, 37.03 points, 44.89 points, and 18.19 points, respectively; those of the specialized courts were 66.59 points, 61.25 points, 32.33 points, 41.67 points, and 31.25 points, respectively. The low average scores suggested the weak judicial openness in these domains.

2.9 *Less Advanced Construction of Judicial Openness Platforms*

In this information age, the website has been billed as the first platform for information disclosure, which has enjoyed great recognition in the transparency of all government affairs. According to Article 7 of the Notice of *the General Office of the State Council on the Preparation for the Implementation of the Regulations of the People's Republic of China on the Disclosure of Government Information promulgated in 2007,* "the websites of the governments at various levels will be the first platforms for government information disclosure." Article 11 of the Key Arrangements of *the General Office of the State Council for Government Information Disclosure issued in 2012 provided that a*ll regions and departments should strengthen the administration of government websites, conduct supervision and examination on a level-by-level basis, and maximize the role of government websites as the first platforms for information disclosure. Pursuant to the Opinions of the General Office of the State Council on Strengthening the Development of Contents of Information on Government Websites issued in 2014, government information should be released in a timely and accurate manner, exchange and interaction should be carried out, the public should be canvassed, a response should be made to public concerns, and public supervision should be welcomed. In this way, government websites will become the primary sources for the public to obtain government information and an important communication channel. Under this document, all regions and departments should treat government websites as primary platforms for government information disclosure and establish and improve information release mechanisms to promptly release information on crucial government conferences, activities, and policies. Over the years, the rapid development of government websites has been based on such understanding. *The Guide of the General Office of the State Council to the Development of Government Websites printed and issued in 2017 proposed that* people's governments at or above the county level and departments under the State Council should set up portals and not close them under normal circumstances. In addition, according to this Guide, authorities should adapt to the internet age, encourage intensive sharing, and keep innovative so that government websites will become more comprehensive and authoritative platforms for publishing and interpreting policies, guiding public opinions, responding to public concerns more efficiently, and providing services for the convenience of the public. The construction of websites is essential to the transparency of government affairs and services hereabout and the judicial openness of courts and various litigation services.

When the judicial transparency assessment was first conducted in 2011, all intermediate people's courts of 10 provinces, autonomous regions, and municipalities directly under the Central Government had websites with valid links. In other assessed 11 provinces, autonomous regions, and municipalities directly under the Central Government, the intermediate people's courts with websites accounted for less than 60%.[9] Comparatively, after many years of the informatization construction of courts, courts nationwide have gained impressive achievements in building their portals. The statistics show that by February 2016, all high people's courts, 358 intermediate people's courts, and 2,747 primary people's courts across the nation had built websites for government affairs.[10]

However, the 2020 Assessment reveals that several primary people's courts have not set up or have closed their websites due to the lack of personnel and funds, making it difficult for the public and the parties involved in a particular case to inquire about the court. With the continuous perfection of various platforms set up by higher courts, much information about primary people's courts may be directly released. It is not practical now for primary courts to carry out judicial openness, totally relying on higher courts, as they still have information entailing independent disclosure. In addition, years of assessments have presented plenty of problems regarding the websites of most courts, such as repeated construction of platforms, non-standard setting of columns, irregular information release locations, and unconfigured or invalid functions of searching the website. On the whole, the construction of the court websites has been far behind that of government agencies, which is inimical to the effect of judicial openness as well.

---

[9] See Li and Tian [1].

[10] See Center for National Index of Rule of Law of CASS & Innovation Project Team for Index of Rule of Law of the Institute of Law of CASS [2].

References

1. Li, L., & Tian, H. (2012). *Blue Book of Rule of Law: Annual Report on Rule of Law in China No.10 (2012).* Social Sciences Academic Press (China), p.260.
2. Center for National Index of Rule of Law of CASS & Innovation Project Team for Index of Rule of Law of the Institute of Law of CASS. (2016). *A Third Party Assessment Report on the Informatization of Chinese Courts.* China Social Sciences Press, p.18.

Chapter 6
Status Quo of Judicial Transparency in Various Fields

Based on the data collected in the judicial transparency index assessments in 2019 and 2020, this chapter will analyze some principal fields and contents regarding judicial openness to explore the achievements and problems in China's enhancement of judicial transparency in recent years.

1 Disclosure of Personnel Information

According to the Several Opinions of the Supreme People's Court on Promoting the Building of the Three Platforms for Judicial Openness, a people's court should disclose to the public members of the judicial committee, names, job titles, and ranks of judges, and other personnel information on the platform for judicial process information disclosure. Disclosing all kinds of court personnel information is one key element of disclosure of trial affairs, a crucial aspect of protecting the parties' rights, and the prerequisite for supervision over the court work. In recent years, assessment and analysis of the disclosure of information on leaders, judges, enforcement judges, judicial assistants, and judicial police has been the focus of our judicial transparency assessments. Leaders include court leaders and department heads. The assessment of the disclosure of information on court leaders focuses on disclosing their names, job titles, ranks, CVs, and affairs in the charge. Department heads include heads of business departments and heads of administrative departments. The assessment of the disclosure of information on business department heads focuses on the disclosure of their names, job titles, ranks, and CVs; the assessment of the disclosure of information on administrative department heads focuses on their names, job titles, and CVs.

Y. Wang and H. Tian, *Judicial Transparency in China*,
https://doi.org/10.1007/978-981-19-7822-7_6

1.1 Overview

The assessment results in 2019 and 2020 reveal that the disclosure of court personnel information on the court websites has developed in a good way. The indicators show that disclosure by the assessed courts has improved year by year. However, disclosure of such information by their divisions is unsatisfactory in terms of the absolute values of these indicators.

In the 2019 Assessment, only eight of the 93 courts disclosed information about the court leaders on the websites, including their names, job titles, ranks, CVs, and affairs in the charge, accounting for 8.60%. Sixteen courts disclosed information on the business department heads, including their names, job titles, ranks, and CVs, accounting for 17.20%. Fifteen courts disclosed information on the administrative department heads, including their names, job titles, and CVs, accounting for 16.13%. Seventeen courts disclosed information on the quota judges, including their names, CVs, and ranks, accounting for 18.28%. Ten courts disclosed information on the enforcement judges, including their names, CVs, and ranks, accounting for 10.75%. Sixteen courts disclosed the roster of judge assistants and court clerks, accounting for 17.20%. Ten courts disclosed the roster of judicial police, accounting for 10.75% (see Fig. 1).

In the 2020 Assessment, 17 of the 93 assessed courts disclosed all the information about the court leaders on their websites, including their names, job titles, ranks, CVs, and affairs in the charge, accounting for 18.28%. Only eight of the 119 primary people's courts, excluding five courts without websites, disclosed all the information mentioned above on the court leaders, accounting for 6.72%. Sixteen of the 93 assessed courts disclosed information on the business department heads, including their names, job titles, ranks, and CVs, accounting for 17.20%. Only eight of the 119 primary people's courts disclosed information on the business department heads, accounting for 6.72%. Eighteen of the 93 assessed courts disclosed information on the administrative department heads, including their names, job titles, and CVs, accounting for 19.35%. Only 13 primary people's courts disclosed all the above information on their administrative department heads, accounting for 10.92%. Seventeen of the 93 assessed courts disclosed information on the quota judges, including their names, CVs, and ranks, accounting for 18.28%. Only six of the 119 primary people's courts disclosed the complete information mentioned above, accounting for 5.05%. Among the original 93 assessed objects, 14 courts disclosed information on the enforcement judges, including their names, CVs, and ranks, accounting for 15.05%. Only five of the 119 primary people's courts disclosed the complete information mentioned above, accounting for 4.20%. Among the 93 assessed objects, 18 courts disclosed the roster of judge assistants and court clerks, accounting for 19.35%. Only eight of the 119 primary people's courts disclosed the roster of judge assistants and court clerks, accounting for 6.72%. Among the original 93 assessed objects, 15 courts disclosed the roster of judicial police, accounting for 16.13%. Only seven of the 119 primary people's courts disclosed the roster of judicial police, accounting for 5.88% (see Fig. 1). Two high people's courts, nine intermediate people's courts, 44

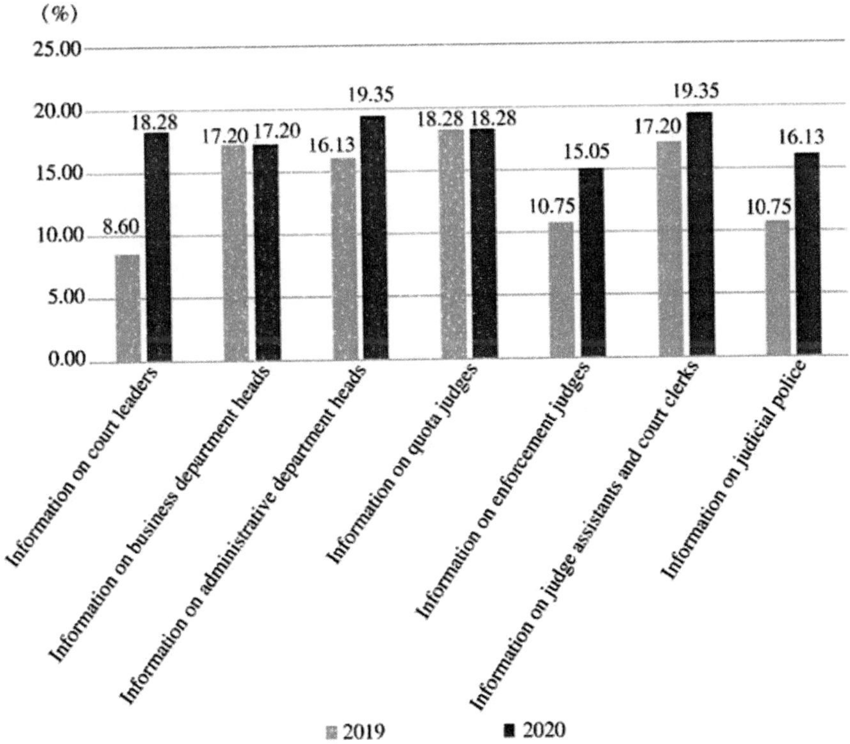

Fig. 1 A comparison of disclosure of court personnel information in 2019 and 2020

primary people's courts, and one free trade zone court did not disclose any personnel information on their websites.

The primary people's courts were assessed for the first time, so there was no comparison. The other 93 courts have improved in disclosing personnel information in the past two years.

The standard of personnel information disclosure varied considerably from court to court. Some courts disclosed very detailed personnel information. For example, the Intermediate People's Court of Chengdu City revealed the names, genders, nationalities, dates of birth, places of birth, CVs, job titles of the court leaders, and the affairs in the charge. However, the disclosure in some courts was simplistic. For instance, some courts disclosed only the names and titles of the leaders. Moreover, the classification of personnel was not uniform. The classification of personnel information disclosed by the Intermediate People's Court of Jilin City was pretty detailed. Its personnel was divided into ten categories: court leaders, judicial committee members, judges, judge assistants, court clerks, people's assessors, heads of administrative departments, judicial assistants, office clerks, and other court personnel. Besides, the Intermediate People's Court of Jilin City made a second classification of its court personnel according to different posts. A majority of courts had a comparatively cursory personnel classification. Some courts disclosed only the "judge catalog," including information on court leaders, judicial committee members, quota judges, enforcement department officials, and other personnel in different posts.

In addition, personnel information was generally not updated in time. Some courts played an exemplary role in updating personnel information. For example, the Intermediate People's Court of Ningbo City updated the personnel information in the same column in chronological order so that the public could compare and understand the personnel changes. Many courts disclosed the personnel information on their portals in 2018, 2017, or even earlier. For instance, in the 2019 Assessment, it was found that the roster of judges of a high people's court was disclosed on its litigation service website on June 26, 2014.

1.2 *Information on Court Leaders*

Court leaders at all levels are leading cadres whose basic personal information, including CVs and affairs in the charge, is part of public officials' public information that should be made public to society. Regarding government transparency, information on leaders of administrative organs at all levels has long been within the extent of the information that should be disclosed or even voluntarily disclosed. It has even been included in the items that governments should voluntarily disclose. Disclosure of such information by courts contributes to the self-discipline of court leaders and strengthens public supervision over them. However, our assessment results have proved a long way to go despite some progress in disclosing such information.

According to the statistics in 2020, the intermediate people's courts performed the best in disclosing information on court leaders on their websites, followed by the specialized courts, the high people's courts, and the primary people's courts, with the primary courts being the least adequate (see Fig. 2). Only three of the 32 high people's courts disclosed the names, job titles, ranks, CVs of the court leaders, and the affairs in the charge, accounting for 9.38%. Among the 49 intermediate people's courts in larger cities, 12 courts disclosed the names, titles, ranks, CVs of the court leaders, and the affairs in the charge, accounting for 24.49%. Only two of the 12 specialized courts disclosed the names, titles, ranks, CVs of the court leaders, and the affairs in the charge, accounting for 16.67%. Among the 119 primary people's courts, excluding the five courts without websites, eight courts disclosed the names, positions, ranks, CVs of the court leaders, and the affairs in the charge, accounting for 6.72%.

Regarding the information on court leaders, their names and positions were highly disclosed on the court websites, while their ranks were rarely disclosed. The leaders' CVs and affairs in the charge were the least disclosed (see Fig. 3). Among the 32 high people's courts, 28 courts disclosed the names of the court leaders, 27 disclosed their positions, 21 disclosed their ranks, 17 disclosed their CVs, and six disclosed the affairs in the charge, accounting for 87.50%, 84.38%, 65.63%, 53.13%, and 18.75%, respectively. Among the 49 intermediate people's courts in larger cities,

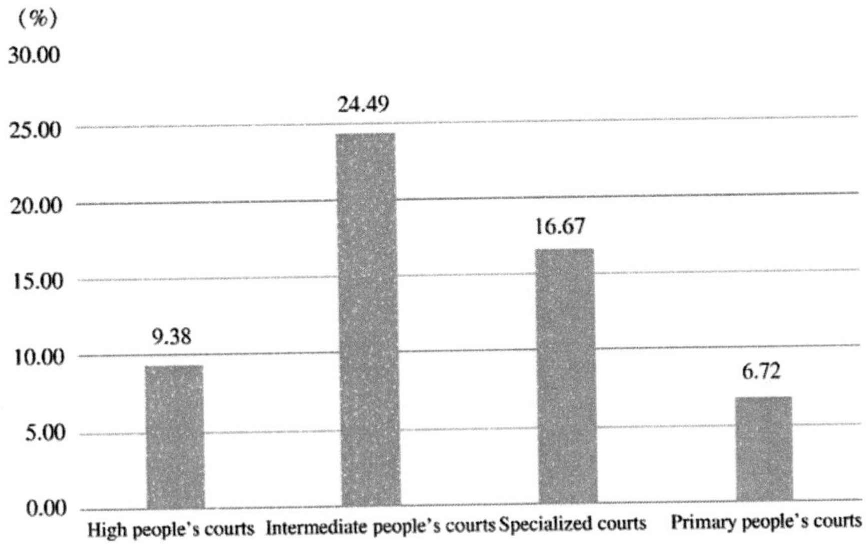

Fig. 2 Disclosure of comprehensive information on court leaders in 2020

38 courts disclosed the names of the court leaders, 37 disclosed their positions, 25 disclosed their ranks, 18 disclosed their CVs, and 15 disclosed the affairs in the charge, accounting for 77.55%, 75.51%, 51.02%, 36.73%, and 30.61%, respectively. Among the 12 specialized courts, 11 courts disclosed the names of the court leaders, 11 disclosed their positions, five disclosed their ranks, five disclosed their CVs, and four disclosed the affairs in the charge, accounting for 91.67%, 91.67%, 41.67%, 41.67%, and 33.33%, respectively. Among the 119 primary people's courts, excluding those without websites, 66 courts disclosed the names of the court leaders, 64 disclosed their positions, 35 disclosed their ranks, 26 disclosed their CVs, and 21 disclosed the affairs in the charge, accounting for 55.46%, 53.78%, 29.41%, 21.85%, and 17.65%, respectively. It can be seen that among the four types of courts, the specialized courts performed the best in disclosing the names, positions of the court leaders, and the affairs in the charge, while the high people's courts performed the best in disclosing the ranks and CVs of the court leaders. The disclosure of the names, positions, ranks, CVs of the court leaders, and the affairs in the charge decreased progressively in the court hierarchy. The disclosure of the court leaders' CVs and the affairs in the charge was the most unsatisfactory.

1.3 Information on Business Department Heads

A business department is a specialized division in the court directly responsible for trial and enforcement. Generally, its head is a quota judge in charge of the department

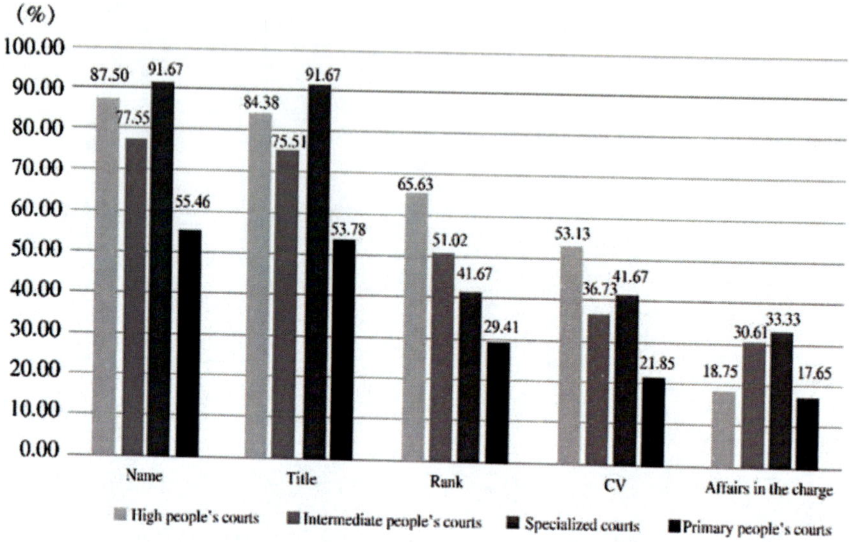

Fig. 3 A comparison of disclosure of information on court leaders in 2020

and a leading cadre with some job title. Disclosing his name, position, rank, and CV is also helpful in subjecting the head to public supervision.

The analysis of the assessment results in 2020 reveals that the specialized courts disclosed the most information on business department heads on their websites, followed by the high people's courts, the intermediate people's courts, and the primary people's courts, with the primary people's courts being the least adequate (see Fig. 4). Among the 32 high people's courts, only six courts disclosed the names, titles, ranks, and CVs of the business department heads on their websites, accounting for 18.75%. Among the 49 intermediate people's courts in larger cities, seven courts disclosed the names, titles, ranks, and CVs of the business department heads on their websites, accounting for 14.29%. Among the 12 specialized courts, only three courts disclosed the names, titles, ranks, and CVs of the business department heads on their websites, accounting for 25.00%. Among the 119 primary people's courts, excluding those without websites, eight courts disclosed the business department heads' names, titles, ranks, and CVs, accounting for 6.72%.

In terms of the contents of information on business department heads, the disclosure of the heads' names and titles was relatively high, while that of their ranks was relatively low. The disclosure of their CVs was the least good (see Fig. 5). Among the 32 high people's courts, 17 courts disclosed the names of the business department heads, 16 disclosed their titles, 11 disclosed their ranks, and six disclosed their CVs, accounting for 53.13%, 50.00%, 34.38%, and 18.75%, respectively. Among the 49 intermediate people's courts in larger cities, 24 courts disclosed the names of the business department heads, 24 disclosed their titles, 18 disclosed their ranks, and eight

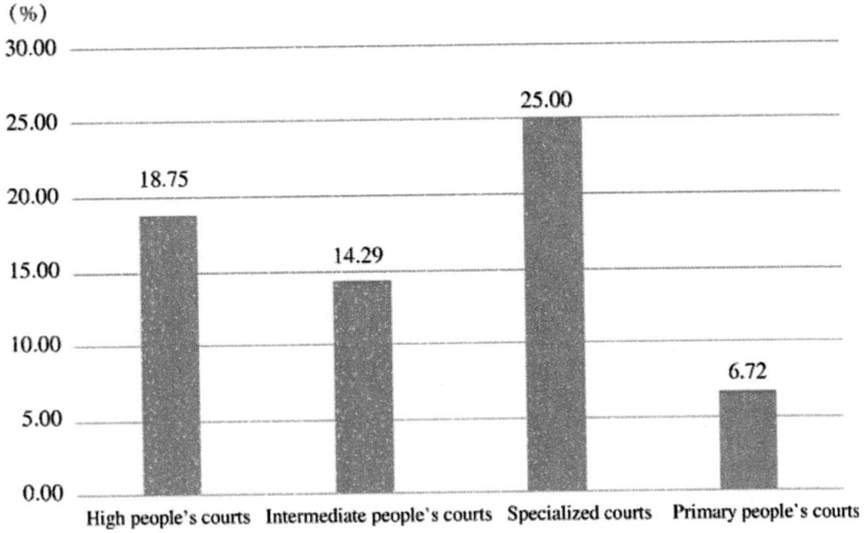

Fig. 4 Disclosure of comprehensive information on business department heads in 2020

disclosed their CVs, accounting for 48.98%, 48.98%, 36.73%, and 16.33%, respectively. Among the 12 specialized courts, seven courts disclosed the names of the business department heads, seven disclosed their titles, five disclosed their ranks, and four disclosed their CVs, accounting for 58.33%, 58.33%, 41.67%, and 33.33%, respectively. Among the 119 primary people's courts, excluding those without websites, 33 courts disclosed the names of the business department heads, 30 disclosed their titles, 25 disclosed their ranks, and eight disclosed their CVs, accounting for 27.73%, 25.21%, 21.01%, and 6.72%, respectively. It can be seen that among the four types of courts, the specialized courts performed the best in disclosing the names, titles, ranks, and CVs of the business department heads. However, on the whole, the disclosure of the business department heads' names, titles, ranks, and CVs decreased progressively in the court hierarchy. The disclosure of their CVs by all the assessed courts was the most unsatisfactory, followed by their ranks.

1.4 Information on Administrative Department Heads

An administrative department is a critical internal division of the court. It does not directly participate in trial and enforcement but is indirectly involved in the exercise of judicial and enforcement powers. Its head also has some power. The basic information on the head, such as his name, title, and CV, should be disclosed so that the public can supervise the court's work. However, the analysis of the assessment results in 2020 reveals that the specialized courts disclosed the most information on administrative department heads on their websites, followed by the high people's

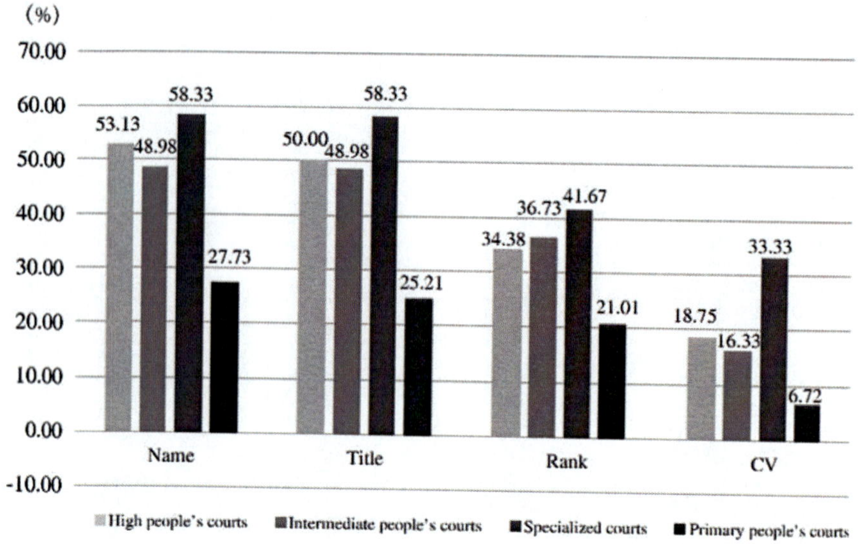

Fig. 5 A comparison of disclosure of information on business department heads in 2020

courts, the intermediate people's courts, and the primary people's courts, with the primary courts being the most unsatisfactory (see Fig. 6). Only seven of the 32 high people's courts disclosed the administrative department heads' names, titles, ranks, and CVs, accounting for 21.88%. Among the 49 intermediate people's courts in larger cities, eight courts disclosed the administrative department heads' names, titles, ranks, and CVs, accounting for 16.33%. Among the 12 specialized courts, only three courts disclosed the administrative department heads' names, titles, ranks, and CVs, accounting for 25.00%. Among the 119 courts, excluding those without websites, 13 courts disclosed the names, titles, ranks, and CVs of the administrative department heads, accounting for 10.92%.

Regarding the contents of information on administrative department heads, the disclosure of their names and titles was relatively high, while that of their CVs was the least good (see Fig. 7). Among the 32 high people's courts, 16 courts disclosed on their websites the names of the administrative department heads, 16 disclosed their titles, and seven disclosed their CVs, accounting for 50.00%, 50.00%, and 21.88%, respectively. Among the 49 intermediate people's courts in larger cities, 21 courts disclosed on their websites the names of the administrative department heads, 21 disclosed their titles, and eight courts disclosed their CVs, accounting for 42.86%, 42.86%, and 16.33%, respectively. Among the 12 specialized courts, five courts disclosed on their websites the names of the administrative department heads, five courts disclosed their titles, and three courts disclosed their CVs, accounting for 41.67%, 41.67%, and 25.00%, respectively. Among the 119 courts, excluding those without websites, 31 courts disclosed the names of the administrative department heads, 30 courts disclosed their titles, and 13 courts disclosed their CVs, accounting for 20.06%, 25.21%, and 10.92%, respectively. It can be seen that among the four types of courts,

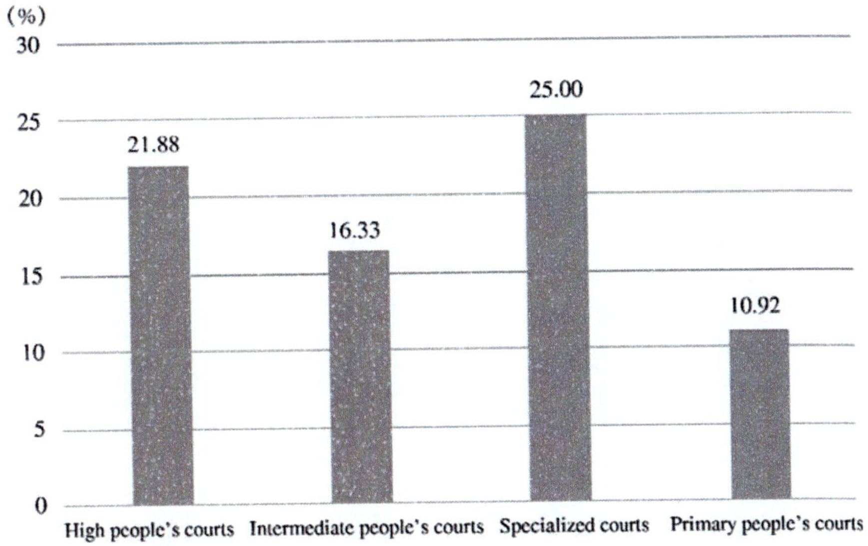

Fig. 6 Disclosure of comprehensive information on administrative department heads in 2020

the high people's courts performed the best in disclosing the names and titles of the administrative department heads, followed by the intermediate people's courts, with the primary people's courts being the most unsatisfactory. The specialized courts performed the best in disclosing the administrative department heads' CVs, followed by the high people's courts, with the primary people's courts being the least satisfactory. The administrative department heads' CVs were the least disclosed by all the assessed courts.

1.5 Information on Quota Judges

Quota judges exercise judicial power following the principle of "whoever tries a case being responsible for it." Their case-handling activities directly affect the realization of the parties' litigation rights and substantive rights. In order to safeguard the parties' litigation rights and effectively supervise quota judges' lawful performance of their trial and enforcement functions, it is necessary to disclose the basic information about them.

According to the assessment results in 2020, the specialized courts disclosed the most information on quota judges on their websites, followed by the intermediate people's courts, the high people's courts, and the primary people's courts in order. The primary courts performed the least desirable (see Fig. 8). Four of the 32 high people's courts disclosed the quota judges' names, ranks, and CVs, accounting for 12.50%. Among the 49 intermediate people's courts in larger cities, nine courts

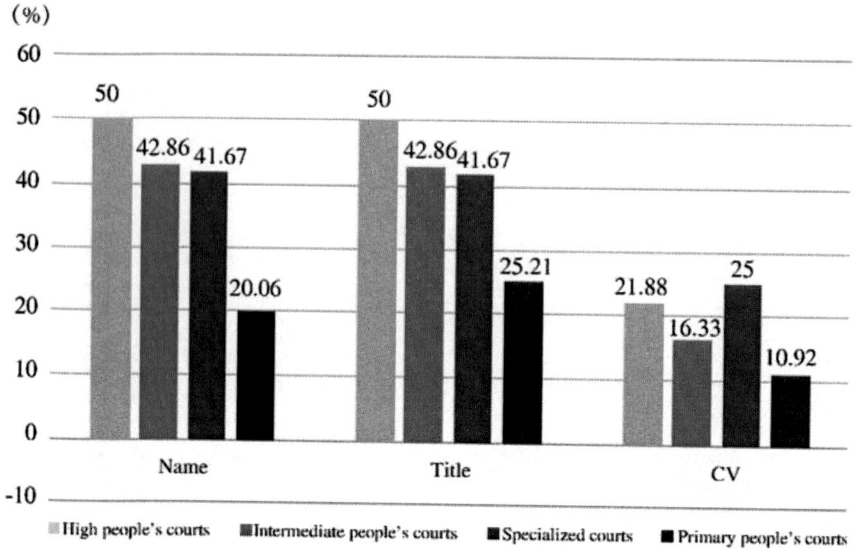

Fig. 7 A comparison of disclosure of information on administrative department heads in 2020

disclosed the quota judges' names, ranks, and CVs, accounting for 18.37%. Among the 12 specialized courts, four courts disclosed the quota judges' names, ranks, and CVs, accounting for 33.3%. Among the 119 courts, excluding the courts without websites, six courts disclosed the quota judges' names, ranks, and CVs, accounting for 5.04%.

Regarding the information on quota judges, their names were much more disclosed than their ranks, and their CVs were the least disclosed on the websites (see Fig. 9). Among the 32 high people's courts, 17 courts disclosed the names of the quota judges, 11 courts disclosed their ranks, and four courts disclosed their CVs, accounting for 53.13%, 34.38%, and 12.50%, respectively. Among the 49 intermediate people's courts in larger cities, 29 courts disclosed the names of the quota judges, 23 courts disclosed their ranks, and nine courts disclosed their CVs, accounting for 59.18%, 46.94%, and 18.38%, respectively. Among the 12 specialized courts, ten courts disclosed the names of the quota judges, seven courts disclosed their ranks, and five courts disclosed their CVs, accounting for 83.33%, 58.33%, and 41.67%, respectively. Among the 119 primary courts, excluding the courts without websites, 41 courts disclosed the names of the quota judges, 25 courts disclosed their ranks, and seven courts disclosed their CVs, accounting for 34.45%, 21.01%, and 5.88%, respectively. It can be seen that among the four types of courts, the specialized courts performed the best in disclosing the names, ranks, and CVs of the quota judges, followed by the intermediate people's courts, with the primary people's courts being the least satisfactory. Furthermore, the disclosure of CVs of the quota judges by all the assessed courts was the most inadequate.

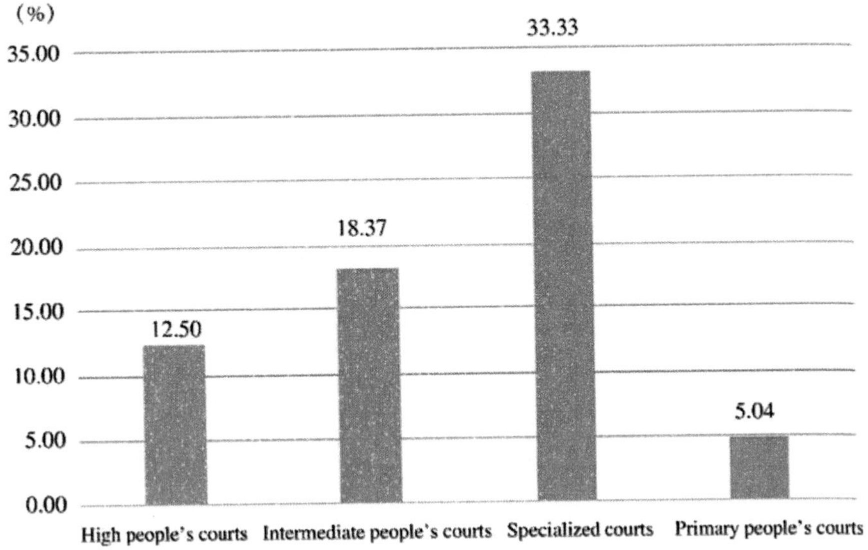

Fig. 8 Disclosure of comprehensive information on quota judges in 2020

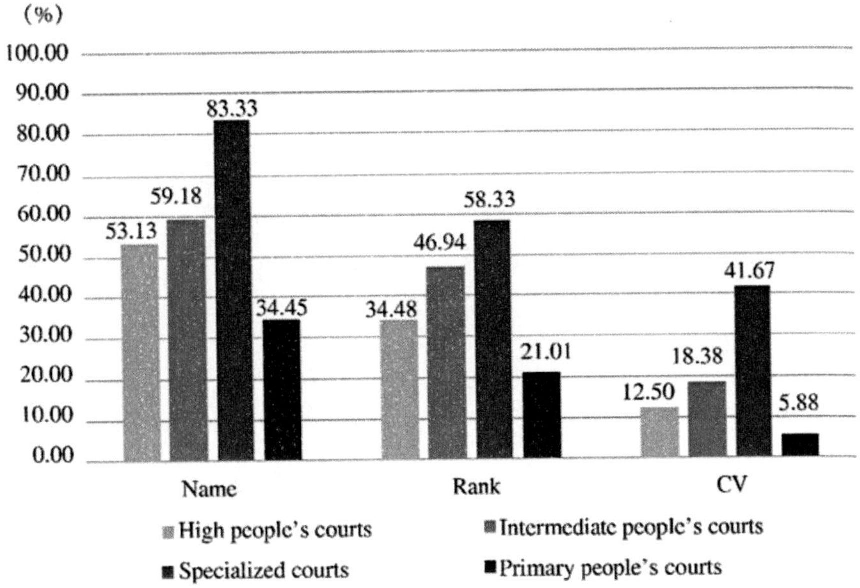

Fig. 9 A comparison of disclosure of information on quota judges in 2020

1.6 Information on the Members of a Judicial Committee

A judicial committee is an organization by which the people's court exercises collective leadership over the judicial work. According to the Organic Law of the People's Courts, the people's courts at all levels shall set up judicial committees. A judicial committee shall sum up the trial experience and deliberate and decide on applying laws in major, difficult, and complicated cases and other major issues relevant to the trial. It is also an essential requirement for judicial openness to disclose information on the members of a judicial committee.

According to the assessment results in 2020, the high people's courts disclosed the most information on judicial committee members, followed by the intermediate people's courts, the specialized courts, and the primary people's courts, with the primary courts being the least satisfactory (see Fig. 10). Among the 32 high people's courts, 23 courts disclosed information on the judicial committee members, accounting for 71.88%. Among the 49 intermediate people's courts in larger cities, 31 courts disclosed information on the judicial committee members, accounting for 63.27%. Among the 12 specialized courts, five courts disclosed information on the judicial committee members, accounting for 41.67%. Among the 119 courts, excluding those without websites, 38 courts disclosed information on the judicial committee members, accounting for 31.93%.

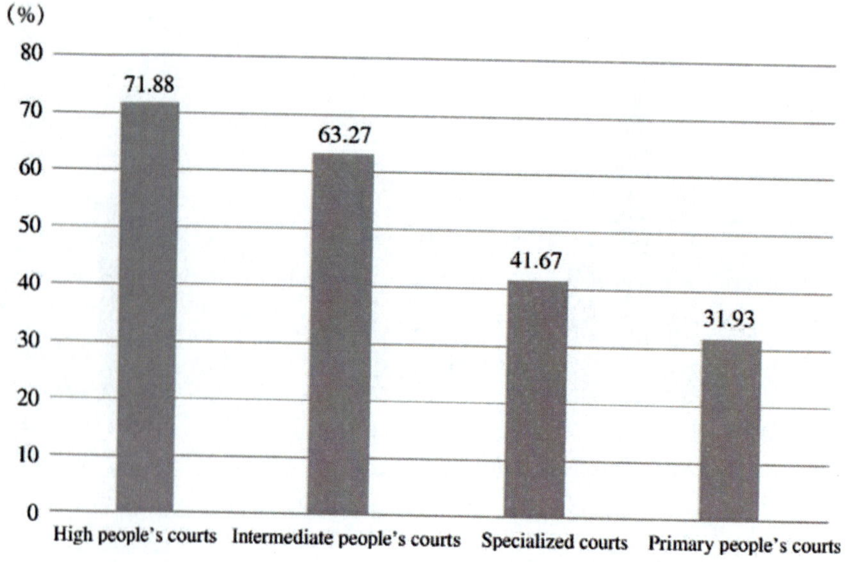

Fig. 10 Disclosure of information on the members of a judicial committee in 2020

1.7 Information on Enforcement Judges

Enforcement is a significant part of the court work, which relates to paying an effective judgment and realizing the parties' determined rights. Disclosing information on enforcement judges also facilitates service for the people and supervision by the people. According to the assessment results in 2020, the specialized courts disclosed the most information on enforcement judges on their websites, followed by the intermediate people's courts, the high people's courts, and the primary people's courts, with the primary people's courts being the least satisfactory (see Fig. 11). Four of the 32 high people's courts disclosed the enforcement judges' names, ranks, and CVs, accounting for 12.50%. Among the 49 intermediate people's courts in larger cities, nine courts disclosed the enforcement judges' names, ranks, and CVs, accounting for 16.33%. Among the 12 specialized courts, two courts disclosed the enforcement judges' names, ranks, and CVs, accounting for 16.67%. Among the 119 primary people's courts, excluding those without websites, five courts disclosed the enforcement judges' names, ranks, and CVs, accounting for 4.20%.

In terms of the information on enforcement judges, the disclosure of their names was high, while that of their ranks was relatively low, with the disclosure of their CVs being the least satisfactory (see Fig. 12). Among the 32 high people's courts, 12 courts disclosed the enforcement judges' names, eight disclosed their ranks, and four disclosed their CVs, accounting for 37.50%, 25.00%, and 12.50%, respectively. Among the 49 intermediate people's courts in larger cities, 22 courts disclosed the enforcement judges' names, 15 disclosed their ranks, and eight disclosed their CVs,

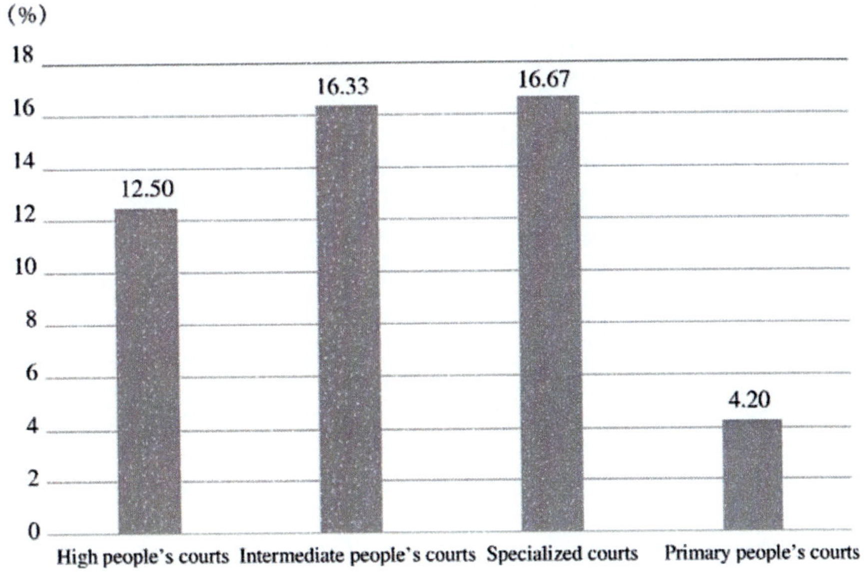

Fig. 11 Disclosure of comprehensive information on enforcement judges in 2020

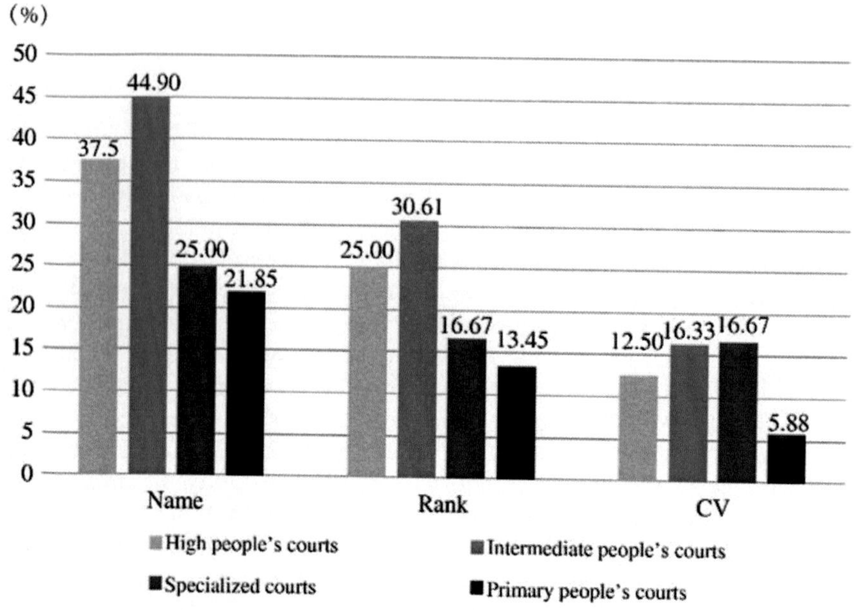

Fig. 12 A comparison of disclosure of information on enforcement judges in 2020

accounting for 44.90%, 30.61%, and 16.33%, respectively. Among the 12 specialized courts, three courts disclosed the enforcement judges' names, two disclosed their ranks, and two disclosed their CVs, accounting for 25.00%, 16.67%, and 16.67%, respectively. Among the 119 primary people's courts, excluding those without websites, 26 courts disclosed the enforcement judges' names, 16 disclosed their ranks, and seven disclosed their CVs, accounting for 21.85%, 13.45%, and 5.88%, respectively. It can be seen that among the four types of courts, the intermediate people's courts performed the best in disclosing the names, ranks, and CVs of the enforcement judges, followed by the high people's courts, with the primary people's courts being the least satisfactory. Moreover, the disclosure of the enforcement judges' CVs by all the assessed courts was the most inadequate.

1.8 Disclosure Channels

As the Internet and e-government prospers, portals have become a leading platform for various organs to disclose information to the public. Information on court personnel is made public mainly on court portals, and the channels for disclosure are still diversified and not unified. According to the assessment results in 2020, it has become the mainstream to disclose various types of information on court personnel on a court portal. However, some information was disclosed on the website of a higher court. The contents were disclosed in different sections of the court website. At the same time, the disclosure of such information on China Judicial Process Information Online built by the Supreme People's Court was not satisfactory.

Regarding disclosing information on court leaders, take names with the highest disclosure rate as an instance. Twenty-eight high people's courts disclosed the names of the court leaders on their portals. Among the 49 intermediate people's courts in larger cities, 36 courts disclosed the names of the court leaders on their court websites, and one disclosed the court leaders' names on the website of the higher court. Moreover, one disclosed the court leaders' names on both its website and the website of the higher court, with the disclosed information inconsistent. Among the 12 specialized courts, ten courts disclosed such information on their websites. One disclosed the court leaders' names on both its website and the website of the higher court, with the disclosed information inconsistent. Among the 119 primary people's courts, 61 courts disclosed such information on their websites, one disclosed the court leaders' names on the website of the higher court, and two disclosed the court leaders' names on both the websites and the higher courts' websites, with the disclosed information inconsistent. Besides, the information on court leaders was disclosed in different website sections. Among the high people's courts, 23 courts disclosed information on the court leaders in a column or related articles, one disclosed such information in the roster of the Party committee members on the website, and four indicated such information in the roster of judges or that of judicial committee members. Among the intermediate people's courts, 31 courts disclosed the court leaders' information in a column or related articles, one disclosed such information in the roster of the Party committee members on the website, and six courts indicated such information in the roster of judges or that of judicial committee members. All the 11 specialized courts disclosed such information in a particular column or related articles on their websites. Among the primary people's courts, 50 courts disclosed such information in a particular column or related articles, one disclosed information in the roster of Party committee members on the website, and 15 indicated such information in the roster of judges or that of judicial committee members. The assessment results show that the disclosure of personnel information on the websites by courts at all levels and of all kinds was highly arbitrary, and there was a lack of a uniform standard.

In addition, the disclosure of personnel information on China Judicial Process Information Online is far from satisfactory. In recent years, the Supreme People's Court has made available China Judicial Process Information Online as a unified platform for disclosing various kinds of judicial process information. It discloses judicial process information to the parties and their agents; it also discloses to the public the basic knowledge about courts nationwide, such as organization settings, the roster of judges, the litigation guide, the announcement of court sessions, and roster information. This approach helps the public and the parties inquire about court information and judicial process information and avoids the difficulties they may be confronted with in searching court websites, making the goal realized that information on courts nationwide can be found on one website. Moreover, disclosing basic information on courts nationwide and judicial process information on China

Judicial Process Information Online has helped to set the standard for disclosing relevant information and effectively solved the long-standing problem of different disclosed contents and disclosure methods in courts across the country in terms of the disclosure of judicial process information. However, the disclosure of personnel information on China Judicial Process Information Online by courts at all levels and of all kinds is not satisfactory.

Regarding disclosing information on court leaders, the assessment results in 2020 show that among the 32 high people's courts, 23 courts disclosed information on the court leaders on China Judicial Process Information Online, accounting for 71.88%. Twenty-one courts disclosed conflicting information on their websites, and two did not disclose such information on their websites. Among the 49 intermediate people's courts in larger cities, 37 courts disclosed information on the court leaders on China Judicial Process Information Online, accounting for 75.51%. Among them, one court disclosed the same information on its website, 29 courts disclosed different information, and seven failed to disclose such information on their websites. Among the 12 specialized courts, seven courts disclosed information on the court leaders on China Judicial Process Information Online, accounting for 58.33%. One court disclosed information consistent with that disclosed on its website, while six courts failed. Among the 119 primary people's courts, 72 courts disclosed information on the court leaders on China Judicial Process Information Online, accounting for 60.50% (see Fig. 13). Among them, two courts disclosed the information in complete agreement with that disclosed on their websites, 35 courts disclosed information inconsistent with that disclosed on their websites, and 35 courts did not disclose such information on their websites. It can be seen from the above facts that the intermediate people's courts performed the best in disclosing information on the court leaders on China Judicial Process Information Online, followed by the high people's courts, with the specialized courts being the worst. Overall, the information consistency between China Judicial Process Information Online and the court websites was unsatisfactory.

In terms of disclosing information on business department heads, according to the assessment results in 2020, among the 32 high people's courts, 26 courts disclosed information on the business department heads on China Judicial Process Information Online, accounting for 81.25%. Thirteen courts disclosed conflicting information on their websites, and 13 did not disclose such information. Among the 49 intermediate people's courts in larger cities, 37 courts disclosed information on the business department heads on China Judicial Process Information Online, accounting for 75.51%. Eighteen courts disclosed conflicting information on their websites, and 19 did not disclose such information. Among the 12 specialized courts, four courts disclosed information on the business department heads on China Judicial Process Information Online, accounting for 33.33%. Two courts disclosed information inconsistent with that on their websites, and two courts did not disclose such information on their websites. Among the 119 primary people's courts, 71 courts disclosed information on the business department heads on China Judicial Process Information Online, accounting for 59.66% (see Fig. 14). Sixteen courts disclosed conflicting information on their websites, and 55 courts did not disclose such information. The above

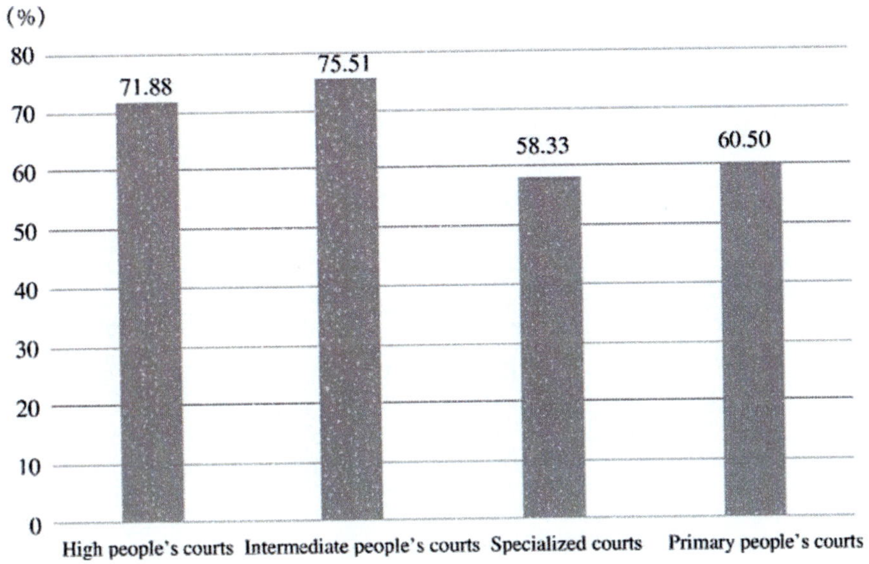

Fig. 13 Disclosure of information on court leaders on China Judicial Process Information Online in 2020

data shows that the high people's courts performed the best in disclosing information on the business department heads on China Judicial Process Information Online, followed by the intermediate people's courts, with the specialized courts being the worst. Furthermore, no court disclosed completely the same information on its business department heads on China Judicial Process Information Online as was disclosed on its website.

Regarding the disclosure of information on quota judges, the assessment results in 2020 show that among the 32 high people's courts, 26 courts disclosed information on the quota judges on China Judicial Process Information Online, accounting for 81.25%. Among them, one court disclosed the same information on its website, 12 courts disclosed conflicting information, and 13 courts did not disclose such information on their websites. Among the 49 intermediate people's courts in larger cities, 37 courts disclosed information on the quota judges on China Judicial Process Information Online, accounting for 75.51%. Twenty-two courts of them disclosed information inconsistent with that on their websites, and 15 courts did not disclose such information. Among the 12 specialized courts, six courts disclosed information on the quota judges on China Judicial Process Information Online, accounting for 50.00%. Unhappily, all the information was inconsistent with that on their websites. Among the 119 primary people's courts, 69 courts disclosed information on the quota judges on China Judicial Process Information Online, accounting for 57.98% (see Fig. 15). Twenty-four courts disclosed conflicting information on their websites, and 45 did not disclose such information. It can be concluded that the high people's courts performed the best in disclosing information on the quota judges on China

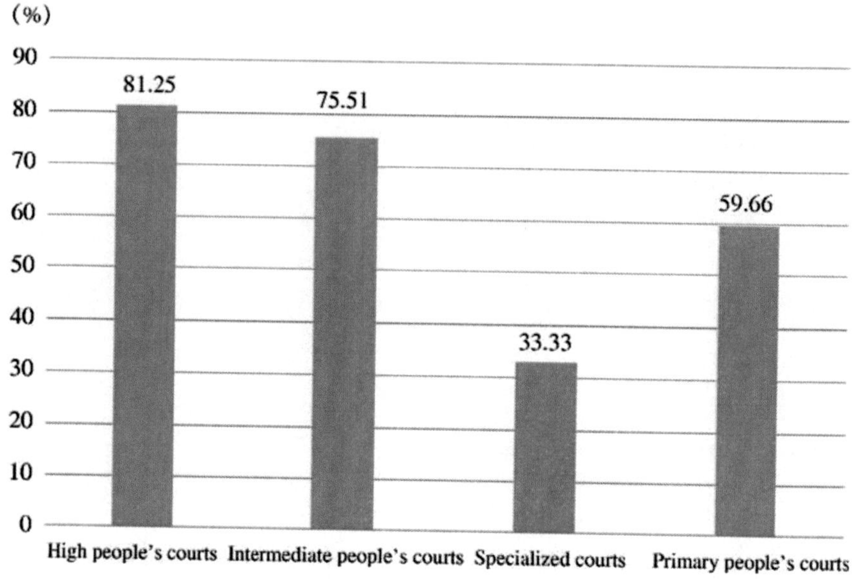

Fig. 14 Disclosure of information on business department heads on China Judicial Process Information Online in 2020

Judicial Process Information Online, followed by the intermediate people's courts, with the specialized courts being the worst. Only one high people's court disclosed the information on the quota judges on China Judicial Process Information Online in complete agreement with that disclosed on its website.

To sum up, the channels for disclosing court personnel information are not unified. Such information cannot be found in fixed sections of the portals, making it harder to inquire about personnel information and damaging the effect of disclosure. In addition, the national unified disclosure platform, China Judicial Process Information Online, has not yet achieved the purpose of collecting all the information on court personnel across the country. Furthermore, the personnel information disclosed on this website is not timely updated. A large amount of data is inaccurate, making the website less attractive and probably misleading the public.

2 Roster Information

2.1 Overview

In the process of trial and enforcement, a people's court often needs the assistance of external experts or institutions to conduct professional work, such as authentication,

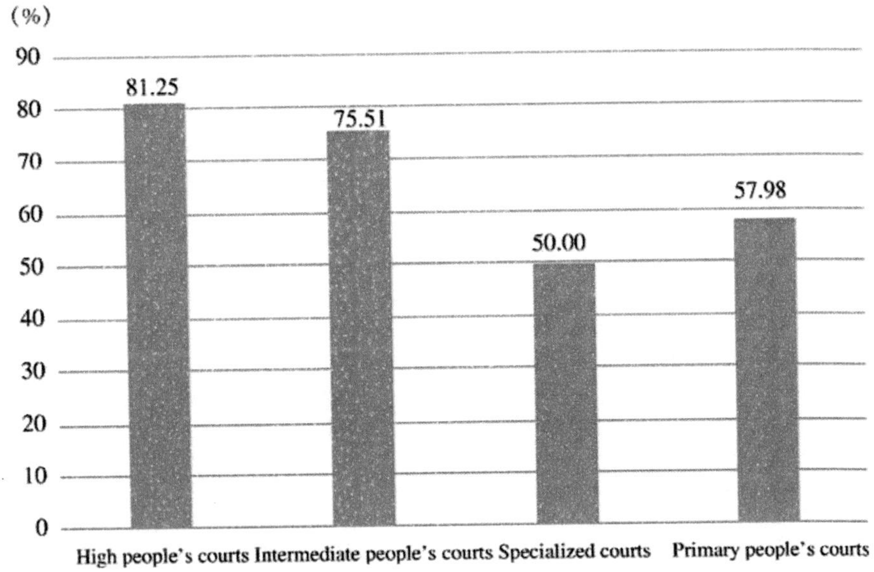

Fig. 15 Disclosure of information on quota judges on China Judicial Process Information Online in 2020

evaluation, bankruptcy administration, and mediation. In order to ensure the impartiality and fairness of entrusting such businesses to outsiders and the professionalism of entrusted institutions and individuals, the people's courts have established the roster system, and any individual or institution included in a roster can be entrusted. Therefore, all kinds of roster information must be disclosed to society. For example, in terms of the roster of bankruptcy administrators, the Supreme People's Court issued the Provisions on Designating the Administrator During the Trial of Enterprise Bankruptcy Cases in 2007, providing that the people's court shall review and determine the roster of administrators and make an announcement through nationally influential media. Regarding strengthening the administration of people's mediation organizations, the Supreme People's Court issued the Provisions on Specially Invited Mediation by the People's Courts in 2016, providing that a people's court shall provide at such a place as the litigation service center the rosters of specially invited mediation organizations and mediators, and publicize the roster information on the bulletin board, the official website, or any other platform of the court to facilitate consultation by the parties.

The relevant documents issued by the Supreme People's Court on judicial openness have further clarified the requirement for roster information disclosure. According to the Several Opinions on Promoting the Building of the Three Platforms for Judicial Openness issued by the Supreme People's Court in 2013, a people's court should disclose to the public on China Judicial Process Information Online the roster of people's assessors, the roster of specially invited mediation organizations, the roster of specially invited mediators, the roster of evaluation institutions, the roster of auction institutions, and the roster of other selected intermediaries. According to the Opinions on Furthering Judicial Openness issued by the Supreme People's Court in 2018, a people's court should take the initiative in disclosing various kinds of information, including but not limited to: information on specialized organizations and professionals engaged in forensic appraisal, evaluation, inspection, and auditing; information on bankruptcy administrators; information on medical appraisal work carried out to diagnose a prisoner's illness or conduct a pregnancy test when a prison is considering the prisoner's temporary service of his sentence outside prison; information on expert pools, specially invited mediators and mediation organizations, resident lawyers, and expert volunteers participating in litigation services.

The provisions on forensic appraisal seem to be slightly vague. For instance, according to the Provisions on the Administration of Externally Entrusted Judicial Appraisals by the People's Courts in 2002 issued by the Supreme People's Court, appraisal experts who have been approved to be included in the roster of forensic appraisal experts of a people's court shall be announced in *People's Court Daily*. Similar provisions also can be found in the Opinions of the Supreme People's Court on Furthering Judicial Openness. According to the Provisions of the Supreme People's Court on Several Issues Concerning the Determination of Reference Prices for Disposition of Property by the People's Courts issued in 2018, the Supreme People's Court shall establish a bank of lists of judicial assessment institutions for the people's courts based on the lists of assessment institutions recommended by various national appraisal industry associations. According to the professional fields of assessment and the practicing scope of the assessment institutions, sub-databases of lists shall be established under which sub-lists at the provincial and municipal levels shall be established according to the administrative divisions. Seemingly, rosters of evaluation authorities have been made public mainly on the platform of the Supreme People's Court. In practice, some courts have disclosed such information, while others have disclosed it on China Judicial Process Information Online.

The assessment results in 2019 show that only six of the 93 courts published rosters on their portals of specially invited mediators and mediation organizations, authentication institutions, evaluation institutions, and bankruptcy administrators, accounting for 6.45%. The roster information disclosed by the six courts on their portals was not exactly the same as that published on China Judicial Process Information Online. In addition, 28 courts did not disclose any roster information on the portals, accounting for 30.11%.

The assessment results in 2020 show that among the original 93 assessed courts, only 15 courts published the rosters of specially invited mediators and mediation organizations, authentication institutions, and evaluation institutions on their websites, accounting for 16.13%. Among the 87 assessed courts, excluding the six specialized courts that did not handle bankruptcy cases, 14 courts published the rosters of specially invited mediators and mediation organizations, authentication institutions, evaluation institutions, and bankruptcy administrators on their websites, accounting for 16.09%. Still, the roster information disclosed on the above courts' portals was not wholly consistent with that on China Judicial Process Information Online. Among the 93 assessed courts, 18 courts did not disclose any roster information on their websites, accounting for 19.35%. Only one primary people's court disclosed such information on its website, and 85 courts did not disclose any such information, accounting for 0.84% and 71.43%, respectively.

2.2 *Mediation Rosters*

Mediation rosters include the roster of specially invited mediation organizations and that of specially invited mediators. According to the assessment results in 2020, seven of the 32 high people's courts, 13 of the 49 intermediate people's courts, two of the 12 specialized courts, and 14 of the 119 primary people's courts disclosed the roster of specially invited mediation organizations, accounting for 21.88%, 26.53%, 16.67%, and 11.76%, respectively.

The assessment results in 2020 show that eight of the 32 high people's courts, 16 of the 49 intermediate people's courts, seven of the 12 specialized courts, and 20 of the 119 primary people's courts disclosed the roster of specially invited mediators, accounting for 25.00%, 32.65%, 58.33%, and 16.81%, respectively (see Fig. 16).

Moreover, only one intermediate people's court disclosed the information on the roster of specially invited mediation organizations on its website in complete

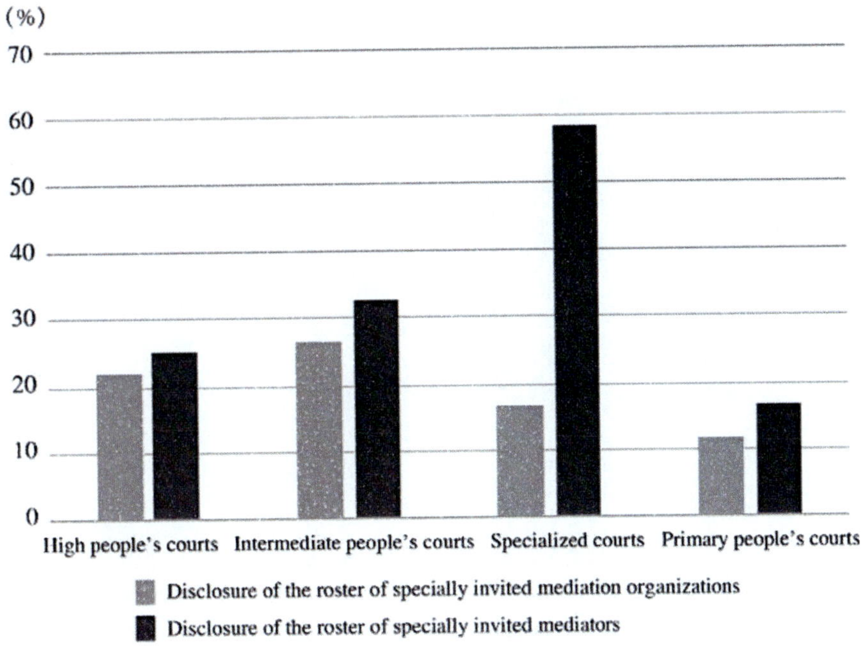

Fig. 16 Disclosure of the roster of specially invited mediation organizations and the roster of specially invited mediators in 2020

agreement with that disclosed on China Judicial Process Information Online. One intermediate people's court and three primary people's courts disclosed exactly the same information on the roster of specially invited mediators on their websites as that on China Judicial Process Information Online.

On the whole, the disclosure of the roster of specially invited mediators was better than that of the roster of specially invited mediation organizations. The disclosure by the primary people's courts was far from satisfactory. The disclosure of mediation roster information on China Judicial Process Information Online was generally inadequate.

2.3 *The Roster of Authentication Institutions*

Twenty-one of the 32 high people's courts, 30 of the 49 intermediate people's courts, four of the 12 specialized courts, and 14 of the 119 primary people's courts disclosed the roster of authentication institutions in 2020, accounting for 65.63%, 61.22%, 33.33%, and 11.76%, respectively (see Fig. 17).

On the whole, the disclosure of the roster of authentication institutions was increasingly worse from the higher people's courts to the lower people's courts. The high people's courts performed the best, followed by the intermediate people's courts, with the primary people's courts being the least satisfactory.

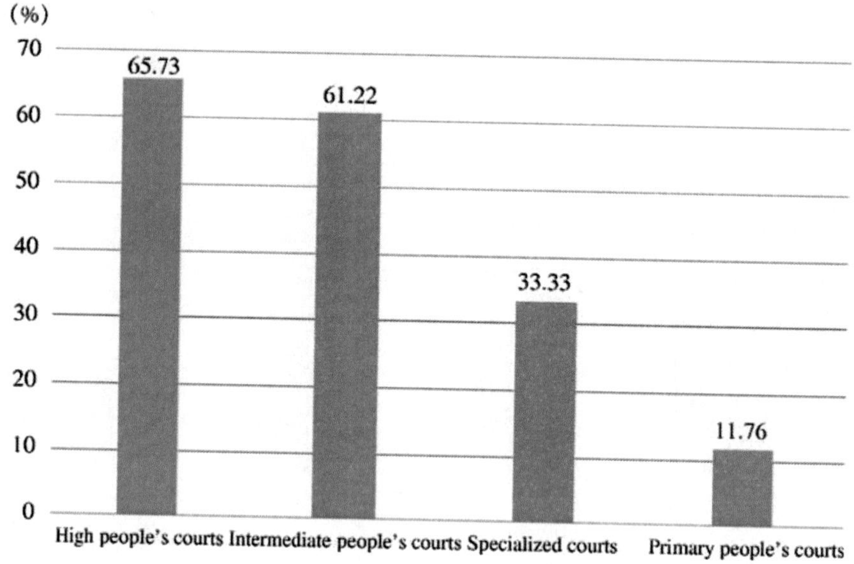

Fig. 17 Disclosure of the roster of authentication institutions in 2020

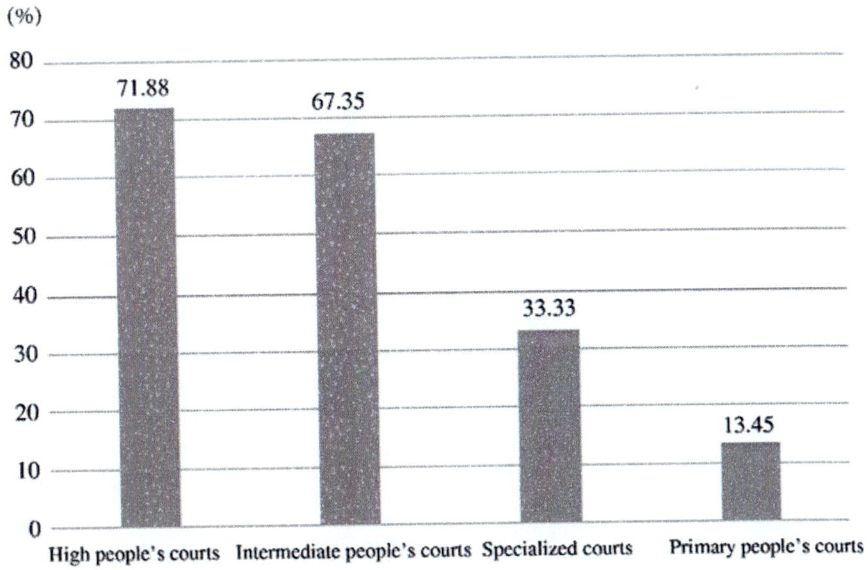

Fig. 18 Disclosure of the roster of evaluation institutions in 2020

2.4 *The Roster of Evaluation Institutions*

Twenty-three of the 32 high people's courts, 33 of the 49 intermediate people's courts, four of the 12 specialized courts, and 16 of the 119 primary people's courts disclosed the roster of evaluation institutions in 2020, accounting for 71.88%, 67.35%, 33.33%, and 13.45%, respectively (see Fig. 18).

Overall, the disclosure of the roster of evaluation institutions was progressively unsatisfactory from the higher people's courts to the lower people's courts. The high people's courts performed the best, followed by the intermediate people's courts, with the primary people's courts being the least desirable.

2.5 *The Roster of Bankruptcy Administrators*

Sixteen of the 32 high people's courts, 21 of the 49 intermediate people's courts, one of the 12 specialized courts, and seven of the 119 primary people's courts disclosed the roster of bankruptcy administrators in 2020, accounting for 50.00%, 42.86%, 8.33%, and 5.88%, respectively (see Fig. 19).

To sum up, the disclosure of the roster of bankruptcy administrators was also gradually inadequate from the higher people's courts to the lower people's courts. The high people's courts performed the best, followed by the intermediate people's

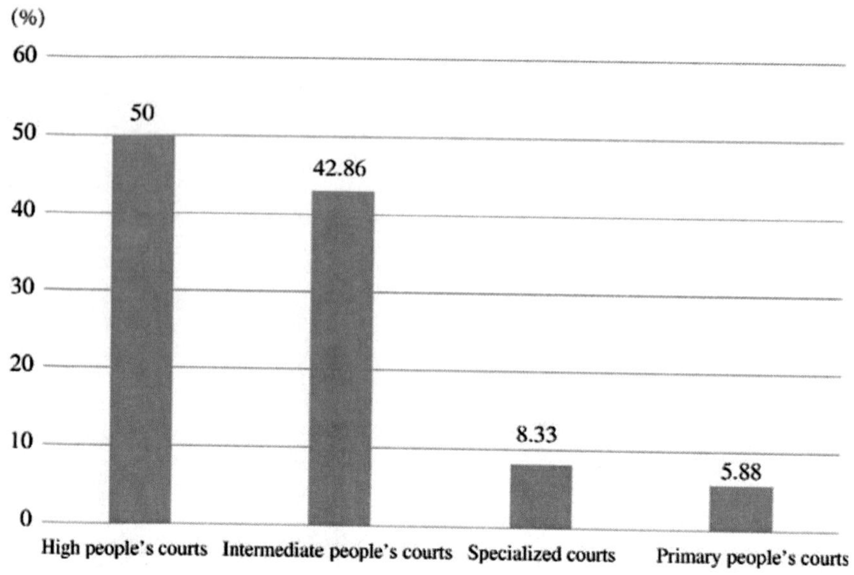

Fig. 19 Disclosure of the roster of bankruptcy administrators in 2020

courts, with the primary people's courts being the least satisfactory. It may be because bankruptcy cases are mainly handled by courts above the intermediate level.

2.6 *Disclosure Channels*

According to law, the roster information must be disclosed on China Judicial Process Information Online. However, the effect practically is not satisfactory. The assessment results in 2020 show that three high people's courts, seven intermediate people's courts, one specialized court, and 14 primary people's courts disclosed information on the specially invited mediation organizations on China Judicial Process Information Online. Only one intermediate people's court disclosed the information on this platform consistent with that published on its portal.

Three high people's courts, ten intermediate people's courts, four specialized courts, and 42 primary people's courts disclosed information on the specially invited mediators on China Judicial Process Information Online. Only one intermediate people's court and three primary people's courts disclosed the information on this platform consistent with that on their portals.

Seventeen high people's courts, 25 intermediate people's courts, two specialized courts, and 34 primary people's courts disclosed information on the roster of authentication institutions on China Judicial Process Information Online. Only two intermediate people's courts and two primary people's courts disclosed the information on this platform consistent with that on their portals.

Eighteen high people's courts, 28 intermediate people's courts, one specialized court, and 42 primary people's courts disclosed information on the evaluation institutions on China Judicial Process Information Online. Only three intermediate people's courts and two primary people's courts disclosed the information on their websites in agreement with that on this platform.

Two high people's courts, six intermediate people's courts, and ten primary people's courts disclosed information on the bankruptcy administrators on China Judicial Process Information Online. Only one intermediate people's court and one primary people's court disclosed the information on their websites in agreement with that on this platform.

In conclusion, the disclosure of roster information on China Judicial Process Information Online was far from satisfactory. In particular, the inconsistency of information on multiple platforms featured prominently.

3 Information on Office Disqualification

It is absolutely imperative that we establish a comprehensive disqualification system to avoid collusion between judges and their immediate family members and maintain judicial credibility. Explicit provisions regarding office disqualification can be found in the Judges Law of the People's Republic of China. However, it was found in the 2019 Assessment that only seven people's courts disclosed such information, accounting for 7.4%, and the information was disclosed in different sections, making it inconvenient to inquire. According to the assessment report in 2020, ten of the high people's courts, the intermediate people's courts, and the specialized courts disclosed such information, accounting for 10.75%. The disclosure rate increased slightly. Among the 119 primary people's courts, only seven made public the roster of judges disqualified, accounting for 5.88%.

4 Results of the Handling of Motions and Proposals

Disclosing the results of the handling of motions by deputies to the people's congresses and proposals by CPPCC members is a powerful means of responding to the concerns of deputies, CPPCC members, and the public. It also helps enhance judicial credibility. Such disclosure has become a part of the disclosure of government affairs. According to the Notice by the General Office of the State Council on Disclosing the Results of the Handling of Motions Made by Deputies to the NPC and Proposals by CPPCC Members, all regions and departments should further promote the disclosure of the full text of response documents in handling motions by deputies to the people's congresses and proposals by CPPCC members. For motions and proposals involving public benefits, public rights and interests, and social concerns, and those requiring to be known by society, the response documents thereof should, in principle, be made public in the full text. Suppose a response document has been approved to be disclosed after the examination. In that case, the people's court should make it public on its own initiative through government bulletins, the website, Weibo and WeChat, press conferences, newspapers, broadcast, television, and other means that are easy for the public to access. In particular, government websites should be well used as information disclosure platforms to display the results of the handling of motions and proposals for the public's convenience to consult. However, such disclosure work is still in its infancy in judicial openness.

The 2019 assessment results show that only 11 courts set up columns, accounting for 11.7% of the 93 courts. Seven courts disclosed their complete responses to the motions and proposals in 2019, and the other four courts had no related content in their columns. Two courts did not set up columns, but they disclosed the responses in the full text in 2019. Four courts did not set up columns, but they disclosed the abstract of their handling results in 2019 in different sections of the websites. Seventy-seven courts neither set up columns nor disclosed the full text of their responses or the abstract of the handling results, accounting for 81.9%.

The 2020 assessment results show that among the original 93 courts, 15 set up columns accounting for 16.13%. Eight courts disclosed the full text of the response documents in handling the motions and proposals, and six disclosed the abstract of the handling results. Eight of the 119 primary people's courts set up columns, accounting for 6.72%, and none disclosed information on the handling results.

It shows that disclosing the results of the handling of the deputies' motions and the members' proposals did not attract enough attention in judicial openness and was far from satisfactory.

5 Litigation Guides

5.1 Overview

A litigation guide can show litigation participants how to participate in the action smoothly. It can help the parties understand litigation procedures and their rights and avoid potential litigation risks. A litigation guide is an essential prerequisite for the parties to accept litigation services, participate in litigation activities, and protect their litigation rights and substantive rights. To this end, the Supreme People's Court issued the Several Opinions on Promoting the Building of the Three Platforms for Judicial Openness. According to the Opinions, a people's court should disclose to the public through the judicial process information disclosure platform the conditions for filing a case, conditions and requirements for applying for a retrial or an appeal, litigation procedures, styles of litigation documents, standards of legal costs, procedures and conditions for suspension, reduction, and exemption thereof, a timely reminder of litigation risks, alternative dispute resolution mechanisms, and other information. According to the Opinions of the Supreme People's Court on Furthering Judicial

Openness, a people's court should use its initiative to disclose the litigation guide, on the best efforts basis improve access to information on litigation services, advance the level of litigation services, and effectively facilitate litigation. The Guiding Opinions of the Supreme People's Court on Comprehensively Promoting the Construction of Litigation Service Centers in the People's Courts put forward that a people's court should provide the parties at the administrative hall with guiding materials such as visit notices, litigation guides, risk statements, and self-service inquiry machines such as electronic touch screens. The litigation service website should be equipped with the function of information inquiry and litigation guidance so that the public can directly log on to the website to inquire about the litigation guidance information. Besides, the website should provide frequently used electronic templates, such as a statement of complaint, a statement of defense, an application for enforcement, and a power of attorney.

According to the assessments, some courts used videos, flow charts, and other means to disclose trial information, which is convenient and easy to understand. For example, the Intermediate People's Court of Zibo City specially produced a flow chart for filing a case during the epidemic, which is straightforward and convenient. The Intermediate People's Court of Xiamen City published both Chinese and English versions of its litigation guide. The High People's Court of Yunnan Province offered detailed instructions with screenshots of each step for the online filing; the Intermediate People's Court of Qiqihar City made an electronic version of the Handbook for Suing Without Asking for Help, which is comprehensive and easy to read. The Intermediate People's Court of Shenzhen City vividly presented its litigation guide through computer animation.

The assessment results in 2019 and 2020 reveal that a litigation guide is a regular part of judicial openness, and courts of all types generally disclose litigation guides on websites. However, a slow updating of litigation guides, inaccurate content, and low popularity all proved poor quality disclosure. For example, the 2020 Assessment shows that one high people's court, five intermediate people's courts, four specialized courts, and 15 primary people's courts did not issue a litigation guide.

5.2 *Adequacy of a Litigation Guide*

The litigation guide disclosed by every court must cover all kinds of cases within its jurisdiction and be equipped with relevant guidelines to assist the parties taking part in litigation. Otherwise, the provided litigation guide is insufficient. It was found in the assessment that many courts disclosed on their websites a litigation guide in respect of some types of cases (such as civil cases) or cases subject to certain levels of jurisdiction (such as first-instance cases).

The 2020 Assessment shows that among the 32 high people's courts, 22 courts issued a litigation guide according to the types of cases within their jurisdiction, such as civil and commercial cases, criminal cases, administrative cases, and state compensation cases, accounting for 68.75%. Nine courts did not publish a complete litigation guide according to the aforementioned types, and one court failed to disclose a litigation guide, accounting for 28.13% and 3.13%, respectively. Among the 49 intermediate people's courts, 25 courts issued a litigation guide for all cases in terms of the types within their jurisdiction, 19 courts did not issue a complete litigation guide, and five courts did not issue a litigation guide, accounting for 51.02%, 38.78%, and 10.20%, respectively. Among the 12 specialized courts, four courts disclosed a litigation guide for all cases according to the types, four did not issue a complete litigation guide, and four did not issue a litigation guide, accounting for 33.33%, 33.33%, and 33.33%, respectively. Among the 119 primary people's courts, 50 courts disclosed a litigation guide for all cases according to the types, 54 courts did not publish a comprehensive litigation guide, and 15 courts did not issue a litigation guide, accounting for 42.02%, 45.38%, and 12.61%, respectively (see Fig. 20). It can be seen that the overall proportion of the courts that issued a litigation guide comprehensively was not high, and the specialized courts and the primary people's courts performed relatively low.

Many cases may enter the appeal, retrial, and other proceedings for any court at every level after the court makes a judgment. Therefore, a litigation guide should provide necessary guidelines on appeals and cases tried by a people's court of second instance and retrials under the trial supervision system subject to and upon the level of jurisdiction to facilitate the participation of the parties involved. However, the

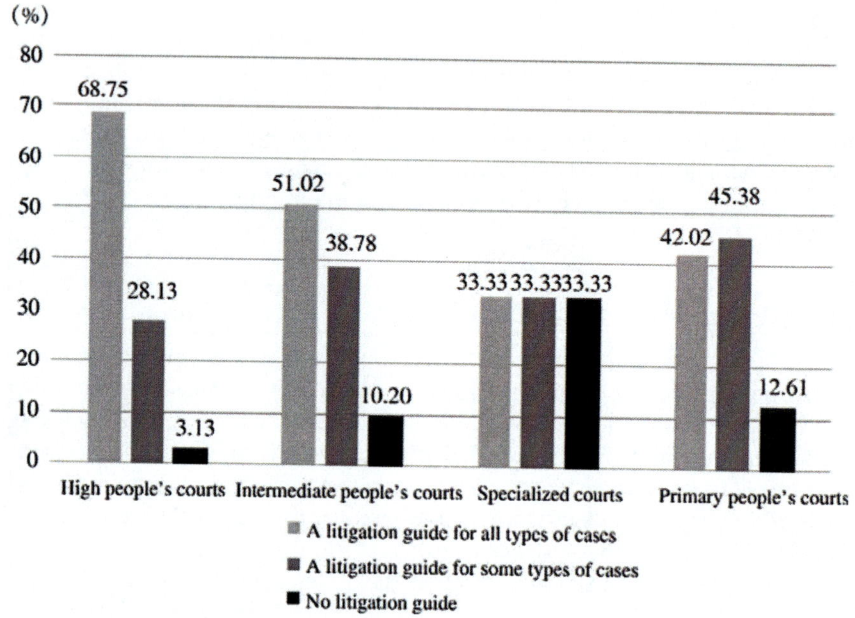

Fig. 20 Litigation guides published pursuant to the types of cases in 2020

assessment shows that the release of litigation guides in respect hereof was unsatisfactory. Among the 32 high people's courts, 17 courts issued a litigation guide for appeals, and cases tried by the people's court of second instance and retrials under the trial supervision system according to the level of jurisdiction, 14 courts did not publish a comprehensive litigation guide under the above procedures, and one court did not disclose any litigation guide, accounting for 53.13%, 43.75%, and 3.13%, respectively. Among the 49 intermediate people's courts, 22 courts issued a litigation guide for appeals, cases tried by the people's court of second instance, and retrials according to the level of jurisdiction, 22 courts did not issue a complete litigation guide following the above procedures, and five courts did not disclose any litigation guide, accounting for 44.90%, 44.90%, and 10.20%, respectively. Among the 12 specialized courts, six courts issued a litigation guide for appeals, cases tried by the people's court of second instance, and retrials according to the level of jurisdiction, two courts did not publish a complete litigation guide under the above procedures, and four courts did not disclose a litigation guide, accounting for 50.00%, 16.67%, and 33.33%, respectively. Among the 119 primary people's courts, 36 courts issued a litigation guide for appeals, cases tried by the people's courts of the second instance, and retrials according to the level of jurisdiction, 68 courts did not comprehensively publish a litigation guide under the above procedures, and 15 courts did not disclose any litigation guide. They accounted for 30.25%, 57.14%, and 12.61%, respectively (see Fig. 21). It can be seen that the work of providing litigation guides according to the trial procedures in which the parties may be involved was far from enough. The performance of the primary people's courts was the worst.

When publishing a litigation guide, the people's court should also disclose litigation risks. Litigation risks refer to the factors that the litigants and their agents *ad litem* may face in legal activities. They have nothing to do with the disputed facts but may affect the trial and enforcement, causing legal rights and interests to be unrealized. The Civil Procedure Law provides that litigants shall be informed of litigation risks, which should be included in a litigation guide as well.[1] According to the assessment, among the 32 high people's courts, five courts made public litigation risks in respect of significant types of cases such as civil and commercial cases, criminal cases, and administrative cases, 24 courts disclosed litigation risks regarding some types of cases, and three courts disclosed no litigation risks to the litigants, accounting for 15.63%, 75%, and 9.38%, respectively. Among the 49 intermediate people's courts, two courts disclosed litigation risks in respect of major types of cases such as civil and commercial cases, criminal cases, and administrative cases, 41 courts disclosed litigation risks regarding some types of cases, and three courts did not make public litigation risks, accounting for 4.08%, 83.67%, and 12.24%, respectively. Among the 12 specialized courts, two courts informed the parties of litigation risks in respect of major types of cases such as civil and commercial cases, criminal cases, and administrative cases, four courts disclosed litigation risks regarding some types of cases, and six courts did not disclose any litigation risks, accounting for 16.67%, 33.33%,

[1] See Zhou and Xie [1].

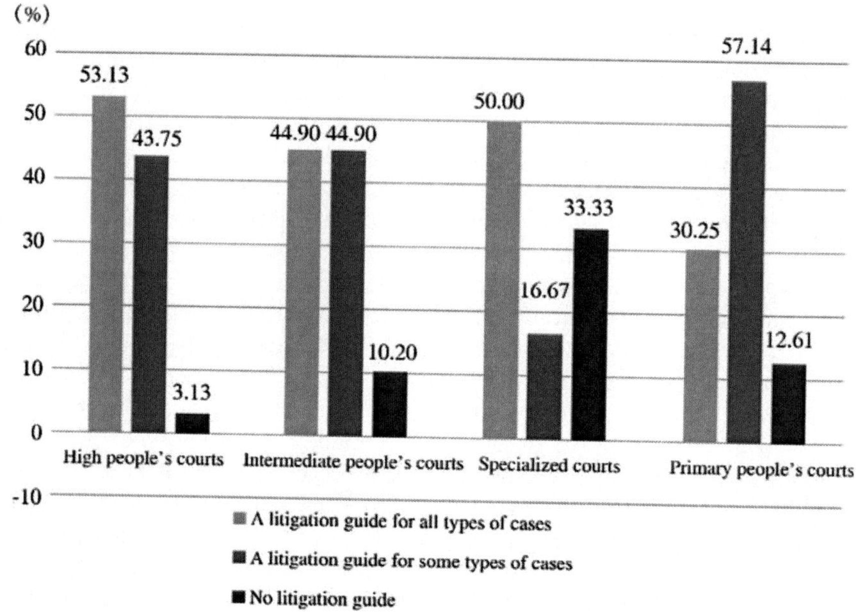

Fig. 21 A litigation guide published pursuant to the level of jurisdiction in 2020

and 50.00%, respectively. Four of the 119 primary people's courts made the litigants aware of litigation risks in respect of major types of cases, 79 courts disclosed litigation risks regarding some types of cases, and 36 courts did not disclose any litigation risks, accounting for 3.36%, 66.39%, and 30.26%, respectively (see Fig. 22). It can be seen that very few courts issued litigation risk alerts as comprehensively as possible. In this regard, the high people's courts and the intermediate people's courts performed the best, and the primary people's courts and the specialized courts had a relatively low issuance rate. Most courts only disclosed some litigation risks, and the intermediate people's courts had the highest disclosure rate among these courts. Overall, the issuance of litigation risk alerts by the primary people's courts was the least satisfactory.

In addition, courts must issue samples of legal instruments for the parties' reference when they are preparing and submitting legal instruments such as pleadings. Instrument samples or guidelines for writing instruments are provided in many courts' case filing halls or litigation service halls. In order to reduce the visits by the parties, it is imperative to furnish the parties with samples of various litigation instruments through the Internet. It was found in the assessment that among the 32 high people's courts, 16 courts provided complete legal instrument samples concerning civil and commercial cases, criminal cases, and administrative cases, 12 courts provided legal instrument samples regarding some types of cases, and four courts did not issue any samples, accounting for 50%, 37.50%, and 12.50%, respectively. Among the 49 intermediate people's courts, 22 courts provided a complete set of legal instrument

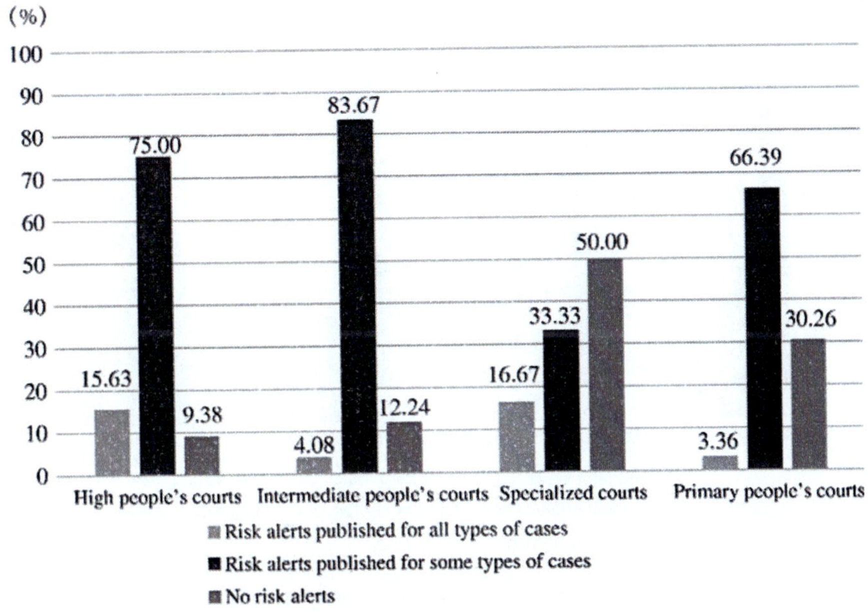

Fig. 22 Litigation risk alerts published pursuant to the types of cases in 2020

samples in respect of civil and commercial cases, criminal cases, and administrative cases, 20 courts provided legal instrument samples regarding some types of cases, and seven courts did not issue any samples, accounting for 44.90%, 40.82%, and 14.29%, respectively. Among the 32 specialized courts, five courts provided a complete set of legal instrument samples in respect of civil and commercial cases, criminal cases, and administrative cases, two courts provided legal instrument samples regarding some types of cases, and five courts did not issue any samples accounting for 41.67%, 16.67%, and 41.67%, respectively. Among the 119 primary people's courts, 35 courts provided a complete set of legal instrument samples, 48 courts provided legal instrument samples regarding some types of cases, and 36 courts did not issue any samples, accounting for 29.41%, 40.34%, and 30.25%, respectively (see Fig. 23). The rate of comprehensively issuing all types of litigation instrument samples decreased in the order of the high people's courts, the intermediate people's courts, the specialized courts, and the primary people's courts. The rate of failing to issue any litigation instrument samples decreased in the order of the specialized courts, the primary people's courts, the intermediate people's courts, and the high people's courts. The above also shows that the lower the court level was, the less satisfactory the issuance of litigation risk alerts was.

In general, according to the analysis of the above four dimensions, it can be concluded that the issuance of the litigation guides by the primary people's courts was the least satisfactory. In primary people's courts, people can receive the most immediate litigation services. The standardization of the issuance of litigation guides

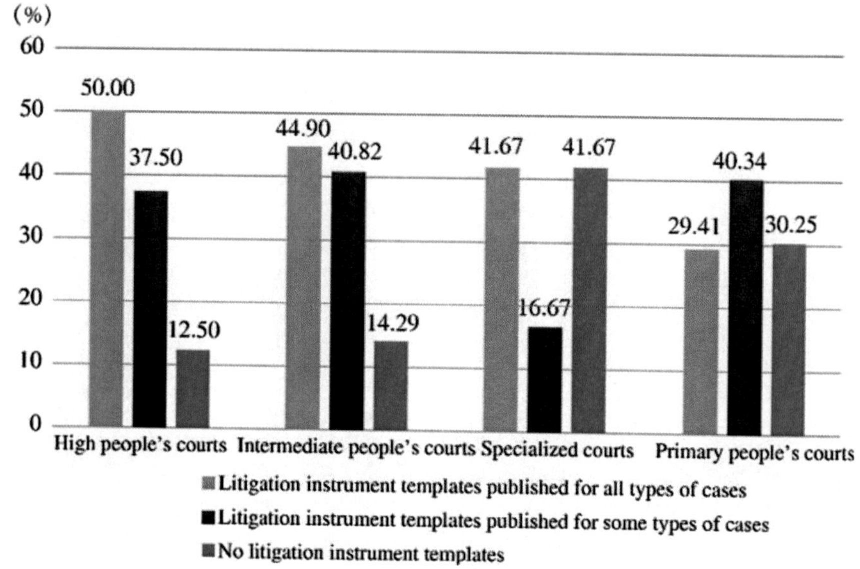

Fig. 23 Litigation instrument templates issued pursuant to the types of cases in 2020

by primary people's courts is directly related to whether the litigants and the general public can be better served.

5.3 *Accuracy of a Litigation Guide*

A litigation guide is an "instruction book" for litigation activities that can guide the public to file a lawsuit and participate in litigation according to law. Only when it is accurate can a litigation guide work effectively, or it will be a mere decoration and even mislead the public. It was found in the assessment that there was a relatively high proportion of errors in the litigation guides. Among all the assessed objects (excluding the Supreme People's Court and the five primary people's courts without websites), 52.82% of the courts had errors in their litigation guides. Among the 32 high people's courts, seven courts did not make apparent errors in their litigation guides, 24 had errors in their litigation guides, and one court did not issue a litigation guide, accounting for 21.88%, 75%, and 3.13%, respectively. Among the 49 intermediate people's courts, 11 courts did not make apparent errors in their litigation guides, 33 had errors in their litigation guides, and five did not issue any litigation guide, accounting for 22.45%, 67.35%, and 10.20%, respectively. Among the 12 specialized courts, six courts did not make apparent errors in their litigation guides, two courts had errors in their litigation guides, and four courts did not issue a litigation guide, accounting for 50.00%, 16.67%, and 33.33%, respectively. Among the 119 primary people's courts, 40 courts had no apparent errors in their litigation

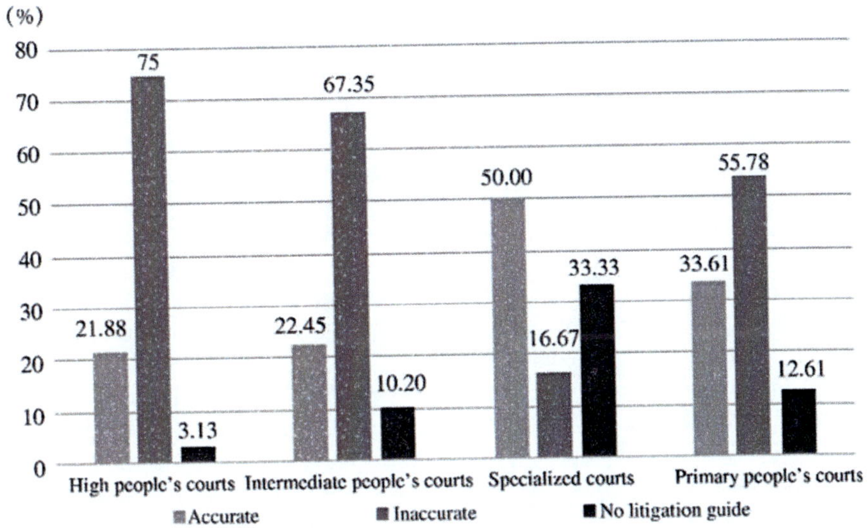

Fig. 24 Accuracy of a litigation guide in 2020

guides, 64 courts had errors in their litigation guides, and 15 courts did not issue any litigation guide, accounting for 33.61%, 53.78%, and 12.61%, respectively (see Fig. 24). Generally, the proportion of the litigation guides with inaccurate content was relatively high. The high people's courts had the highest rate of errors in the litigation guides, followed by the intermediate people's courts and the primary people's courts.

There are many types of specific errors. The following is a summary of the instances found in the assessment.

5.3.1 Copying Litigation Guides of Other Courts

Some courts copied other courts' litigation guides and made no modifications to place names, units, and other details. On the portal of the Primary People's Court of Taihe County of Anhui Province, the content of the "About Suing" page in the sub-column of "Case Filing Guide" under the column of "Litigation Guide" almost copied the content of an intermediate people's court of Beijing Municipality. For instance, "B. Cases having a significant impact within the jurisdiction include in the nine districts and counties under the jurisdiction of the Court (Xicheng District, Xuanwu District, Haidian District, Shijingshan District, Mentougou District, Changping District, Fangshan District, Daxing District, Yanqing County), a civil case with the subject matter at a value of at least 2.5 million yuan; an economic case with the subject matter at a value of at least 5 million yuan; all intellectual property cases except those of first-instance accepted by the Primary People's Court of Haidian

District; and cases determined by the Supreme People's Court to be within the jurisdiction of intermediate people's courts." Another example is, "The manager of an electronic accessories company located in Shijingshan District came to the Court to sue Hongda Computer Company. The Court ruled not to accept the case. In the manager's opinion, the Computer Company owed him tens of millions of yuan in payment for goods, so the case involving such a tremendous amount of money should be tried by the intermediate court. The Court explained that the case should be tried by an intermediate court, which is determined by the level of jurisdiction. However, this case should be tried by the Second Intermediate People's Court rather than the First Intermediate People's Court, which is determined by the territorial jurisdiction provisions. In this case, the defendant is located in Fengtai District, which is subject to the Second Intermediate People's Court."

The Litigation Guide of the Intermediate People's Court of Fushun City of Liaoning Province copied the content of a court in Chongqing. An example was found on the "Litigation Notice" page under its portal's "Legal Knowledge" column. "1. The primary people's court has the jurisdiction over civil cases as a court of first instance, except as otherwise provided by law. The primary people's courts under the jurisdiction of the First Intermediate People's Court of Chongqing Municipality and the two primary people's courts in Wanzhou District and Fuling District as courts of first instance accept civil cases with the amount in dispute less than 2 million yuan, and foreign-related cases, and Hong Kong, Macao, and Taiwan-related cases with the amount in dispute less than 1 million yuan. Other primary people's courts under the jurisdiction of the Second Intermediate People's Court, the Third Intermediate People's Court, and the Fourth Intermediate People's Court of Chongqing Municipality as courts of first instance accept civil cases with the amount in dispute less than 1 million yuan, and foreign-related, and Hong Kong, Macao, and Taiwan-related cases."

5.3.2 Errors in the Provisions on the Time Limit of Trial

Revised procedure law provisions were used in the litigation guides of some courts to describe the time limit of trial. For example, in terms of the time limit of the trial of criminal cases, according to the latest Criminal Procedure Law, a people's court shall announce a sentence for a case of public prosecution within two months, or three months at the latest, after accepting the case; for a case with the possibility of a death penalty or a case with an incidental civil action or under any of the circumstances set forth in Article 158 of this Law, the time limit of trial may be extended for three months with the approval of the people's court at the next higher level; and, if more extension is needed under exceptional circumstances, the extension shall be reported to the Supreme People's Court for approval. However, old expressions were still found in some courts' litigation guides. For instance, in the "Litigation Guide" subcolumn under the "Justice for the People" column of the portal of the High People's Court of Shaanxi Province, "according to the first paragraph of Article 168 of this Law, a people's court shall announce a sentence for a case of public prosecution within one month or, one and a half months at the latest, after accepting it." In the sub-column of "Litigation Procedures" under the "Legal Knowledge" column of the portal of the High People's Court of Jilin Province, "the procedures at first instance in the Criminal Procedure Law" was stated as "a people's court as a court of first instance shall announce a sentence for a case of public prosecution within one month or, one and a half months at the latest, after accepting it; under any of the circumstances set forth in Article 126 of the Criminal Procedure Law, the time limit may be extended for one more month with the approval of or decision by the high people's court of a province, autonomous region, or municipality directly under the Central Government; if the jurisdiction of a people's court over a case is altered, the time limit for handling the case shall be calculated from the date on which another people's court receives the case as of the alteration." Besides, similar errors were discovered in the litigation guides published on the portals of some courts, such as the High People's Court of Qinghai Province, the Intermediate People's Court of Jilin City, the Intermediate People's Court of Xi'an City, the Intermediate People's Court of Zhuhai City, the Intermediate People's Court of Hohhot City, the Ganzhou Primary People's Court of Zhangye City.

5.3.3 Errors in the Provisions on Jurisdiction

The litigation guides of some courts followed old provisions, resulting in errors in the provisions on jurisdiction. For example, the Administrative Procedure Law revised in 2014 changed the original Article 14 to Article 15, "An Intermediate People's Court shall have jurisdiction over the following administrative cases as a court of first instance: (1) A case filed against an administrative action taken by a department of the State Council or by a people's government at or above the county level. (2) A case handled by the Customs. (3) A major or complicated case within its territorial jurisdiction. (4) Other cases under the jurisdiction of an Intermediate People's Court as prescribed by the law." However, many courts, such as the Intermediate People's Court of Shijiazhuang City and the Intermediate People's Court of Haikou City, still stated that the administrative cases under the jurisdiction of an intermediate people's court as a court of first instance include "a case filed against a specific administrative action taken by a department of the State Council or by a people's government of a province, autonomous region or municipality directly under the Central Government."

5.3.4 Errors in the Provisions on the Time Limit for Applying for Enforcement

According to Article 239 of the Civil Procedure Law in force, the time limit for applying for enforcement shall be two years. The suspension or interruption of the time limitation for applying for enforcement shall be governed by legal provisions regarding the suspension or interruption of the time limitations for instituting an action. The exact time limit applies to the application for enforcement in administrative cases under the judicial interpretations of the Supreme People's Court. However, some courts stated that "(1) the time limit for the application for the enforcement of a civil instrument in force shall be one year if one or both of the parties are citizens; it shall be six months if both parties are legal persons or other organizations. (2) the time limit for the application for the enforcement of an administrative instrument in force shall be three months". The High People's Court of Hainan Province and the Intermediate People's Court of Nanchang City were among such courts.

5.3.5 Errors in the Provisions on the Limitation of Actions

The litigation guides of some courts mixed the limitation of actions for civil cases with that for administrative cases. According to the law in effect, the limitation of actions for civil cases generally is three years. However, many courts followed the outdated provision in their litigation guides, according to which the limitation of actions is two years, such as the High People's Court of Hui Autonomous Region of Ningxia Province, the Intermediate People's Court of Wuxi City, the Intermediate People's Court of Changchun City, and Shanghai Intellectual Property Court.

The law in force provides that the limitation of actions for administrative cases is six months. However, some courts followed the old provision in their litigation guides. According to the litigation guide for administrative cases of the Primary People's Court of Hengqin New Area of Zhuhai City, "if a citizen, a legal person, or any other organization brings a suit before a people's court, that shall be done within three months since he or it is aware that a specific administrative act has been conducted, except as otherwise provided for by law."

To sum up, errors in the litigation guides were mainly due to the direct copying of other courts' litigation guides without any modification according to the situation of the court and the region where the court is located. After the relevant procedure laws and judicial interpretations had been amended, the litigation guides were not modified accordingly, resulting in errors in content.

5.4 *Popularity of a Litigation Guide*

A "guide" should accurately inform the public about how to participate in litigation and rely on legal means to protect their rights and interests. It should also be designed to be popular and easy to catch. Otherwise, there is no need to go to great lengths to compile and disclose it, and all we have to do is post the relevant laws and judicial interpretations as they are. Accordingly, a litigation guide should include flowcharts for different cases to inform the public of the procedures they need to follow when filing a lawsuit and what needs to be paid attention to in each procedure. Copying the provisions of the laws or judicial interpretations should be avoided, and "legal language" should be translated into words familiar to the public and easy to understand.

The assessment shows a relatively low proportion of disclosing flowcharts in a litigation guide. Among the 32 high people's courts, ten courts had flowcharts for all major types of cases, eight had flowcharts for some types of cases, 13 did not have any flowchart, and one did not disclose a litigation guide, accounting for 31.25%, 25.00%, 40.63%, and 3.13%, respectively. Among the 49 intermediate people's courts, 13 courts had flowcharts for major types of cases, 11 had flowcharts for some types of cases, 20 did not have any flowchart, and five did not disclose a litigation guide, accounting for 26.53%, 22.45%, 40.82%, and 10.20%, respectively. Among the 12 specialized courts, one court had flowcharts for main types of cases, one had flowcharts for some types of cases, six did not have any flowchart, and four did not disclose a litigation guide, accounting for 8.33%, 8.33%, 50.00%, and 33.33%, respectively. Among the 119 primary people's courts, 18 courts had flowcharts for main types of cases, 14 had flowcharts for some types of cases, 72 did not have any flowchart, and 15 did not post a litigation guide, accounting for 15.13%, 11.76%, 60.50%, and 12.61% respectively (see Fig. 25). It can be seen that the lower the court level was, the less satisfactory the litigation guide with flowcharts was.

A relatively low standard was adopted during our investigation into and assessment of whether some courts had copied the provisions of relevant laws or judicial interpretations. Only those who copied such provisions without any change were

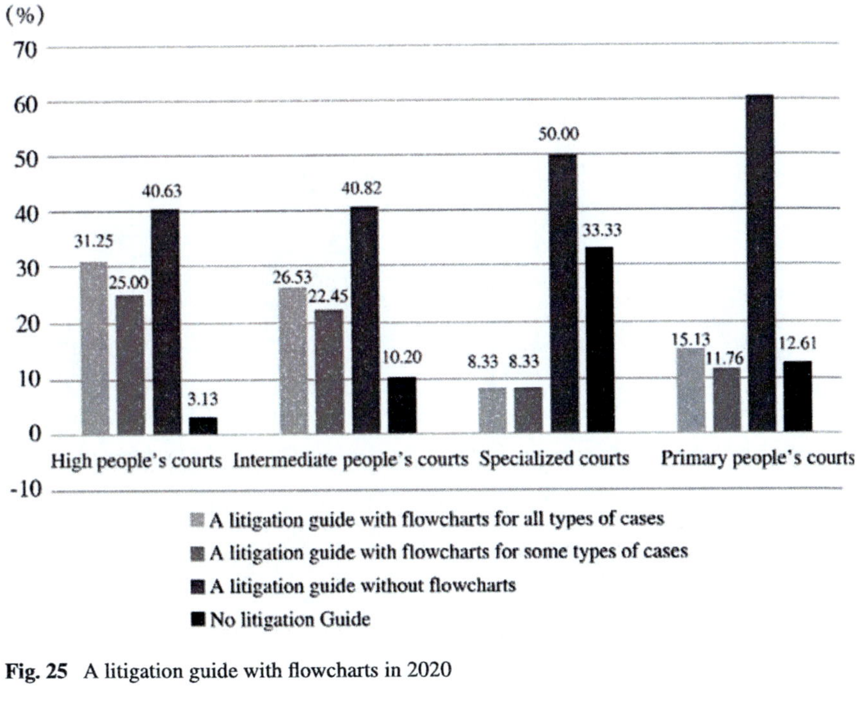

Fig. 25 A litigation guide with flowcharts in 2020

deemed to have copied the provisions. Some slight modifications to the laws or judicial interpretations were beyond our consideration. The assessment shows that three courts of the 32 high people's courts copied the provisions, 28 did not, and one did not disclose any litigation guide, accounting for 9.38%, 87.50%, and 3.13%, respectively. Among the 49 intermediate people's courts, six courts copied the provisions, 38 did not, and five did not post any litigation guide, accounting for 12.24%, 77.55%, and 10.20%, respectively. Among the 12 specialized courts, eight courts did not copy the provisions, and four did not disclose any litigation guide, accounting for 66.67% and 33.33%, respectively. Among the 119 primary people's courts, 20 courts copied the provisions, 84 did not, and 15 did not disclose a litigation guide, accounting for 16.81%, 70.59%, and 12.61%, respectively (see Fig. 26). The lower the court level is and the closer the relationship with the general public is, the more popular a litigation guide should be. Then, the public can, without any difficulty, understand the procedures and risks of case handling. However, in practice, the lower the court level was, the less accessible its litigation guide was. Copying was found in many primary and intermediate people's courts rather than in the specialized courts. It can be concluded that the primary and intermediate people's courts should have cared more about the public's participation in litigation in compiling a litigation guide and avoided blindly copying the laws and judicial interpretations.

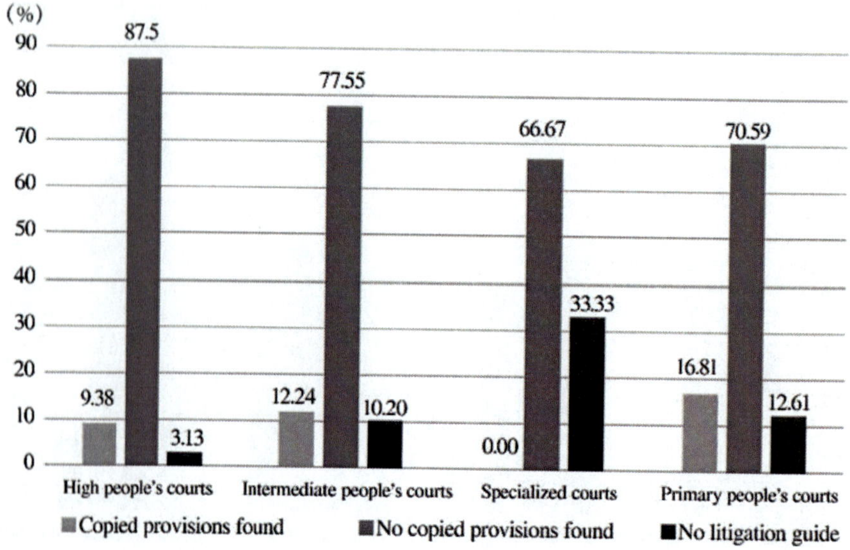

Fig. 26 A litigation guide copying the provisions of relevant laws or judicial interpretations in 2020

5.5 *Disclosure of the Guidelines in Response to the Epidemic*

Since the sudden outbreak of COVID-19 at the beginning of 2020, courts' trial and enforcement work in various places has been affected to varying degrees. The routine handling of cases by courts and the guarantee of the parties' litigation rights and substantive rights have been affected. In such exceptional circumstances, courts should ensure the routine disclosure and maintenance of litigation guides and provide guidelines for the public by timely disclosing information on activities such as instituting and defending legal proceedings during the epidemic. In response, a new item was added to the assessment in 2020, namely whether the court had released relevant service guidelines and other information for the inconvenience caused by the epidemic.

The assessment shows that some courts released information and news reports on their portals to address the inconvenience caused by the COVID-19. For example, guides to the case- filing process during the epidemic were explicitly posted on the websites of the High People's Court of Yunnan Province, the Primary People's Court of Hengqin New Area of Zhuhai City, the Intermediate People's Court of Zibo City, and the Intermediate People's Court of Wuxi City. Service guidelines during the epidemic were found on the websites of the High People's Court of Shandong Province, the Intermediate People's Court of Guangzhou City of Guangdong Province, and the Intermediate People's Court of Datong City of Shanxi Province. Although the Beijing Intellectual Property Court did not disclose any litigation guide, service guidelines of the Intellectual Property Court during the epidemic were released on the website of the High People's Court of Beijing Municipality.

The data shows that among the 32 high people's courts, ten courts posted a litigation guide on their websites and also released relevant information in response to the epidemic, one did not post a litigation guide but released relevant information in response to the epidemic, and 21 disclosed a litigation guide but did not release relevant information in response to the epidemic, accounting for 31.25%, 3.13%, and 65.63%, respectively. Among the 49 intermediate people's courts, 16 courts posted a litigation guide on their websites and released relevant information in response to the epidemic, and 28 disclosed a litigation guide but did not release relevant information, accounting for 32.65% and 57.14%, respectively. Among the 12 specialized courts, three courts posted a litigation guide on their websites and also released relevant information in response to the epidemic, three did not post a litigation guide but released relevant information, five disclosed a litigation guide but failed to release relevant information, and one court disclosed neither a litigation guide nor relevant information in response to the epidemic on its website, accounting for 25.00%, 25.00%, 41.67%, and 8.33%, respectively. Among the 119 primary people's courts, 51 courts posted a litigation guide on their websites and also released relevant information in response to the epidemic, five did not post a litigation guide but released relevant information, 53 published a litigation guide but failed to release relevant information, and ten released neither a litigation guide nor relevant information in response to the epidemic on their websites, accounting for 42.86%, 4.20%, 44.54%,

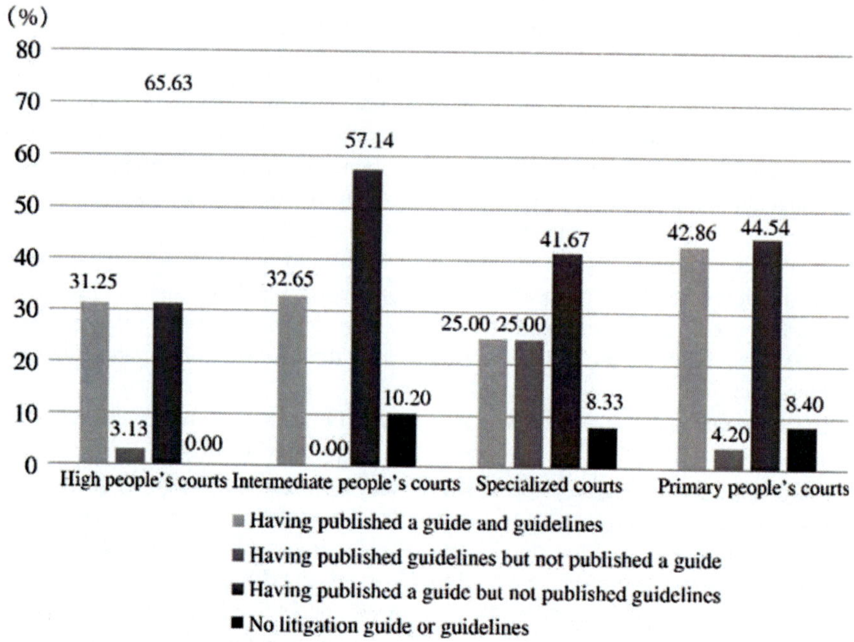

Fig. 27 Guidelines during COVID-19 in 2020

and 8.40% respectively (see Fig. 27). The difference in the release of service guidelines during the epidemic by various courts was not substantial. Still, the disclosure proportion was not high in general. That indicates that in the face of similar emergencies, the courts must promptly release relevant service guidelines to facilitate the public's participation in litigation and guarantee their rights.

5.6 *Places of a Litigation Guide*

A litigation guide should be posted in a conspicuous place so that the public can quickly notice it. However, it is found in the assessment that the guides were published on the websites without regularity, and there was a lack of uniform publication channels, making it difficult to inquire about information.

Some courts posted the litigation guide on several platforms. For example, the Intermediate People's Court of Wuxi City had two websites where its litigation guide was published. However, the discrepancy in the information posted in the two places was quite wide. The Intermediate People's Court of Lanzhou City managed the Lanzhou Court Online, the Lanzhou Court Litigation Service Center Online, and the Lanzhou Court Justice Administration Online. Its litigation guide was posted on all of these websites, and the content differed on every website. The same case was with the Primary People's Court of Yanji City of Jilin Province.

Some courts posted the litigation guide in a column that did not match the guide. Website columns are where relevant information is intensively disclosed, and the collection and disclosure of information about similar topics are helpful for public inquiries. However, the assessment shows that some courts posted the litigation guide in a column dealing with other issues, which was not conducive to the inquiry into litigation guides. For instance, the litigation guide of the Primary People's Court of Meilan District of Haikou City was placed under the "Legal Knowledge" column instead of the "Litigation Guide" column. The Intermediate People's Court of Suzhou City posted the guide information on appeal cases, cases tried by a people's court of second instance, and retrial cases on the same website under different columns such as "Litigation Guide" and "Judicial Openness".

Some courts piled up the guide information in just one column irregularly, making it extremely difficult to search. Some courts did not set up sub-columns, and the information was piled up under the "Litigation Guide" column. Some courts set up sub-columns, but they did not exert the function. For example, there was no sub-column under the "Litigation Guide" column of the Intermediate People's Court of Changchun City, leading to a clutter of the litigation guide, instrument templates, litigation risk alerts, flowcharts, and other documents. No sub-column was found under the "Litigation Guide" column on the Primary People's Court of Changji City website; thus, relevant information, the list of judges, and the list of mediators were shown on the same web page. There were sub-columns under the "Litigation Guide" column on the Primary People's Court of Yumen City website. Still, all the contents crowded the "Hotline" sub-column under the "Litigation Guide" column with a highly confusing classification. The guide information of the Primary People's Court of Lanshan District of Linyi City was stacked and hard to find. The litigation guides of the Primary People's Court of Nankai District of Tianjin Municipality and the Primary People's Court of Tianjin Binhai New Area were posted in the "Litigation Service" column in a disorderly pile.

It can be concluded that the website construction level of courts at all levels has not been advanced, and the courts should strengthen the awareness of improving information disclosure on the websites. The understanding of judicial openness and the user-oriented website construction is waiting to be raised. The website construction, column design, and information release have not been as convenient as possible for the public to inquire about and obtain information.

6 Disclosure of Judgments

6.1 Overview

Judgments are the products of trial activities, the most important texts related to legitimate rights and interests of the parties concerned, and one of the essential outcomes of the case handling by people's courts according to the law. In a judgment, fact determination, law application, and the final result are the critical basis of judicial fairness. It is an integral part of judicial openness and contemporary judicial civilization that judgments should be delivered to the parties and disclosed to the public at the same time. Disclosing judgments to the public, a reflection of judicial progress over a decade, helps regulate judges' exercise of judicial power, improve the ability to handle cases, facilitate social supervision and review, collect judicial big data, and unify criteria for judgment. Previously, judgment disclosure was not a routine procedure but an exception. By the end of 2013, the courts nationwide had gradually explored the release of judgments online. However, most courts had done so spontaneously and voluntarily, resulting in a relatively low figure in the number and proportion of disclosed judgments. According to the Provisions of the Supreme People's Court on the Publication of Judgments on the Internet by People's Courts issued in 2013, against the background that the publication of judgments was not comprehensive, timely, accurate, and convenient for inquiries due to the absence of a unified platform and express criteria for the online disclosure of judgments, "China Judgements Online" was established for publishing effective judgments. It is a milestone in China's judicial openness as it has laid the institutional and technical foundations for the systematic, comprehensive, and standardized disclosure of judgments in the information age.

Since the establishment by the Supreme People's Court of this unified national platform for judgment disclosure, the effective judgments made by people's courts nationwide have been disclosed on "China Judgements Online". With the help of information technology, the disclosure of judgments has made a great leap. By February 29, 2016, the people's courts at all levels had published more than 15.707 million judgments in force, with nearly 40,000 new ones added every day, including judgments written in five ethnic languages—Uyghur, Mongolian, Tibetan, Korean, and Kazakh. The total number of visits reached 478 million, with an average of 580,000 visits per day. Online judgments have achieved the "full coverage of all courts and all types of cases across the country".[2] By December 31, 2016, more than 25.5 million judgments had been uploaded to China Judgements Online, with the cumulative number of visits exceeding 4.72 billion.[3] By December 31, 2018, 61.79 million judgments had been published on China Judgements Online, with the cumulative number of visits exceeding 21.3 billion and users covering more than

[2] See Center for National Index of Rule of Law of CASS [2].

[3] See Li and Tian [3].

210 countries and regions.[4] By 6 p.m. on August 30, 2020, the total number of judgments on China Judgements Online had exceeded 100 million, with nearly 48 billion visits.[5]

As stated above, in the 2020 Assessment, the project team obtained information on the online judgments disclosed by the assessed courts between January 1 and September 30, 2020, through the Trial Administration Office of the Supreme People's Court.

According to the results of the 2020 Assessment, China has achieved remarkable progress in judgment disclosure. However, existing problems deserve careful consideration. The trend that many courts are stagnating or even regressing should not be ignored. The data analysis shows that a large proportion of published judgments were not disclosed in the complete text, although the number increased. Of all the obtained judgments, 22.28% only disclosed information items, 51.22% of which were not made public for other reasons. The ratio was even higher in some courts. The ratio in many courts exceeded 90%. On the contrary, the proportion of those judgments not disclosed in the full text for statutory causes was relatively low.

6.2 *Disclosure of the Data on Judgment Disclosure*

Disclosing the data on judgment disclosure is key to the management of and supervision over judgment disclosure and also an integral part of the mechanism of ensuring judgment disclosure. Sadly, the mechanism's operation is not satisfactory. For instance, the number of the high people's and intermediate people's courts that made public the data on judgment disclosure and analysis reports in 2020 is considerably less than that in the previous year. Eight high people's courts, nine intermediate people's courts, and nine primary people's courts disclosed statistics on judgment disclosure, accounting for 25.00%, 18.37%, and 7.56%, respectively. No specialized courts disclosed such data. In addition, some of them disclosed the data on a monthly or seasonal basis. Only four intermediate people's courts and two primary people's courts made their analysis reports on judgment disclosure publicly available.

6.3 *Judgments Disclosed in the Full Text*

The number of judgments disclosed online between 1 January to 30 September 2020 reveals that judgment disclosure differed from court to court. During this period, 218 courts, including the Supreme People's Court, disclosed on China Judgements Online a total of 2,917,783 judgments, with 2,267,819 judgments disclosed in the full text accounting for 77.72% and 649,963 not disclosed in the full text accounting

[4] See Chen and Tian [4].

[5] See *People's Court Daily* [5].

for 22.28%. Two courts disclosed the full text of less than 20% of the published judgments, accounting for 0.92%; four courts disclosed the full text of more than 20% but less than or equal to 40% of the published judgments, accounting for 1.83%; 13 courts disclosed the full text of over 40%, but less than or equal to 60% of the published judgments, accounting for 5.96%; 64 courts disclosed the full text of over 60% but less than or equal to 80% of the published judgments, accounting for 29.36%; and 135 courts disclosed the full text of more than 80% of the published judgments, accounting for 61.93% (see Fig. 28). Eight courts made public on China Judgements Online the full text of all their published judgments, namely the Production and Construction Corps Branch of the High People's Court of Xinjiang Uygur Autonomous Region, the Primary People's Court of Guangdong Free Trade Zone (Nansha) of Guangdong Province, the Intermediate People's Court of Haikou City of Hainan Province, the Intermediate People's Court of Guiyang City of Guizhou Province, the Primary People's Court of Chengmai County of Hainan Province, the Primary People's Court of Yunyan District of Guiyang City, Guizhou Province, the Primary People's Court of Nanming District of Guiyang City, Guizhou Province, the Primary People's Court of Xishui County of Guizhou Province. Ten courts disclosed less than 50% of all the published judgments in the full text, namely the Primary People's Court of Huangzhong District of Xining City, Qinghai Province, the Primary People's Court of Hejin City of Shanxi Province, the Primary People's Court of Longxi County of Gansu Province, Beijing Internet Court, the Primary People's Court of Huangdao District of Qingdao City, Shandong Province, the Primary People's Court of Zhenxiong County of Yunnan Province, the Primary People's Court of Xuanwei City of Yunnan Province, the Primary People's Court of Ulanhot City of Inner Mongolia Autonomous Region, the Primary People's Court of Kuqa City of Aksu Prefecture, Xinjiang Uygur Autonomous Region, Guangzhou Internet Court. Overall, the percentage of those judgments not disclosed in the full text was relatively high.

The high people's courts made public a relatively higher proportion of their judgments in the full text among the courts at all levels. Statistics show that, among the assessed high people's courts, only two courts made public less than 90% of their judgments in the full text, while the rest disclosed more than 90%, accounting for 93.75%. All of the assessed intermediate people's courts disclosed more than 60% of the judgments in the full text. Among them, four courts disclosed over 60% but less than or equal to 80%, accounting for 8.16%; ten courts disclosed over 80% but less than or equal to 90%, accounting for 20.41%; and 35 courts made public more than 90%, accounting for 71.43%. Among the 12 specialized courts, two courts disclosed less than 60%, accounting for 16.67%; three courts disclosed over 60% but less than or equal to 80%, accounting for 25.00%; and seven courts disclosed more than 90%, accounting for 58.33%. Among the 124 primary people's courts, 17 courts disclosed less than 60%, accounting for 13.71%; 57 courts disclosed over 60% but less than or equal to 80%, accounting for 45.97%; 36 courts disclosed over 80% but less than or equal to 90%, accounting for 29.03%; and 14 courts disclosed more than 90%, accounting for 11.29% (see Table 1). Overall, the high people's courts performed

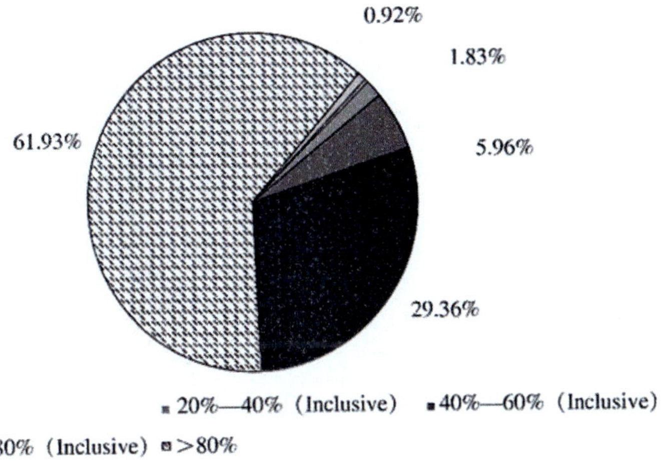

Fig. 28 Distribution of the courts in the light of the proportion of the judgments disclosed in the full text

the best in disclosing judgments in the full text, and the primary people's courts had a poor performance. The courts across the country performed differently.

6.3.1 Civil Judgments Disclosed in the Full Text

According to the data on civil judgments disclosed online, the total number of civil judgments online was 1,868,028, with 1,353,665 civil judgments disclosed in the full text, accounting for 72.46%. Among those judgments, three courts made public less than 20% (inclusive) of their judgments in the full text, accounting for 1.38%; nine courts disclosed over 20% but less than 40% (inclusive) of their judgments in the full text, accounting for 4.13%; 24 courts disclosed over 40% but less than 60% (inclusive) of their judgments in the full text, accounting for 11.01%; 71 courts disclosed over 60% but less than 80% (inclusive) of their judgments in the full text, accounting for 32.57%, 111 courts disclosed more than 80%, accounting for 50.92%; and 101 courts disclosed over 80% but less than 100% (see Fig. 29). Ten courts made public the full text of all their published civil judgments, namely the High People's Court of Liaoning Province, the Production and Construction Corps Branch of the High People's Court of Xinjiang Uygur Autonomous Region, the Primary People's Court of Guangdong Free Trade Zone (Nansha) of Guangdong Province, the Intermediate People's Court of Haikou City of Hainan Province, the Intermediate People's Court of Guiyang City of Guizhou Province, the Primary People's Court of Yuexiu District of Guangzhou City, Guangdong Province, the Primary People's Court of Chengmai County of Hainan Province, the Primary People's Court of Yunyan District of Guiyang City, Guizhou Province, the Primary People's Court of Nanming District of Guiyang City, Guizhou Province, the Primary People's Court

Table 1 The number of judgments disclosed online between January 1 to September 30, 2020 (ranking by the proportion of judgments disclosed in the full text)

Court	The total number of judgments disclosed	The number of judgments disclosed in the full text	Proportion (%)	The number of judgments not published in the full text but with information items disclosed	Proportion (%)	The number of judgments only with information items disclosed for "other reasons"	Proportion (%)
The Production and Construction Corps Branch of the High People's Court of Xinjiang Uygur Autonomous Region	315	315	100.00	0	0.00	0	0.00
The Primary People's Court of Guangdong Free Trade Zone (Nansha) of Guangdong Province	3574	3574	100.00	0	0.00	0	0.00
The Intermediate People's Court of Haikou City of Hainan Province	2130	2130	100.00	0	0.00	0	0.00

(continued)

Table 1 (continued)

Court	The total number of judgments disclosed	The number of judgments disclosed in the full text	Proportion (%)	The number of judgments not published in the full text but with information items disclosed	Proportion (%)	The number of judgments only with information items disclosed for "other reasons"	Proportion (%)
The Intermediate People's Court of Guiyang City of Guizhou Province	16,516	16,516	100.00	0	0.00	0	0.00
The Primary People's Court of Chengmai County of Hainan Province	889	889	100.00	0	0.00	0	0.00
The Primary People's Court of Yunyan District of Guiyang City, Guizhou Province	8756	8756	100.00	0	0.00	0	0.00
The Primary People's Court of Nanming District of Guiyang City, Guizhou Province	8994	8994	100.00	0	0.00	0	0.00

(continued)

Table 1 (continued)

Court	The total number of judgments disclosed	The number of judgments disclosed in the full text	Proportion (%)	The number of judgments not published in the full text but with information items disclosed	Proportion (%)	The number of judgments only with information items disclosed for "other reasons"	Proportion (%)
The Primary People's Court of Xishui County of Guizhou Province	6496	6496	100.00	0	0.00	0	0.00
The Primary People's Court of Longhua District of Haikou City, Hainan Province	7781	7778	99.96	3	0.04	0	0.00
The Primary People's Court of Yuexiu District of Guangzhou City, Guangdong Province	71,175	71,147	99.96	28	0.04	0	0.00
The High People's Court of Jilin Province	3779	3776	99.92	3	0.08	2	66.67
Guangzhou Intellectual Property Court	7136	7130	99.92	6	0.08	6	100.00

(continued)

Table 1 (continued)

Court	The total number of judgments disclosed	The number of judgments disclosed in the full text	Proportion (%)	The number of judgments not published in the full text but with information items disclosed	Proportion (%)	The number of judgments only with information items disclosed for "other reasons"	Proportion (%)
The Primary People's Court of Yumen City of Gansu Province	653	652	99.85	1	0.15	0	0.00
The High People's Court of Shandong Province	16,019	15,990	99.82	29	0.18	0	0.00
The Intermediate People's Court of Guangzhou City of Guangdong Province	25,368	25,313	99.78	55	0.22	40	72.73
The High People's Court of Tianjin Municipality	3137	3128	99.71	9	0.29	0	0.00
The High People's Court of Chongqing Municipality	5452	5435	99.69	17	0.31	0	0.00

(continued)

Table 1 (continued)

Court	The total number of judgments disclosed	The number of judgments disclosed in the full text	Proportion (%)	The number of judgments not published in the full text but with information items disclosed	Proportion (%)	The number of judgments only with information items disclosed for "other reasons"	Proportion (%)
The High People's Court of Liaoning Province	10,546	10,502	99.58	44	0.42	29	65.91
The High People's Court of Guizhou Province	6747	6712	99.48	35	0.52	0	0.00
The Supreme People's Court	19,592	19,474	99.40	118	0.60	114	96.61
The High People's Court of Anhui Province	5435	5396	99.28	39	0.72	25	64.10
The High People's Court of Hainan Province	976	968	99.18	8	0.82	2	25.00
The High People's Court of Guangxi Zhuang Autonomous Region	5000	4958	99.16	42	0.84	0	0.00

(continued)

Table 1 (continued)

Court	The total number of judgments disclosed	The number of judgments disclosed in the full text	Proportion (%)	The number of judgments not published in the full text but with information items disclosed	Proportion (%)	The number of judgments only with information items disclosed for "other reasons"	Proportion (%)
The Intermediate People's Court of Baotou City of Inner Mongolia Autonomous Region	2050	2027	98.88	23	1.12	18	78.26
The High People's Court of Henan Province	5776	5701	98.70	75	1.30	26	34.67
The High People's Court of Beijing Municipality	13,832	13,601	98.33	231	1.67	952	61.47
The High People's Court of Inner Mongolia Autonomous Region	4750	4670	98.32	80	1.68	74	92.50
The High People's Court of Fujian Province	8858	8685	98.05	173	1.95	64	36.99

(continued)

Table 1 (continued)

Court	The total number of judgments disclosed	The number of judgments disclosed in the full text	Proportion (%)	The number of judgments not published in the full text but with information items disclosed	Proportion (%)	The number of judgments only with information items disclosed for "other reasons"	Proportion (%)
The High People's Court of Sichuan Province	7910	7752	98.00	158	2.00	33	20.89
The High People's Court of Zhejiang Province	11,490	11,257	97.97	233	2.03	20	8.58
The Intermediate People's Court of Zhuhai City of Guangdong Province	2000	1958	97.90	42	2.10	27	64.29
The Intermediate People's Court of Datong City of Shanxi Province	2418	2364	97.77	54	2.23	7	12.96
The High People's Court of Qinghai Province	1203	1175	97.67	28	2.33	5	17.86
The High People's Court of Yunnan Province	7582	7400	97.60	182	2.40	142	78.02

(continued)

Table 1 (continued)

Court	The total number of judgments disclosed	The number of judgments disclosed in the full text	Proportion (%)	The number of judgments not published in the full text but with information items disclosed	Proportion (%)	The number of judgments only with information items disclosed for "other reasons"	Proportion (%)
Beijing Intellectual Property Court	15,424	14,985	97.15	439	2.85	66	15.03
The High People's Court of Jiangsu Province	7349	7129	97.01	220	2.99	0	0.00
The High People's Court of Guangdong Province	14,598	14,159	96.99	439	3.01	240	54.67
The High People's Court of Hebei Province	8930	8657	96.94	273	3.06	184	67.40
The Intermediate People's Court of Shenzhen City of Guangdong Province	19,815	19,178	96.79	637	3.21	189	29.67
The High People's Court of Hunan Province	11,526	11,148	96.72	378	3.28	3	0.79

(continued)

Table 1 (continued)

Court	The total number of judgments disclosed	The number of judgments disclosed in the full text	Proportion (%)	The number of judgments not published in the full text but with information items disclosed	Proportion (%)	The number of judgments only with information items disclosed for "other reasons"	Proportion (%)
The Intermediate People's Court of Lanzhou City of Gansu Province	5393	5215	96.70	178	3.30	70	39.33
The Primary People's Court of Futian District of Shenzhen City, Guangdong Province	50,624	48,900	96.59	1724	3.41	84	4.87
The High People's Court of Ningxia Hui Autonomous Region	888	857	96.51	31	3.49	19	61.29
The Primary People's Court of Huidong County of Guangdong Province	6514	6267	96.21	247	3.79	98	39.68

(continued)

Table 1 (continued)

Court	The total number of judgments disclosed	The number of judgments disclosed in the full text	Proportion (%)	The number of judgments not published in the full text but with information items disclosed	Proportion (%)	The number of judgments only with information items disclosed for "other reasons"	Proportion (%)
The Intermediate People's Court of Nanning City of Guangxi Zhuang Autonomous Region	7471	7163	95.88	308	4.12	0	0.00
The Intermediate People's Court of Changchun City of Jilin Province	9268	8877	95.78	391	4.22	48	12.28
The Primary People's Court of Shenzhen Qianhai Cooperation Zone of Guangdong Province	8091	7745	95.72	346	4.28	4	1.16
The Intermediate People's Court of Xining City of Qinghai Province	6305	6029	95.62	276	4.38	61	22.10

(continued)

Table 1 (continued)

Court	The total number of judgments disclosed	The number of judgments disclosed in the full text	Proportion (%)	The number of judgments not published in the full text but with information items disclosed	Proportion (%)	The number of judgments only with information items disclosed for "other reasons"	Proportion (%)
The Intermediate People's Court of Qiqihar City of Heilongjiang Province	6095	5825	95.57	270	4.43	83	30.74
The High People's Court of Jiangxi Province	2604	2487	95.51	117	4.49	93	79.49
The High People's Court of Gansu Province	2354	2248	95.50	106	4.50	41	38.68
The High People's Court of Xizang Autonomous Region	303	289	95.38	14	4.62	4	28.57
The Intermediate People's Court of Chengdu City of Sichuan Province	35,198	33,180	94.27	2018	5.73	252	12.49

(continued)

Table 1 (continued)

Court	The total number of judgments disclosed	The number of judgments disclosed in the full text	Proportion (%)	The number of judgments not published in the full text but with information items disclosed	Proportion (%)	The number of judgments only with information items disclosed for "other reasons"	Proportion (%)
The Intermediate People's Court of Shantou City of Guangdong Province	1500	1414	94.27	86	5.73	65	75.58
The Intermediate People's Court of Yinchuan City of Ningxia Hui Autonomous Region	5815	5480	94.24	335	5.76	88	26.27
The Intermediate People's Court of Xiamen City of Fujian Province	7071	6658	94.16	413	5.84	72	17.43
The Intermediate People's Court of Jinan City of Shandong Province	22,854	21,489	94.03	1365	5.97	112	8.21

(continued)

Table 1 (continued)

Court	The total number of judgments disclosed	The number of judgments disclosed in the full text	Proportion (%)	The number of judgments not published in the full text but with information items disclosed	Proportion (%)	The number of judgments only with information items disclosed for "other reasons"	Proportion (%)
The Intermediate People's Court of Ningbo City of Zhejiang Province	11,694	10,991	93.99	703	6.01	42	5.97
The Primary People's Court of Qingxiu District of Nanning City, Guangxi Zhuang Autonomous Region	19,050	17,890	93.91	1160	6.09	0	0.00
The Intermediate People's Court of Hohhot City of Inner Mongolia Autonomous Region	6564	6151	93.71	413	6.29	15	3.63
The Intermediate People's Court of Anshan City of Liaoning Province	6083	5699	93.69	384	6.31	196	51.04

(continued)

Table 1 (continued)

Court	The total number of judgments disclosed	The number of judgments disclosed in the full text	Proportion (%)	The number of judgments not published in the full text but with information items disclosed	Proportion (%)	The number of judgments only with information items disclosed for "other reasons"	Proportion (%)
The High People's Court of Shanghai Municipality	5865	5488	93.57	377	6.43	358	94.96
The Primary People's Court of Meilan District of Haikou City, Hainan Province	3814	3563	93.42	251	6.58	60	23.90
The Intermediate People's Court of Hangzhou City of Zhejiang Province	22,448	20,955	93.35	1493	6.65	151	10.11
The Intermediate People's Court of Shijiazhuang City of Hebei Province	14,146	13,199	93.31	947	6.69	148	15.63
The Intermediate People's Court of Nanchang City of Jiangxi Province	12,311	11,432	92.86	879	7.14	186	21.16

(continued)

Table 1 (continued)

Court	The total number of judgments disclosed	The number of judgments disclosed in the full text	Proportion (%)	The number of judgments not published in the full text but with information items disclosed	Proportion (%)	The number of judgments only with information items disclosed for "other reasons"	Proportion (%)
The Intermediate People's Court of Zibo City of Shandong Province	8523	7893	92.61	630	7.39	556	88.25
Hangzhou Internet Court	15,007	13,875	92.46	1132	7.54	18	1.59
The High People's Court of Xinjiang Uygur Autonomous Region	2435	2248	92.32	187	7.68	90	48.13
The Intermediate People's Court of Qingdao City of Shandong Province	18,237	16,804	92.14	1433	7.86	94	6.56
The High People's Court of Heilongjiang Province	3931	3620	92.09	311	7.91	284	91.32

(continued)

Table 1 (continued)

Court	The total number of judgments disclosed	The number of judgments disclosed in the full text	Proportion (%)	The number of judgments not published in the full text but with information items disclosed	Proportion (%)	The number of judgments only with information items disclosed for "other reasons"	Proportion (%)
The Intermediate People's Court of Kunming City of Yunnan Province	10,506	9669	92.03	837	7.97	11	1.31
The Primary People's Court of Zhuhai Hengqin New Area	1414	1299	91.87	115	8.13	112	97.39
The Intermediate People's Court of Jilin City of Jilin Province	4280	3921	91.61	359	8.39	219	61.00
The Intermediate People's Court of Xuzhou City of Jiangsu Province	11,106	10,140	91.30	966	8.70	0	0.00

(continued)

Table 1 (continued)

Court	The total number of judgments disclosed	The number of judgments disclosed in the full text	Proportion (%)	The number of judgments not published in the full text but with information items disclosed	Proportion (%)	The number of judgments only with information items disclosed for "other reasons"	Proportion (%)
The Primary People's Court of Zhengzhou High-Tech Industrial Development Zone of Henan Province	41,372	37,715	91.16	3657	8.84	453	12.39
The Primary People's Court of Siming District of Xiamen City, Fujian Province	19,876	18,081	90.97	1795	9.03	0	0.00
The Intermediate People's Court of Taiyuan City of Shanxi Province	6942	6304	90.81	638	9.19	214	33.54
The Primary People's Court of Chongqing Pilot Free Trade Zone	7601	6892	90.67	709	9.33	30	4.23

(continued)

Table 1 (continued)

Court	The total number of judgments disclosed	The number of judgments disclosed in the full text	Proportion (%)	The number of judgments not published in the full text but with information items disclosed	Proportion (%)	The number of judgments only with information items disclosed for "other reasons"	Proportion (%)
The Intermediate People's Court of Tangshan City of Hebei Province	10,975	9948	90.64	1027	9.36	517	50.34
The Intermediate People's Court of Wuhan City of Hubei Province	15,565	14,108	90.64	1457	9.36	1207	82.84
The Intermediate People's Court of Suzhou City of Jiangsu Province	13,983	12,674	90.64	1309	9.36	0	0.00
The Primary People's Court of Wuhua District of Kunming City, Yunnan Province	13,380	12,094	90.39	1286	9.61	0	0.00
The High People's Court of Shaanxi Province	5396	4876	90.36	520	9.64	434	83.46

(continued)

Table 1 (continued)

Court	The total number of judgments disclosed	The number of judgments disclosed in the full text	Proportion (%)	The number of judgments not published in the full text but with information items disclosed	Proportion (%)	The number of judgments only with information items disclosed for "other reasons"	Proportion (%)
The Intermediate People's Court of Handan City of Hebei Province	9131	8246	90.31	885	9.69	356	40.23
The Intermediate People's Court of Luoyang City of Henan Province	7656	6907	90.22	749	9.78	392	52.34
The Intermediate People's Court of Wuxi City of Jiangsu Province	9293	8376	90.13	917	9.87	0	0.00
The Intermediate People's Court of Fuzhou City of Fujian Province	11,378	10,233	89.94	1145	10.06	329	28.73
The Intermediate People's Court of Huainan City of Anhui Province	2324	2081	89.54	243	10.46	31	12.76

(continued)

Table 1 (continued)

Court	The total number of judgments disclosed	The number of judgments disclosed in the full text	Proportion (%)	The number of judgments not published in the full text but with information items disclosed	Proportion (%)	The number of judgments only with information items disclosed for "other reasons"	Proportion (%)
The Primary People's Court of Yingde City of Guangdong Province	3058	2736	89.47	322	10.53	14	4.35
The Primary People's Court of Yanji City of Jilin Province	12,515	11,155	89.13	1360	10.87	1	0.07
The High People's Court of Hubei Province	3351	2983	89.02	368	10.98	345	93.75
The High People's Court of Shanxi Province	1921	1709	88.96	212	11.04	188	88.68
The Primary People's Court of Donghu District of Nanchang City, Jiangxi Province	16,456	14,634	88.93	1822	11.07	595	32.66

(continued)

Table 1 (continued)

Court	The total number of judgments disclosed	The number of judgments disclosed in the full text	Proportion (%)	The number of judgments not published in the full text but with information items disclosed	Proportion (%)	The number of judgments only with information items disclosed for "other reasons"	Proportion (%)
The Intermediate People's Court of Changsha City of Hunan Province	20,649	18,231	88.29	2418	11.71	407	16.83
The Primary People's Court of Danzhou City of Hainan Province	3269	2884	88.22	385	11.78	3	0.78
The Intermediate People's Court of Xi'an City of Shaanxi Province	14,646	12,899	88.07	1747	11.93	513	29.36
The Primary People's Court of Yiwu City of Zhejiang Province	36,251	31,916	88.04	4335	11.96	76	1.75
The Intermediate People's Court of Dalian City of Liaoning Province	15,273	13,406	87.78	1867	12.22	764	40.92

(continued)

Table 1 (continued)

Court	The total number of judgments disclosed	The number of judgments disclosed in the full text	Proportion (%)	The number of judgments not published in the full text but with information items disclosed	Proportion (%)	The number of judgments only with information items disclosed for "other reasons"	Proportion (%)
The Intermediate People's Court of Benxi City of Liaoning Province	2776	2436	87.75	340	12.25	97	28.53
The Primary People's Court of Wuchang District of Wuhan City, Hubei Province	13,836	12,065	87.20	1771	12.80	591	33.37
The Primary People's Court of Chaoyang District of Changchun City, Jilin Province	8800	7665	87.10	1135	12.90	86	7.58
The Intermediate People's Court of Hefei City of Anhui Province	16,995	14,732	86.68	2263	13.32	438	19.35

(continued)

Table 1 (continued)

Court	The total number of judgments disclosed	The number of judgments disclosed in the full text	Proportion (%)	The number of judgments not published in the full text but with information items disclosed	Proportion (%)	The number of judgments only with information items disclosed for "other reasons"	Proportion (%)
The Primary People's Court of Saihan District of Hohhot City, Inner Mongolia Autonomous Region	7739	6692	86.47	1047	13.53	3	0.29
The Primary People's Court of Yangxin County of Hubei Province	2428	2083	85.79	345	14.21	37	10.72
The Intermediate People's Court of Zhengzhou City of Henan Province	24,438	20,962	85.78	3476	14.22	1290	37.11
The Primary People's Court of Xihu District of Nanchang City, Jiangxi Province	11,548	9900	85.73	1648	14.27	956	58.01

(continued)

Table 1 (continued)

Court	The total number of judgments disclosed	The number of judgments disclosed in the full text	Proportion (%)	The number of judgments not published in the full text but with information items disclosed	Proportion (%)	The number of judgments only with information items disclosed for "other reasons"	Proportion (%)
The Primary People's Court of Yaohai District of Hefei City, Anhui Province	13,687	11,726	85.67	1961	14.33	68	3.47
The Primary People's Court of Jiangbei District of Chongqing Municipality	25,821	22,015	85.26	3806	14.74	439	11.53
The Primary People's Court of Ningjiang District of Songyuan City, Jilin Province	9689	8233	84.97	1456	15.03	155	10.65
The Primary People's Court of Yuzhong District of Chongqing Municipality	22,849	19,386	84.84	3463	15.16	0	0.00

(continued)

Table 1 (continued)

Court	The total number of judgments disclosed	The number of judgments disclosed in the full text	Proportion (%)	The number of judgments not published in the full text but with information items disclosed	Proportion (%)	The number of judgments only with information items disclosed for "other reasons"	Proportion (%)
The Primary People's Court of Xixiangtang District of Nanning City, Guangxi Zhuang Autonomous Region	6992	5908	84.50	1084	15.50	1	0.09
The Primary People's Court of Huli District of Xiamen City, Fujian Province	11,455	9678	84.49	1777	15.51	3	0.17
The Primary People's Court of Cangnan County of Zhejiang Province	13,884	11,709	84.33	2175	15.67	1	0.05

(continued)

Table 1 (continued)

Court	The total number of judgments disclosed	The number of judgments disclosed in the full text	Proportion (%)	The number of judgments not published in the full text but with information items disclosed	Proportion (%)	The number of judgments only with information items disclosed for "other reasons"	Proportion (%)
The Intermediate People's Court of Lhasa City of Xizang Autonomous Region	1335	1123	84.12	212	15.88	49	23.11
The Primary People's Court of Chaohu City of Anhui Province	8322	6999	84.10	1323	15.90	1	0.08
The Primary People's Court of Sanhe City of Hebei Province	7471	6261	83.80	1210	16.20	71	5.87
The Primary People's Court of Baohe District of Hefei City, Anhui Province	25,792	21,558	83.58	4234	16.42	1011	23.88

(continued)

Table 1 (continued)

Court	The total number of judgments disclosed	The number of judgments disclosed in the full text	Proportion (%)	The number of judgments not published in the full text but with information items disclosed	Proportion (%)	The number of judgments only with information items disclosed for "other reasons"	Proportion (%)
The Primary People's Court of Chengdu High-Tech Industrial Development Zone of Sichuan Province	19,579	16,364	83.58	3215	16.42	0	0.00
The Primary People's Court of Yanhu District of Yuncheng City, Shanxi Province	10,519	8742	83.11	1777	16.89	22	1.24
The Primary People's Court of Weichang Manchu and Mongolia Autonomous County of Hebei Province	7945	6596	83.02	1349	16.98	119	8.82

(continued)

Table 1 (continued)

Court	The total number of judgments disclosed	The number of judgments disclosed in the full text	Proportion (%)	The number of judgments not published in the full text but with information items disclosed	Proportion (%)	The number of judgments only with information items disclosed for "other reasons"	Proportion (%)
The Primary People's Court of Qian Gorlos Mongolia Autonomous County of Jilin Province	8412	6919	82.25	1493	17.75	15	1.00
The Primary People's Court of Xingyi City of Guizhou Province	9933	8146	82.01	1787	17.99	0	0.00
The Primary People's Court of Ar Horqin Banner of Inner Mongolia Autonomous Region	949	772	81.35	177	18.65	4	2.26

(continued)

Table 1 (continued)

Court	The total number of judgments disclosed	The number of judgments disclosed in the full text	Proportion (%)	The number of judgments not published in the full text but with information items disclosed	Proportion (%)	The number of judgments only with information items disclosed for "other reasons"	Proportion (%)
The Primary People's Court of Nankai District of Tianjin Municipality	14,681	11,938	81.32	2743	18.68	2743	100.00
The Primary People's Court of Binyang County of Guangxi Zhuang Autonomous Region	3571	2903	81.29	668	18.71	32	4.79
The Primary People's Court of Yanta District of Xi'an City, Shaanxi Province	27,121	21,946	80.92	5175	19.08	1630	31.50

(continued)

Table 1 (continued)

Court	The total number of judgments disclosed	The number of judgments disclosed in the full text	Proportion (%)	The number of judgments not published in the full text but with information items disclosed	Proportion (%)	The number of judgments only with information items disclosed for "other reasons"	Proportion (%)
The Primary People's Court of Nanchang County of Jiangxi Province	5774	4668	80.85	1106	19.15	13	1.18
The Primary People's Court of Lanshan District of Linyi City, Shandong Province	24,052	19,425	80.76	4627	19.24	209	4.52
The Primary People's Court of Huaxian County of Henan Province	14,128	11,410	80.76	2718	19.24	372	13.69
The Primary People's Court of Shuyang County of Jiangsu Province	25,259	20,388	80.72	4871	19.28	0	0.00

(continued)

Table 1 (continued)

Court	The total number of judgments disclosed	The number of judgments disclosed in the full text	Proportion (%)	The number of judgments not published in the full text but with information items disclosed	Proportion (%)	The number of judgments only with information items disclosed for "other reasons"	Proportion (%)
The Intermediate People's Court of Harbin City of Heilongjiang Province	8619	6946	80.59	1673	19.41	1386	82.85
The Primary People's Court of Liuyang City of Hunan Province	21,728	17,442	80.27	4286	19.73	74	1.73
The Primary People's Court of Yubei District of Chongqing Municipality	26,579	21,291	80.10	5288	19.90	252	4.77
The Primary People's Court of Jiaozhou City of Shandong Province	11,920	9537	80.01	2383	19.99	27	1.13

(continued)

Table 1 (continued)

Court	The total number of judgments disclosed	The number of judgments disclosed in the full text	Proportion (%)	The number of judgments not published in the full text but with information items disclosed	Proportion (%)	The number of judgments only with information items disclosed for "other reasons"	Proportion (%)
The Intermediate People's Court of Urumqi City of Xinjiang Uygur Autonomous Region	5245	4184	79.77	1061	20.23	369	34.78
The Primary People's Court of Feixian County of Shandong Province	7051	5563	78.90	1488	21.10	16	1.08
The Primary People's Court of Xingqing District of Yinchuan City, Ningxia Hui Autonomous Region	19,563	15,428	78.86	4135	21.14	13	0.31

(continued)

Table 1 (continued)

Court	The total number of judgments disclosed	The number of judgments disclosed in the full text	Proportion (%)	The number of judgments not published in the full text but with information items disclosed	Proportion (%)	The number of judgments only with information items disclosed for "other reasons"	Proportion (%)
The Primary People's Court of Xishan District of Kunming City, Yunnan Province	20,260	15,975	78.85	4285	21.15	159	3.71
Shanghai Financial Court	4137	3237	78.25	900	21.75	629	69.89
The Primary People's Court of Xinzheng City of Henan Province	13,930	10,863	77.98	3067	22.02	222	7.24
The Primary People's Court of Nehe City of Heilongjiang Province	3058	2381	77.86	677	22.14	29	4.28

(continued)

Table 1 (continued)

Court	The total number of judgments disclosed	The number of judgments disclosed in the full text	Proportion (%)	The number of judgments not published in the full text but with information items disclosed	Proportion (%)	The number of judgments only with information items disclosed for "other reasons"	Proportion (%)
The Primary People's Court of Doilungdêqên County of Xizang Autonomous Region	1470	1142	77.69	328	22.31	1	0.30
The Primary People's Court of Haicheng City of Liaoning Province	15,190	11,765	77.45	3425	22.55	1985	57.96
The Primary People's Court of Lhünzhub County of Xizang Autonomous Region	84	65	77.38	19	22.62	0	0.00

(continued)

Table 1 (continued)

Court	The total number of judgments disclosed	The number of judgments disclosed in the full text	Proportion (%)	The number of judgments not published in the full text but with information items disclosed	Proportion (%)	The number of judgments only with information items disclosed for "other reasons"	Proportion (%)
The Primary People's Court of Lingwu City of Ningxia Hui Autonomous Region	6516	5040	77.35	1476	22.65	5	0.34
The Primary People's Court of Xinshi District of Urumqi City, Xinjiang Uygur Autonomous Region	6810	5251	77.11	1559	22.89	49	3.14
Shanghai Intellectual Property Court	2359	1815	76.94	544	23.06	475	87.32
The Primary People's Court of Zhuji City of Zhejiang Province	27,654	21,124	76.39	6530	23.61	652	9.98

(continued)

Table 1 (continued)

Court	The total number of judgments disclosed	The number of judgments disclosed in the full text	Proportion (%)	The number of judgments not published in the full text but with information items disclosed	Proportion (%)	The number of judgments only with information items disclosed for "other reasons"	Proportion (%)
The Primary People's Court of Jinjiang City of Fujian Province	17,366	13,120	75.55	4246	24.45	107	2.52
The Primary People's Court of Ganzhou District of Zhangye City, Gansu Province	10,484	7916	75.51	2568	24.49	3	0.12
The Primary People's Court of Sayibak District of Urumqi City, Xinjiang Uygur Autonomous Region	5226	3922	75.05	1304	24.95	81	6.21

(continued)

Table 1 (continued)

Court	The total number of judgments disclosed	The number of judgments disclosed in the full text	Proportion (%)	The number of judgments not published in the full text but with information items disclosed	Proportion (%)	The number of judgments only with information items disclosed for "other reasons"	Proportion (%)
The Primary People's Court of Jinfeng District of Yinchuan City, Ningxia Hui Autonomous Region	14,591	10,947	75.03	3644	24.97	3	0.08
The Primary People's Court of Hui'an County of Fujian Province	4083	3061	74.97	1022	25.03	23	2.25
The Primary People's Court of Songshan District of Chifeng City, Inner Mongolia Autonomous Region	2320	1720	74.14	600	25.86	0	0.00

(continued)

Table 1 (continued)

Court	The total number of judgments disclosed	The number of judgments disclosed in the full text	Proportion (%)	The number of judgments not published in the full text but with information items disclosed	Proportion (%)	The number of judgments only with information items disclosed for "other reasons"	Proportion (%)
The Primary People's Court of Chengguan District of Lhasa City, Xizang Autonomous Region	2239	1659	74.10	580	25.90	53	9.14
The Primary People's Court of Shenmu City of Shaanxi Province	12,848	9518	74.08	3330	25.92	16	0.48
The Primary People's Court of Golmud City of Qinghai Province	6378	4663	73.11	1715	26.89	102	5.95
The Primary People's Court of Youxian County of Hunan Province	6388	4648	72.76	1740	27.24	189	10.86

(continued)

Table 1 (continued)

Court	The total number of judgments disclosed	The number of judgments disclosed in the full text	Proportion (%)	The number of judgments not published in the full text but with information items disclosed	Proportion (%)	The number of judgments only with information items disclosed for "other reasons"	Proportion (%)
The Primary People's Court of Jinshui District of Zhengzhou City, Henan Province	50,059	36,412	72.74	13,647	27.26	9337	68.42
The Primary People's Court of Guiping City of Guangxi Zhuang Autonomous Region	3136	2268	72.32	868	27.68	0	0.00
The Primary People's Court of Weiyang District of Xi'an City, Shaanxi Province	23,483	16,852	71.76	6631	28.24	1947	29.36
The Primary People's Court of Wujiang District of Suzhou City, Jiangsu Province	23,514	16,869	71.74	6645	28.26	11	0.17

(continued)

Table 1 (continued)

Court	The total number of judgments disclosed	The number of judgments disclosed in the full text	Proportion (%)	The number of judgments not published in the full text but with information items disclosed	Proportion (%)	The number of judgments only with information items disclosed for "other reasons"	Proportion (%)
The Primary People's Court of Qingyang District of Chengdu City, Sichuan Province	24,245	17,320	71.44	6925	28.56	0	0.00
The Intermediate People's Court of Nanjing City of Jiangsu Province	29,027	20,633	71.08	8394	28.92	3412	40.65
The Primary People's Court of Yuhang District of Hangzhou City, Zhejiang Province	30,586	21,722	71.02	8864	28.98	233	2.63
The Primary People's Court of Binxian County of Heilongjiang Province	4764	3376	70.86	1388	29.14	716	51.59

(continued)

Table 1 (continued)

Court	The total number of judgments disclosed	The number of judgments disclosed in the full text	Proportion (%)	The number of judgments not published in the full text but with information items disclosed	Proportion (%)	The number of judgments only with information items disclosed for "other reasons"	Proportion (%)
The Primary People's Court of Furong District of Changsha City, Hunan Province	24,035	16,944	70.50	7091	29.50	5054	71.27
The Primary People's Court of Chengbei District of Xining City, Qinghai Province	8271	5771	69.77	2500	30.23	3	0.12
The Primary People's Court of Linyi County of Shanxi Province	3927	2733	69.60	1194	30.40	4	0.34
The Primary People's Court of Helan County of Ningxia Hui Autonomous Region	6046	4204	69.53	1842	30.47	91	4.94

(continued)

Table 1 (continued)

Court	The total number of judgments disclosed	The number of judgments disclosed in the full text	Proportion (%)	The number of judgments not published in the full text but with information items disclosed	Proportion (%)	The number of judgments only with information items disclosed for "other reasons"	Proportion (%)
The Primary People's Court of Jing'an District of Shanghai Municipality	66,584	46,040	69.15	20,544	30.85	18,900	92.00
The Intermediate People's Court of Fushun City of Liaoning Province	4242	2920	68.84	1322	31.16	1209	91.45
The Primary People's Court of Langzhong City of Sichuan Province	9652	6614	68.52	3038	31.48	0	0.00
The Primary People's Court of Xicheng District of Beijing Municipality	28,305	19,317	68.25	8988	31.75	8988	100.00

(continued)

Table 1 (continued)

Court	The total number of judgments disclosed	The number of judgments disclosed in the full text	Proportion (%)	The number of judgments not published in the full text but with information items disclosed	Proportion (%)	The number of judgments only with information items disclosed for "other reasons"	Proportion (%)
The Primary People's Court of Yuelu District of Changsha City, Hunan Province	28,052	19,143	68.24	8909	31.76	5617	63.05
The Primary People's Court of Binhai New Area of Tianjin Municipality	22,167	15,018	67.75	7149	32.25	2771	38.76
The Primary People's Court of Sichuan Pilot Free Trade Zone	5047	3418	67.72	1629	32.28	368	22.59
The Intermediate People's Court of Shenyang City of Liaoning Province	30,367	20,558	67.70	9809	32.30	9020	91.96

(continued)

Table 1 (continued)

Court	The total number of judgments disclosed	The number of judgments disclosed in the full text	Proportion (%)	The number of judgments not published in the full text but with information items disclosed	Proportion (%)	The number of judgments only with information items disclosed for "other reasons"	Proportion (%)
The Primary People's Court of Hongkou District of Shanghai Municipality	36,625	24,787	67.68	11,838	32.32	10,944	92.45
The Primary People's Court of Dingbian County of Shaanxi Province	8626	5784	67.05	2842	32.95	911	32.05
The Primary People's Court of Minhang District of Shanghai Municipality	61,721	41,072	66.54	20,649	33.46	17,835	86.37
The Primary People's Court of Xiaodian District of Taiyuan City, Shanxi Province	7271	4806	66.10	2465	33.90	1296	52.58

(continued)

Table 1 (continued)

Court	The total number of judgments disclosed	The number of judgments disclosed in the full text	Proportion (%)	The number of judgments not published in the full text but with information items disclosed	Proportion (%)	The number of judgments only with information items disclosed for "other reasons"	Proportion (%)
The Primary People's Court of Haigang District of Qinhuangdao City, Hebei Province	4593	3024	65.84	1569	34.16	19	1.21
The Primary People's Court of Wuqing District of Tianjin Municipality	9755	6419	65.80	3336	34.20	3336	100.00
The Primary People's Court of Pidu District of Chengdu City, Sichuan Province	9739	6384	65.55	3355	34.45	0	0.00
The Primary People's Court of Jiang'an District of Wuhan City, Hubei Province	7993	5211	65.19	2782	34.81	1351	48.56

(continued)

Table 1 (continued)

Court	The total number of judgments disclosed	The number of judgments disclosed in the full text	Proportion (%)	The number of judgments not published in the full text but with information items disclosed	Proportion (%)	The number of judgments only with information items disclosed for "other reasons"	Proportion (%)
The Primary People's Court of Chengdong District of Xining City, Qinghai Province	6571	4277	65.09	2294	34.91	547	23.84
The Primary People's Court of Nangang District of Harbin City, Heilongjiang Province	8589	5588	65.06	3001	34.94	1955	65.14
The Primary People's Court of Chaoyang District of Beijing Municipality	53,212	34,571	64.97	18,641	35.03	18,641	100.00
The Primary People's Court of Gao'an City of Jiangxi Province	8488	5513	64.95	2975	35.05	1325	44.54

(continued)

Table 1 (continued)

Court	The total number of judgments disclosed	The number of judgments disclosed in the full text	Proportion (%)	The number of judgments not published in the full text but with information items disclosed	Proportion (%)	The number of judgments only with information items disclosed for "other reasons"	Proportion (%)
The Primary People's Court of Haidian District of Beijing Municipality	42,670	27,682	64.87	14,987	35.12	14,987	100.00
The Primary People's Court of Kunshan City of Jiangsu Province	16,580	10,728	64.70	5852	35.30	0	0.00
The Primary People's Court of Enshi City of Hubei Province	6657	4284	64.35	2373	35.65	416	17.53
The Primary People's Court of Fengtai District of Beijing Municipality	28,609	18,337	64.10	10,272	35.90	10,272	100.00

(continued)

Table 1 (continued)

Court	The total number of judgments disclosed	The number of judgments disclosed in the full text	Proportion (%)	The number of judgments not published in the full text but with information items disclosed	Proportion (%)	The number of judgments only with information items disclosed for "other reasons"	Proportion (%)
The Primary People's Court of Jiangyin City of Jiangsu Province	21,583	13,752	63.72	7831	36.28	0	0.00
The Primary People's Court of Chengguan District of Lanzhou City, Gansu Province	9876	6211	62.89	3665	37.11	1774	48.40
The Primary People's Court of Chang'an District of Shijiazhuang City, Hebei Province	10,811	6760	62.53	4051	37.47	2566	63.34
The Primary People's Court of Taihe County of Anhui Province	13,000	8071	62.08	4929	37.92	2360	47.88

(continued)

Table 1 (continued)

Court	The total number of judgments disclosed	The number of judgments disclosed in the full text	Proportion (%)	The number of judgments not published in the full text but with information items disclosed	Proportion (%)	The number of judgments only with information items disclosed for "other reasons"	Proportion (%)
The Primary People's Court of Suizhong County of Liaoning Province	7991	4791	59.95	3200	40.05	1981	61.91
The Primary People's Court of Hexi District of Tianjin Municipality	10,889	6306	57.91	4583	42.09	4583	100.00
The Primary People's Court of Heping District of Shenyang City, Liaoning Province	44,246	25,360	57.32	18,886	42.68	11,332	60.00
The Primary People's Court of Shenhe District of Shenyang City, Liaoning Province	32,724	18,639	56.96	14,085	43.04	11,641	82.65

(continued)

Table 1 (continued)

Court	The total number of judgments disclosed	The number of judgments disclosed in the full text	Proportion (%)	The number of judgments not published in the full text but with information items disclosed	Proportion (%)	The number of judgments only with information items disclosed for "other reasons"	Proportion (%)
The Primary People's Court of Changji City of Changji Hui Autonomous Prefecture, Xinjiang Uygur Autonomous Region	5514	3076	55.79	2438	44.21	10	0.41
The Primary People's Court of Pudong New Area of Shanghai Municipality	129,169	69,796	54.03	59,373	45.97	54,754	92.22
The Primary People's Court of Gar County of Xizang Autonomous Region	146	76	52.05	70	47.95	0	0.00

(continued)

Table 1 (continued)

Court	The total number of judgments disclosed	The number of judgments disclosed in the full text	Proportion (%)	The number of judgments not published in the full text but with information items disclosed	Proportion (%)	The number of judgments only with information items disclosed for "other reasons"	Proportion (%)
The Primary People's Court of Daoli District of Harbin City, Heilongjiang Province	1690	851	50.36	839	49.64	695	82.84
The Primary People's Court of Yunyang County of Chongqing Municipality	8046	4044	50.26	4002	49.74	65	1.62
The Primary People's Court of Huangzhong District of Xining City, Qinghai Province	4931	2460	49.89	2471	50.11	96	3.89
The Primary People's Court of Hejin City of Shanxi Province	5649	2500	44.26	3149	55.74	1946	61.80

(continued)

Table 1 (continued)

Court	The total number of judgments disclosed	The number of judgments disclosed in the full text	Proportion (%)	The number of judgments not published in the full text but with information items disclosed	Proportion (%)	The number of judgments only with information items disclosed for "other reasons"	Proportion (%)
The Primary People's Court of Longxi County of Gansu Province	5561	2379	42.78	3182	57.22	80	2.51
Beijing Internet Court	23,871	10,071	42.19	13,800	57.81	10,533	76.33
The Primary People's Court of Huangdao District of Qingdao City, Shandong Province	31,155	12,352	39.65	18,803	60.35	17,021	90.52
The Primary People's Court of Zhenxiong County of Yunnan Province	9575	3108	32.46	6467	67.54	2415	37.34
The Primary People's Court of Xuanwei City of Yunnan Province	14,776	4724	31.97	10,052	68.03	4815	47.90

(continued)

Table 1 (continued)

Court	The total number of judgments disclosed	The number of judgments disclosed in the full text	Proportion (%)	The number of judgments not published in the full text but with information items disclosed	Proportion (%)	The number of judgments only with information items disclosed for "other reasons"	Proportion (%)
The Primary People's Court of Ulanhot City of Inner Mongolia Autonomous Region	6545	2000	30.56	4545	69.44	3175	69.86
The Primary People's Court of Kuqa City of Aksu Prefecture, Xinjiang Uygur Autonomous Region	2068	407	19.68	1661	80.32	482	29.02
Guangzhou Internet Court	42,073	7992	19.00	34,081	81.00	18,805	55.18

of Xishui County of Guizhou Province. Twenty-one primary people's courts and specialized courts disclosed less than 50% of their judgments in the full text, namely in descending order, the Primary People's Court of Hexi District of Tianjin Municipality, the Primary People's Court of Jiangyin City of Jiangsu Province, the Primary People's Court of Binxian County of Heilongjiang Province, the Primary People's Court of Linyi County of Shanxi Province, the Primary People's Court of Longxi County of Gansu Province, the Primary People's Court of Changji City of Changji Hui Autonomous Prefecture, Xinjiang Uygur Autonomous Region, the Primary People's Court of Shenmu City of Shaanxi Province, the Primary People's Court of Furong District of Changsha City, Hunan Province, the Primary People's Court of Ganzhou District of Zhangye City, Gansu Province, the Primary People's Court of Yunyang County of Chongqing Municipality, the Primary People's Court of Ulanhot City of Inner Mongolia Autonomous Region, the Primary People's Court of Gar County of Xizang Autonomous Region, the Primary People's Court of Xuanwei City of Yunnan Province, the Primary People's Court of Zhenxiong County of Yunnan Province, the Primary People's Court of Huangzhong District of Xining City, Qinghai Province, the Primary People's Court of Daoli District of Harbin City, Heilongjiang Province, the Primary People's Court of Hejin City of Shanxi Province, Beijing Internet Court, Beijing Intellectual Property Court, the Primary People's Court of Kuqa City of Aksu Prefecture, Xinjiang Uygur Autonomous Region, Guangzhou Internet Court.

The statistics show that the disclosure of the full text of civil judgments varied considerably among the courts at different levels. Among the high people's courts, two courts disclosed the full text of all their judgments, one court disclosed the full text of more than 80% but less than 90% of its judgments, and the rest disclosed the full text of more than 90% of their judgments, accounting for 96.88%. Among the specialized courts, two courts disclosed the full text of less than 20% (inclusive) of their judgments; one court disclosed that of over 20% but less than 30% (inclusive)

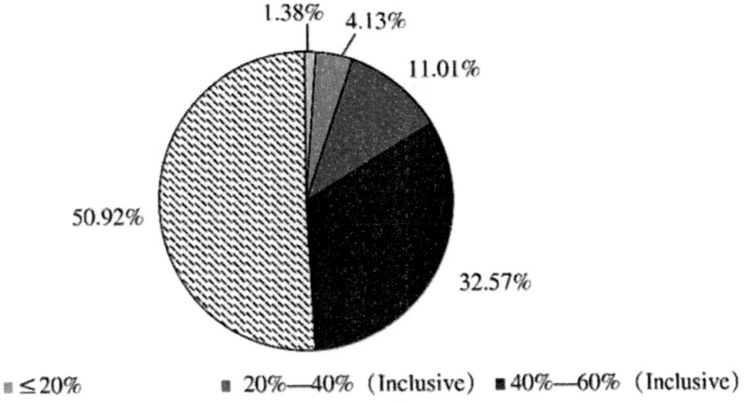

Fig. 29 The proportion of courts that made public the full text of civil judgments

of its judgments; two courts disclosed that of over 60% but less than 80% (inclusive) of their judgments; one court disclosed that of over 80% but less than 90% (inclusive) of its judgments. Six courts disclosed that of more than 90% of their judgments, one of which made public the full text of all its judgments. The courts that disclosed the full text of more than 90% of the judgments accounted for 50%. More than 60% of the judgments of the intermediate people's courts were made public in the full text. Two of them disclosed over 60% but less than 80% (inclusive) of the judgments in the full text, accounting for 4.08%; 17 courts disclosed over 80% but less than 90% (inclusive) of the judgments in the full text, accounting for 34.69%. Thirty courts disclosed more than 90% of the judgments in the full text, accounting for 61.22%, of which two courts disclosed all the judgments in the full text. Judgment disclosure varied greatly among the 124 primary people's courts. Five of them disclosed less than 20% (inclusive) of the judgments in the full text, accounting for 4.04%; four courts disclosed over 20% but less than 40% (inclusive) of the judgments in the full text, accounting for 3.22%; 24 courts disclosed over 40% but less than 60% (inclusive) of the judgments in the full text, accounting for 19.35%; 68 courts disclosed over 60% but less than 80% (inclusive) of the judgments in the full text, accounting for 56.20%; 15 courts disclosed over 80% but less than 90% (inclusive) of the judgments in the full text, accounting for 12.10%. Nine courts disclosed more than 90% of the judgments in the full text, accounting for 7.26%, of which five courts disclosed all the judgments in the full text (see Fig. 30).

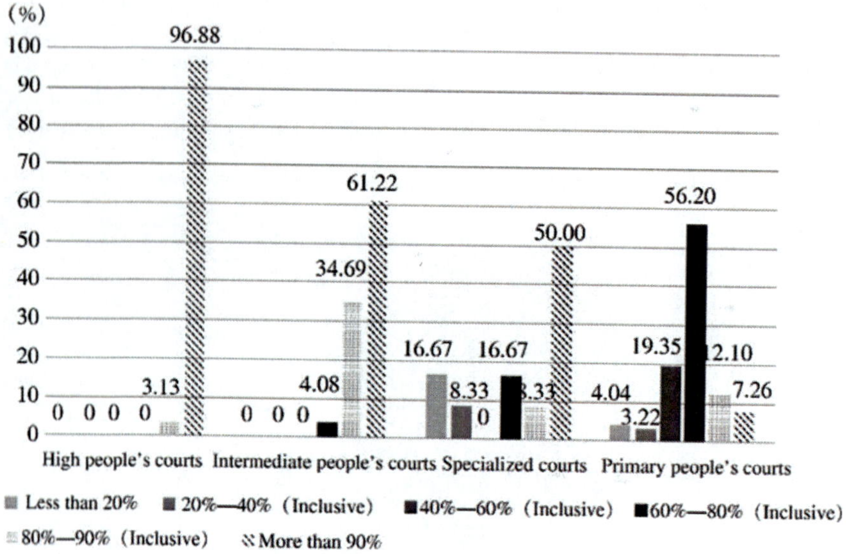

Fig. 30 Disclosure of civil judgments in the full text by courts at all levels

6.3.2 Criminal Judgments Disclosed in the Full Text

The disclosure of criminal judgments in the full text was significantly better than that of civil ones. The total number of criminal judgments disclosed online was 196,562, with 179,812 judgments disclosed in the complete text, accounting for 91.46%.

Eleven courts disclosed no criminal judgments online within nine months, including ten specialized courts and one primary people's court, namely Beijing Intellectual Property Court, Guangzhou Intellectual Property Court, the Primary People's Court of Shenzhen Qianhai Cooperation Zone of Guangdong Province, Shanghai Intellectual Property Court, the Primary People's Court of Guangdong Free Trade Zone (Nansha) of Guangdong Province, Hangzhou Internet Court, Shanghai Financial Court, Beijing Internet Court, Guangzhou Internet Court, the Primary People's Court of Chongqing Pilot Free Trade Zone, and the Primary People's Court of Gar County of Xizang Autonomous Region. That may be because the Primary People's Court of Gar County of Xizang Autonomous Region has a small caseload, and the other ten specialized courts have no jurisdiction over criminal cases. Among the 207 courts that disclosed criminal judgments online, 29 disclosed the full text of all their criminal judgments, accounting for 14.01%, including five high people's courts, five intermediate people's courts, two specialized courts, and 17 primary people's courts. Among the 207 courts, 115 disclosed over 90% of their criminal judgments in the full text but less than 100% (inclusive), accounting for 55.56%; 37 courts disclosed over 80% but less than 90% (inclusive) of their criminal judgments in the full text, accounting for 17.87%; 12 courts disclosed over 70% but less than 80% (inclusive), accounting for 5.80%; three courts disclosed over 60% but less than 70% (inclusive), accounting for 1.45%; and 11 courts disclosed less than 60% (inclusive), accounting for 5.31% (see Fig. 31).

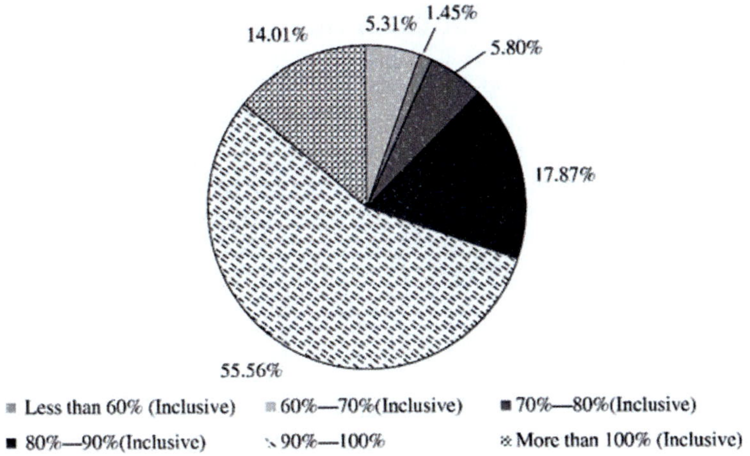

Fig. 31 The proportion of courts that made public the full text of criminal judgments

The statistics show that the disclosure of the full text of criminal judgments varied widely among the courts at different levels. Among the high people's courts, five courts disclosed less than 60% (inclusive) of the criminal judgments in the full text, accounting for 15.63%; two courts disclosed over 70% but less than 80% of the criminal judgments in the full text, accounting for 6.25%; six courts disclosed over 80% but less than 90% of the criminal judgments in the full text, accounting for 18.75%; 14 courts disclosed over 90% but less than 100% of the criminal judgments in the full text, accounting for 43.75%. Five courts made public the full text of all their criminal judgments, accounting for 15.63%.

Among the intermediate people's courts, three courts disclosed less than 60% (inclusive) of the criminal judgments in the full text, accounting for 6.12%; one court disclosed over 60% but less than 70% of the criminal judgments in the full text, accounting for 2.04%; two courts disclosed over 70% but less than 80% of the criminal judgments in the full text, accounting for 4.08%; six courts disclosed over 80% but less than 90% of the criminal judgments in the full text, accounting for 12.24%; 28 court disclosed more than 90% but less than 100% of the criminal judgments in the full text, accounting for 57.14%. Five courts made public the full text of all their criminal judgments, accounting for 10.20%.

Among the specialized courts, only two courts disclosed their criminal judgments, and both published them in the full text.

Among the primary people's courts, one court did not disclose any criminal judgment during this period. Among the 123 courts that disclosed criminal judgments, three courts disclosed less than 60% of their judgments in the full text, accounting for 2.44%; two courts disclosed over 60% but less than 70% of their judgments in the full text, accounting for 1.63%; seven courts disclosed over 70% but less than 80% of their judgments in the full text, accounting for 5.69%; 24 courts disclosed over 80% but less than 90% of their judgments in the full text, accounting for 19.51%; 70 courts disclosed over 90% but less than 100% (not included) of their judgments in the full text, accounting for 56.91%; and 17 courts disclosed all their criminal judgments in the full text, accounting for 13.82% (see Fig. 32). In terms of the distribution of the courts that disclosed more than 90% of their criminal judgments in the full text, the primary people's courts performed better.

In conclusion, in terms of the disclosure of criminal judgments in the complete text, seen from the distribution of courts that disclosed more than 60, 70, 80, or 90% of their criminal judgments, the disclosure by the primary people's courts was comparatively better, while that by the high people's courts was far beyond satisfaction.

6.3.3 Administrative Judgments Disclosed in the Full Text

On the whole, the proportion of administrative judgments disclosed in the full text was vastly better than that of civil and criminal judgments. The total number of administrative judgments published online was 104,674, with 101,468 judgments disclosed in the full text, accounting for 96.94%. Among them, 14 courts disclosed no administrative judgments within nine months, including one intermediate people's

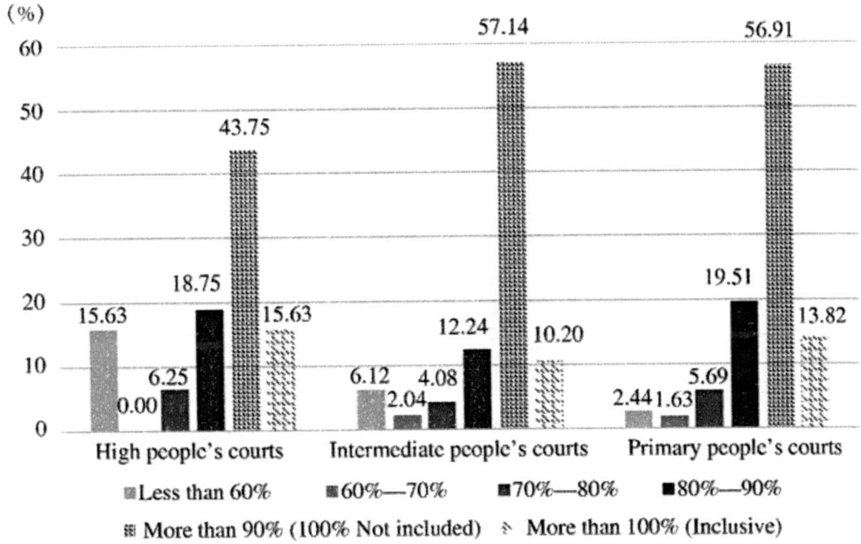

Fig. 32 Disclosure of criminal judgments in the full text by courts at all levels

court, five specialized courts and eight primary people's courts, namely the Intermediate People's Court of Guangzhou City of Guangdong Province, the People's Court of Zhuhai Hengqin New Area of Guangdong Province, the Primary People's Court of Shenzhen Qianhai Cooperation Zone of Guangdong Province, Shanghai Intellectual Property Court, the Primary People's Court of Guangdong Free Trade Zone (Nansha) of Guangdong Province, the Primary People's Court of Chongqing Pilot Free Trade Zone, the Primary People's Court of Shuyang County of Jiangsu Province, the Primary People's Court of Hui'an County of Fujian Province, the Primary People's Court of Huidong County of Guangdong Province, the Primary People's Court of Yingde City of Guangdong Province, the Primary People's Court of Lhünzhub County of Xizang Autonomous Region, the Primary People's Court of Gar County of Xizang Autonomous Region, the Primary People's Court of Lingwu City of Ningxia Hui Autonomous Region, the Primary People's Court of Sayibak District of Urumqi City, Xinjiang Uygur Autonomous Region. Among those courts mentioned above, some primary people's courts might not have received administrative cases or made administrative judgments during and before the assessment. Other courts might not have the power to accept administrative cases according to certain provisions. Among the remaining 204 courts, two courts disclosed less than 20% (inclusive) of the administrative judgments in the full text, accounting for 0.98%, one of which made two administrative judgments, neither of which was made public in the full text. Three courts disclosed over 20% but less than 40% of the administrative judgments in the full text, accounting for 1.47%; two courts disclosed over 40% but less than 60%, accounting for 0.98%; ten courts disclosed over 60% but less than 80%, accounting for 4.90%; nine courts disclosed over 80% but less than 90%,

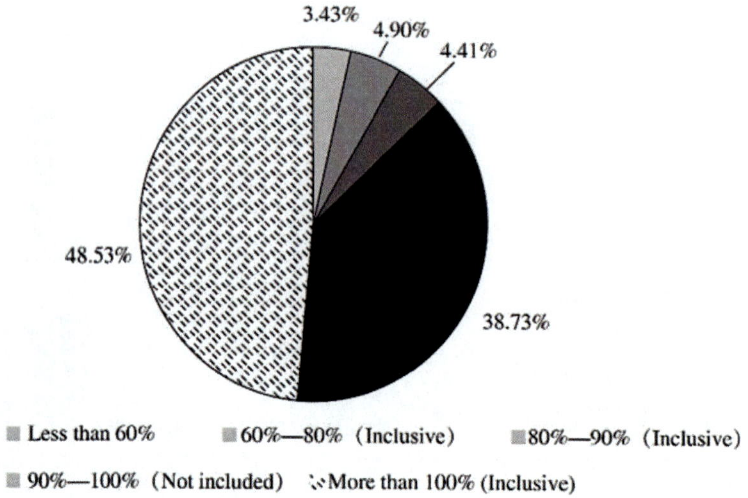

Fig. 33 The proportion of courts that made public the full text of administrative judgments

accounting for 4.41%; 79 courts disclosed over 90% but less than 100%, accounting for 38.73%; and 99 courts disclosed all their administrative judgments in the full text, accounting for 48.53% (see Fig. 33). Totally, 87.25% of all the assessed courts disclosed over 90% of the administrative judgments in the full text.

Regarding the proportion of the disclosure of administrative judgments in the full text by courts at all levels, the high people's courts performed the best. The 32 high people's courts disclosed over 90% of their administrative judgments in the full text, with 93.53% being the lowest proportion; 17 disclosed over 90% but less than 100%, accounting for 53.13%; 15 disclosed all the administrative judgments in the full text, accounting for 46.88%. Among the 48 intermediate people's courts, six disclosed less than 90% of their administrative judgments in the full text, accounting for 12.50%, with 72.6% being the lowest proportion; 23 disclosed over 90% but less than 100%, accounting for 47.92%; 19 disclosed all the administrative judgments in the full text, accounting for 39.58%. Among the seven specialized courts, one court disclosed 51.72% of its administrative judgments in the full text, the lowest proportion; one court disclosed 88.24%, and the other 5 disclosed all the administrative judgments in the full text. Among the 116 primary people's courts, the lowest disclosure proportion was zero; six courts disclosed less than 60% (inclusive), accounting for 5.17%; 12 disclosed over 60% but less than 90%, accounting for 10.34%; 38 disclosed over 90% but less than 100%, accounting for 32.76%; 60 disclosed all their administrative judgments in the full text, accounting for 51.72% (see Fig. 34).

Regarding the courts that disclosed over 90% of their administrative judgments in the complete text, the high people's courts performed the best, followed by the intermediate people's courts and the specialized courts, with the primary people's courts being the least satisfactory.

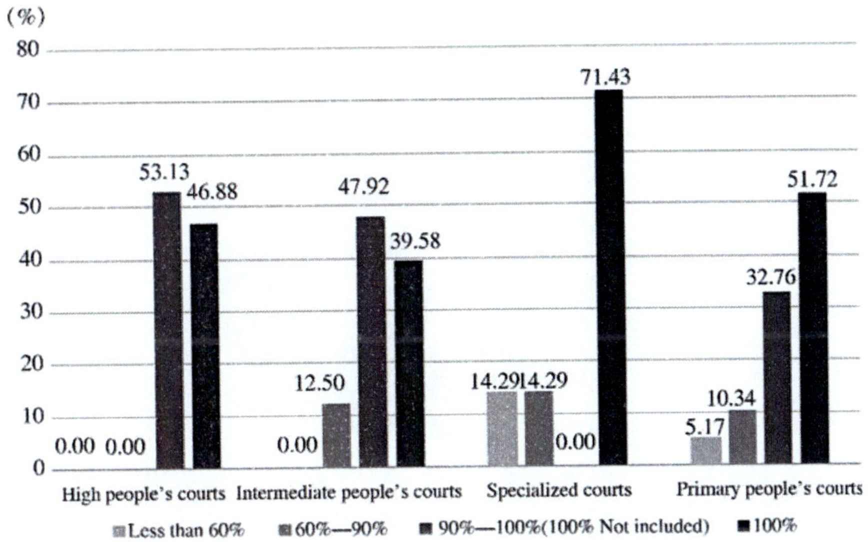

Fig. 34 Disclosure of administrative judgments in the full text by courts at all levels

6.3.4 Enforcement Judgments Disclosed in the Full Text

Overall, the disclosure of enforcement judgments in the full text was less adequate than that of civil, criminal, and administrative ones. The total number of enforcement judgments disclosed online was 709,196, with 597,155 disclosed in the full text, accounting for 84.20%. Of this sum, nine courts did not make available enforcement judgments to the public during this period, including one high people's court, four specialized courts, and four primary people's courts, namely the High People's Court of Inner Mongolia Autonomous Region, Beijing Intellectual Property Court, Guangzhou Intellectual Property Court, Shanghai Intellectual Property Court, the Primary People's Court of Guangdong Free Trade Zone (Nansha) of Guangdong Province, the Primary People's Court of Songshan District of Chifeng City, Inner Mongolia Autonomous Region, the Primary People's Court Ar Horqin Banner of Inner Mongolia Autonomous Region, the Primary People's Court of Yingde City of Guangdong Province, the Primary People's Court of Yumen City of Gansu Province. Among the 209 courts that disclosed enforcement judgments, 18 courts disclosed less than 60% (inclusive) of the enforcement judgments in the full text, accounting for 8.61%; 25 disclosed over 60% but less than 80%, accounting for 11.96%; 13 disclosed over 80% but less than 90%, accounting for 6.22%; 73 disclosed over 90% but less than 100%, accounting for 34.93%; 80 disclosed all their enforcement judgments in the full text, accounting for 38.28% (see Fig. 35).

The specialized courts performed the best in disclosing enforcement judgments in the full text among courts at all levels. One court did not release any enforcement judgment among the high people's courts during this period. One of the remaining

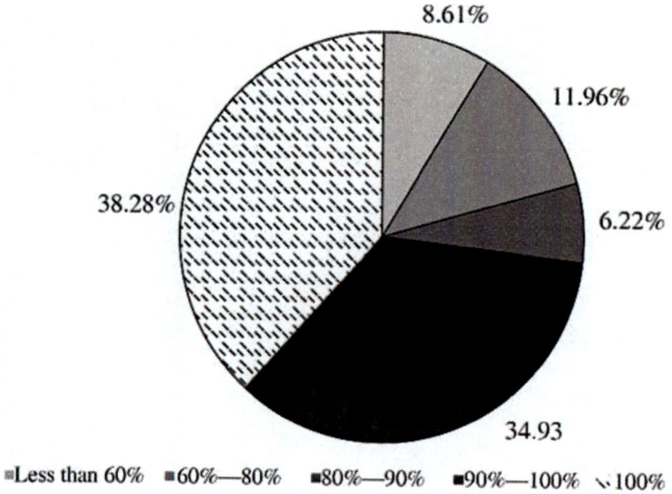

Fig. 35 The proportion of courts that made public the full text of enforcement judgments

31 high people's courts disclosed 24.45% (less than 60% inclusive) of its enforcement judgments in the full text, accounting for 3.23%; 4 disclosed over 60% but less than 90%, accounting for 12.90%; five disclosed over 90% but less than 100%, accounting for 16.13%; 21 disclosed all their enforcement judgments in the full text, accounting for 67.74%. Among the intermediate people's courts, two disclosed less than 60% (inclusive), accounting for 4.08%; ten disclosed over 60% but less than 90%, accounting for 20.41%; 18 disclosed over 90% but less than 100%, accounting for 36.73%; 19 disclosed all their enforcement judgments in the full text, accounting for 38.78%. Among the eight specialized courts which published enforcement judgments, one disclosed less than 60% (inclusive) of the enforcement judgments in the full text, accounting for 12.50%; one disclosed over 60% but less than 90%, accounting for 12.50%; two disclosed over 90% but less than 100%, accounting for 25.00%; four disclosed all their enforcement judgments in the full text, accounting for 50.00%. Among the 120 primary people's courts that disclosed enforcement judgments, 14 disclosed less than 60% (inclusive) of the enforcement judgments in the full text, accounting for 11.67%; 23 disclosed over 60% but less than 90%, accounting for 19.17%; 48 disclosed over 90% but less than 100%, accounting for 40.00%; 35 disclosed all their enforcement judgments in the full text, accounting for 29.17% (see Fig. 36).

Judging from the proportion of the courts that disclosed more than 90% of enforcement judgments in the complete text, the specialized courts performed the best, followed by the high people's courts, with the primary people's courts being the least satisfactory. Against the status quo that primary people's courts handle a disproportionate number of enforcement cases, the disclosure of enforcement judgments

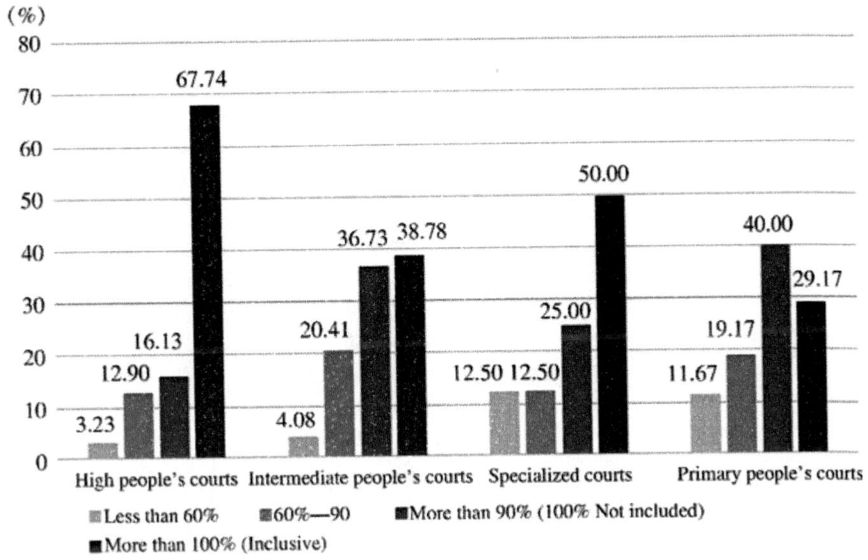

Fig. 36 Disclosure of enforcement judgments in the full text by courts at all levels

did not conform to the actual needs. Besides, the disclosure of enforcement judgments in the full text further shows that there is still a gap between the disclosure of enforcement information and judicial openness in other fields.

6.3.5 Summary

According to the above statistics, the proportion of judgments disclosed in the full text still needs to be improved. A system for disclosing information items on judgments has been established in the Provisions of the Supreme People's Court on the Publication of Judgments on the Internet by People's Courts issued in 2016. It contributes to the revelation of those judgments that have not been disclosed for various reasons and provides an institutional basis for the courts to get a clear picture of the actual situation of judgment disclosure and implement the principle of openness as a rule and non-disclosure as an exception. Online disclosure is not suitable for some judgments, and accordingly, they will not be disclosed in the full text. However, if most judgments are not disclosed in the complete text, it will inevitably affect the purpose of judgment disclosure and the effect hereof. From the above statistics, the overall situation and the disclosure proportion have shown the necessity for some courts to increase the proportion of judgments disclosed in the entire text in the cases concerning some causes of action. In particular, half of the judgments in some courts were not disclosed online in the full text, the reasons behind which deserve attention. That also implies that there is still much room for improvement in judgment disclosure.

6.4 *Reasons for Not Disclosing the Full Text of Judgments*

According to the Provisions of the Supreme People's Court on the Publication of Judgments on the Internet by People's Courts, in the process of uploading judgments on the Internet, under any of the following circumstances, a judgment rendered by a people's court shall not be published on the Internet but its case number, grounds for non-disclosure and other information: it involves divorce proceedings or support and guardianship of underaged children; it involves any state secret; the case is closed by mediation, or the effect of a people's mediation agreement is confirmed; it involves any juvenile delinquency. In case of "any other circumstance under which the people's court holds it inappropriate to publish the judgment on the Internet", the court can disclose only the information on the judgment. Unlike the aforesaid statutory circumstances, "any other circumstance under which the people's court holds it inappropriate to publish the judgment on the Internet" is subject to the court's discretion. In order to standardize the court's application of discretionary causes, the Supreme People's Court has been granting courts at all levels to examine and approve those judgments that are not intended to be made public online since it established the mechanism for publishing judgments online. The application of this system has been gradually regulated.

According to the Zhejiang Court Judicial Transparency Index Assessment results, in applying the examination and approval system for not disclosing judgments online in 2015, some courts did not strictly apply the examination and approval procedures; some did not give specific reasons for non-disclosure. In addition to the statutory causes such as state secrets and personal privacy, the statistics reveal a lot of far-fetched reasons for non-disclosure. For example, the case had a sensitive nature. The parties strongly requested non-disclosure. The case was remanded for retrial. The original judgment was overruled. The case was tried in camera. There were deep divisions between the judgment and the mediation results. It was a bankruptcy case. The judgment failed to be uploaded. The judgment had some errors, and some system operation errors resulted in non-availability.[6]

The revised *Provisions of the Supreme People's Court on the Publication of Judgments on the Internet by People's Court* has clarified the categories of reasons for not disclosing judgments online and simplified the examination and approval process. That is to say, only in case of "any other circumstance under which the people's court holds it inappropriate to publish the judgment on the Internet" is the examination and approval process required. However, the 2018 Third Party Assessment of National Judicial Openness results show that there were still many problems in examining and approving discretionary reasons, including irregularity in the process and too broad or inaccurate reasons.[7]

The statistics in 2020 show a high proportion of the application of discretionary reasons for not disclosing the full text of judgments. Of all the judgments disclosed

---

[6] See Tian and Lv [6].

[7] Center for National Index of Rule of Law of CASS & Innovation Project Team for Index of Rule of Law of the Institute of Law of CASS [7].

by 218 courts between January to September 2020, 649,963 judgments were not published in the full text but with only information items. Among them, 332,892 judgments were not disclosed in the full text due to "other circumstances under which the people's court holds it inappropriate to publish the judgment on the Internet", accounting for a relatively high proportion of 51.22%. Eight courts cited "other circumstances under which the people's court holds it inappropriate to publish the judgment on the Internet" as the only reason for not disclosing the full text of their judgments: the Primary People's Court of Hexi District of Tianjin Municipality, the Primary People's Court of Fengtai District of Beijing Municipality, the Primary People's Court of Haidian District of Beijing Municipality, the Primary People's Court of Chaoyang District of Beijing Municipality, the Primary People's Court of Wuqing District of Tianjin Municipality, the Primary People's Court of Xicheng District of Beijing Municipality, the Primary People's Court of Nankai District of Tianjin Municipality, Guangzhou Intellectual Property Court. Moreover, the proportion of the judgments not disclosed in the full text was high in the above eight courts. Only Guangzhou Intellectual Property Court and the Primary People's Court of Nankai District of Tianjin Municipality had a low proportion, with 0.08% and 18.68%, respectively. The remaining courts all had a higher proportion, with the Primary People's Court of Hexi District of Tianjin Municipality having the highest proportion of 42.09%.

The courts that did not disclose over 90% of their judgments in the full text were as follows: the Primary People's Court of Zhuhai Hengqin New Area of Guangdong Province, the Supreme People's Court, the High People's Court of Shanghai Municipality, the High People's Court of Hubei Province, the High People's Court of Inner Mongolia Autonomous Region, the Primary People's Court of Hongkou District of Shanghai Municipality, the Primary People's Court of Pudong New Area of Shanghai Municipality, the Primary People's Court of Jing'an District of Shanghai Municipality, the Intermediate People's Court of Shenyang City of Liaoning Province, the Intermediate People's Court of Fushun City of Liaoning Province, the High People's Court of Heilongjiang Province, the Primary People's Court of Huangdao District of Qingdao City, Shandong Province (see Table 1). The Supreme People's Court had the lowest proportion of 0.60% among the courts mentioned above. The Primary People's Court of Huangdao District of Qingdao City, Shandong Province, had the highest proportion of 60.35%.

It appears to stand out that some courts did not disclose the full text of the judgments for reasons other than statutory causes, which deserves attention.

6.4.1 Application of Discretionary Reasons in Civil Cases

The courts did not disclose the full text of civil judgments mainly for discretionary reasons. Of the 1,868,028 civil judgments selected in this assessment, 514,363 were not published in the full text, 213,664 of which were not disclosed in the full text for discretionary reasons, accounting for 41.54%.

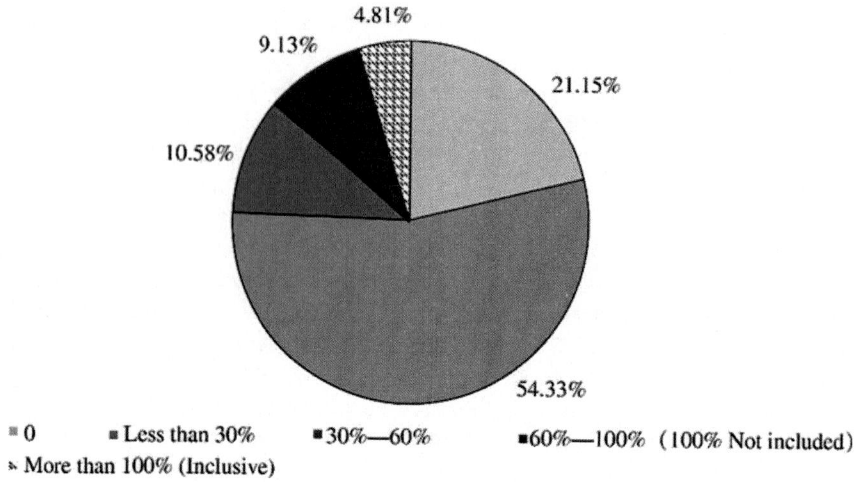

Fig. 37 The proportion of courts that did not disclose the civil judgments in the full text for discretionary reasons

Ten courts disclosed the full text of all the published judgments and raised no legal causes or discretionary reasons for not publishing the full text. Of the remaining 208 courts that did not disclose the full text of the judgments, 44 did not cite discretionary reasons for withholding the full text, accounting for 21.15%. One hundred and thirteen courts had discretionary grounds for not publishing the full text of the judgments, the proportion of which was less than 30% (inclusive), accounting for 54.33%. Twenty-two courts had discretionary grounds for not publishing the full text of the judgments, the proportion of which was 30–60%, accounting for 10.58%. Twenty-nine courts had discretionary grounds for not publishing the full text of the judgments, the proportion of which was over 60%, accounting for 13.94% (see Fig. 37). Ten of them completely cited discretionary reasons for not disclosing the full text of the judgments.

Among the assessed high people's courts, two courts disclosed the full text of all the published judgments. Of the 30 courts that did not fully disclose the full text of all the judgments, 12 did not cite discretionary reasons, accounting for 40.00%. Seven cited discretionary reasons for not publishing the full text of the judgments, the proportion of which was less than 30% (inclusive), accounting for 23.33%. Five cited discretionary reasons for not publishing the full text of the judgments, the proportion of which was 30–60%, accounting for 16.67%. Six cited discretionary reasons for not publishing the full text of the judgments, the proportion of which was over 60%, accounting for 20.00%.

Among the assessed intermediate people's courts, two courts published judgments in the full text during this period. Of the forty-seven courts that did not disclose the full text of judgments, five did not cite discretionary reasons, accounting for 10.64%. Thirty-four courts had discretionary reasons for not releasing the complete text of the judgments, the proportion of which was less than 30% (inclusive), accounting for 72.34%. Four cited discretionary reasons for not publishing the full text of the judgments, the proportion of which was 30–60%, accounting for 8.51%; four cited discretionary grounds for not publishing the full text of the judgments, the proportion of which was over 60%, accounting for 20.00%.

Of the specialized courts, one court disclosed the full text of all the published judgments during this period. Among the eleven courts that did not disclose the full text of some judgments for discretionary reasons, five cited discretionary reasons for not publishing the full text of the judgments, the proportion of which was less than 30% (inclusive), accounting for 45.45%. One court cited discretionary reasons for not publishing the full text of the judgments, the proportion of which was 30–60%, accounting for 9.10%; five had discretionary reasons for not publishing the full text of the judgments, the proportion of which was over 60%, accounting for 45.45%. Two courts of the assessed specialized courts failed to disclose the full text of some judgments entirely for discretionary grounds.

Of all the primary people's courts, five courts disclosed the full text of all the published judgments. Among the 119 courts that did not disclose the full text of some judgments, twenty-seven did not cite discretionary reasons, accounting for 22.69% Sixty-seven courts cited discretionary grounds for not publishing the full text of the judgments, the proportion of which was less than 30% (inclusive), accounting for 56.30%. Twelve cited such reasons for not publishing the full text of the judgments, the proportion of which was 30–60%, accounting for 10.08%; 13 cited discretionary grounds for not publishing the full text of the judgments, the proportion of which was over 60%, accounting for 10.92%. Seven of the assessed primary courts failed to disclose the full text of the judgments entirely for discretionary grounds (see Fig. 38), which were the Primary People's Court of Hexi District of Tianjin Municipality (51.87%), the Primary People's Court of Haidian District of Beijing Municipality (48.73%), the Primary People's Court of Fengtai District of Beijing Municipality (47.04%), the Primary People's Court of Wuqing District of Tianjin Municipality (40.21%), the Primary People's Court of Chaoyang District of Beijing Municipality (38.77%), the Primary People's Court of Xicheng District of Beijing Municipality (36.45%), and the Primary People's Court of Nankai District of Tianjin Municipality (28.29%).

In conclusion, more than 40% of the civil judgments were not disclosed in the full text due to discretionary reasons. The nondisclosure of the full text of civil judgments for discretionary reasons differed from court to court. Generally, a high proportion of the higher courts failed to disclose the full text of civil judgments for discretionary reasons. Maybe it is because the higher courts handled relatively complex civil cases.

6.4.2 Application of Discretionary Reasons in Criminal Cases

Overall, the courts did not disclose the full text of some criminal judgments primarily for discretionary reasons. Of the 196,592 criminal judgments selected in this assessment, 16,780 were not published in the full text, 11,408 of which were not disclosed

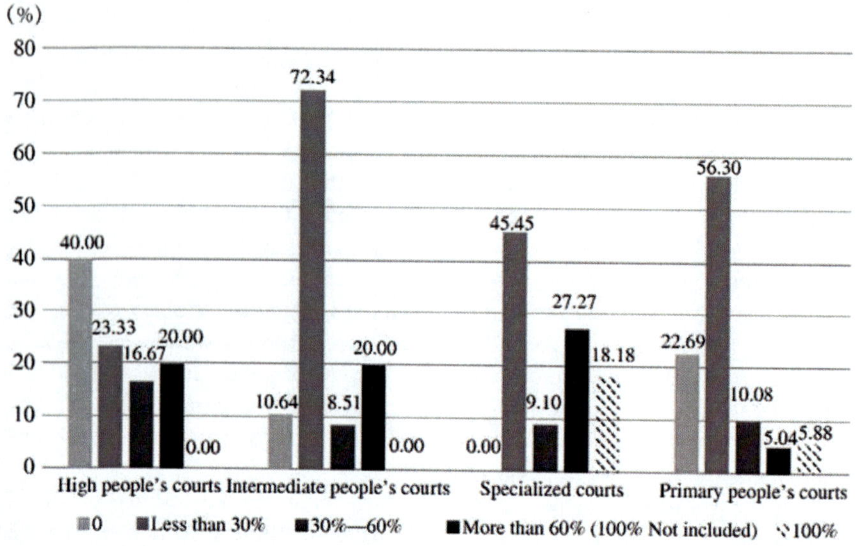

Fig. 38 Application of discretionary reasons by courts of various types in the nondisclosure of the full text of civil judgments

for discretionary grounds, accounting for 67.99 %. This figure is higher than that of civil judgments. It can be seen that the courts relied more on discretionary grounds for not publishing the full text of the criminal judgments, although the proportion of the criminal judgments not published in the complete text, was lower than that of civil judgments.

Eleven courts failed to disclose any criminal judgment. The judgments published by twenty-nine courts were all in the full text. Among the remaining 178 courts, twenty-four never cited discretionary reasons for their nondisclosure of the full text of the judgments, accounting for 13.48%; twenty courts had discretionary grounds for not publishing the full text of the judgments, the proportion of which was less than 30% (inclusive), accounting for 11.24%. Twenty-eight had discretionary grounds for not publishing the full text of the judgments, the proportion of which was 30–60%, accounting for 15.73%. One hundred and six courts cited such grounds for not publishing the full text of the judgments, the proportion of which was over 60%, accounting for 59.55% (see Fig. 39). Twenty-seven courts did not publish the full text of the criminal judgments entirely for discretionary reasons, accounting for 15.17% of the 178 courts.

Four of the assessed high people's courts disclosed the criminal judgments, all in the full text. Four of the remaining 28 courts did not cite discretionary reasons for not publishing the complete text, accounting for 14.28%. Eight courts cited discretionary reasons for not publishing the complete text of the judgments, the proportion of which was less than 30% (inclusive), accounting for 3.57%. Two courts had such reasons for not publishing the complete text of the judgments, the proportion of which was 30–60%, accounting for 7.14%. Nineteen courts had discretionary reasons for not

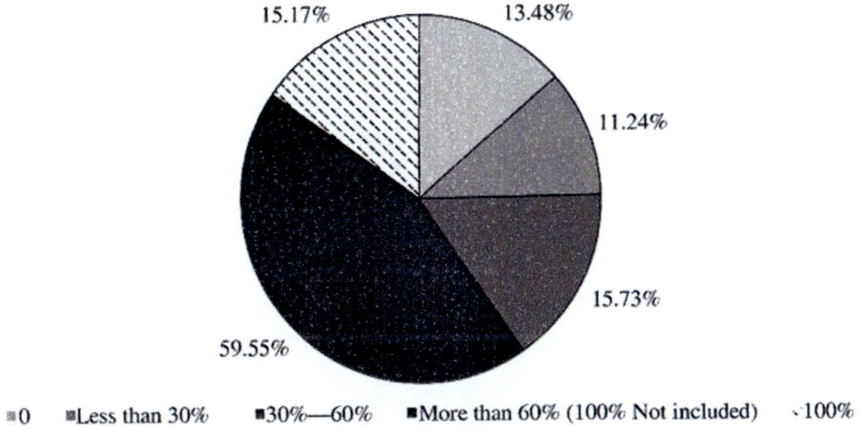

Fig. 39 The proportion of courts that did not disclose the criminal judgments in the full text for discretionary reasons

publishing the complete text of the judgments, the proportion of which was over 60%, accounting for 67.86%. Five courts did not disclose the full text of the criminal judgments totally for discretionary reasons.

Among the assessed intermediate people's courts, the criminal judgments disclosed by five courts were all in the full text. One of the remaining 44 courts did not cite discretionary reasons for not disclosing the full text of the judgments, accounting for 2.27%. Eight courts cited discretionary reasons for not publishing the complete text of the judgments, the proportion of which was less than 30% (inclusive), accounting for 18.18%. Nine courts had such grounds for not publishing the complete text of the judgments, the proportion of which was 30–60%, accounting for 20.45%; 26 courts had discretionary reasons for not publishing the complete text of the judgments, the proportion of which was over 60%, accounting for 50.09%. Five courts did not publish the full text of the criminal judgments entirely for discretionary reasons.

Of the assessed primary people's courts, the criminal judgments published by eighteen courts were all in the full text. Nineteen of the remaining 106 courts never cited discretionary reasons for not disclosing the full text of the judgments, accounting for 17.92%. Eleven courts cited discretionary reasons for not publishing the complete text of the judgments, the proportion of which was less than 30% (inclusive), accounting for 10.38%. Sixteen courts had such grounds for not publishing the full text of the judgments, the proportion of which was 30–60%, accounting for 15.09%; 60 had discretionary reasons for not publishing the complete text of the judgments, the proportion of which was over 60%, accounting for 56.60%. Seventeen courts did not publish the full text of the criminal judgments entirely for discretionary reasons (see Fig. 40).

To sum up, almost 60% of all the assessed courts withheld the full text of the criminal judgments for discretionary grounds, the proportion of which was over

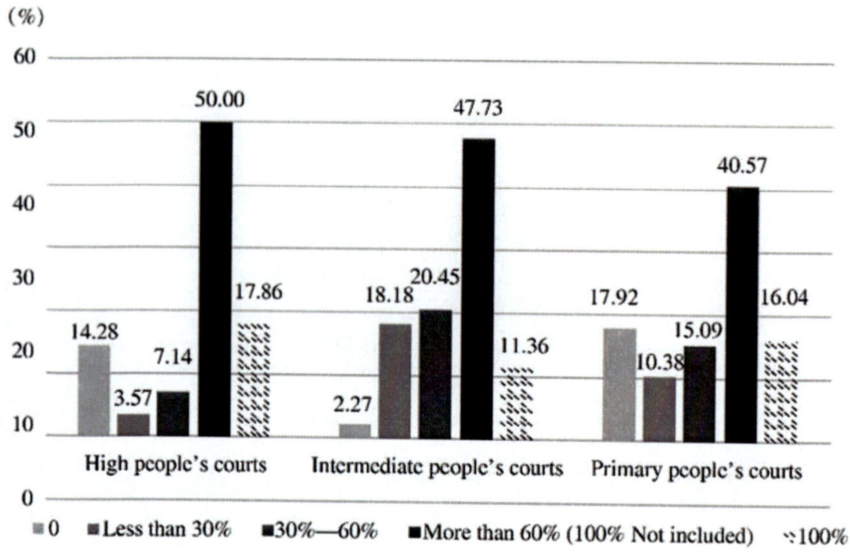

Fig. 40 Application of discretionary reasons by courts of various types in the nondisclosure of the full text of criminal judgments

60%. Many courts did not release the full text of criminal judgments for discretionary reasons. Failure for discretionary grounds to disclose the full text of criminal judgments by courts at all levels was commonly seen, especially by the high people's courts.

6.4.3 Application of Discretionary Reasons in Administrative Cases

Regarding administrative cases, the courts did not disclose the full text of the administrative judgments primarily for discretionary reasons. Of the assessed 104,674 administrative judgments, 3,206 were not published in the complete text, 3,001 of which were not disclosed for discretionary reasons, accounting for 93.61%, higher than other types of judgments.

Fourteen courts never published any administrative judgment, while 99 courts disclosed the administrative judgments all in the full text. Among the remaining 105 courts, nineteen did not cite discretionary reasons for not publishing the full text of the administrative judgments, accounting for 18.10%. Eight courts cited discretionary reasons for not publishing the complete text of the judgments, the proportion of which was less than 60% (inclusive), accounting for 7.62%; 78 courts had discretionary grounds for not publishing the complete text of the judgments, the proportion of which was over 60%, accounting for 74.29% (see Fig. 41). Fifty-nine courts did not publish the full text of the administrative judgments entirely for discretionary reasons.

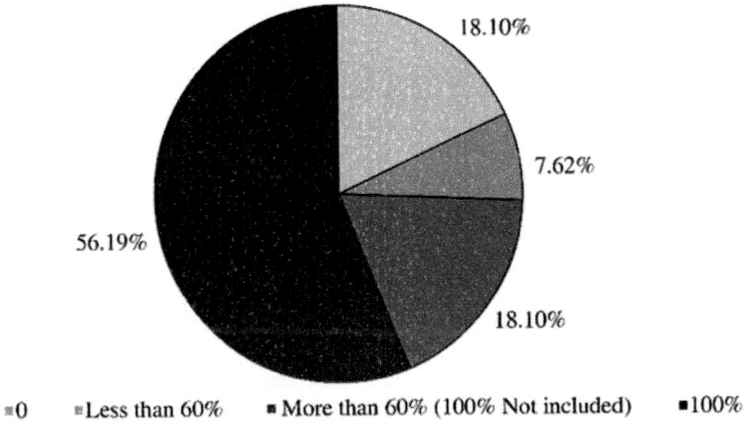

Fig. 41 The proportion of courts that did not disclose the administrative judgments in the full text for discretionary reasons

Among the high people's courts, 15 courts disclosed the published administrative judgments, all in full-text. Of the remaining 17 courts, five never cited discretionary reasons for the nondisclosure of the full text of the administrative judgments, accounting for 29.41%. One court had discretionary reasons for not publishing the complete text of the judgments, the proportion of which was less than 60% (inclusive), accounting for 5.88%; eleven had discretionary grounds for not publishing the complete text of the judgments, the proportion of which was over 60%, accounting for 64.71%. Nine courts did not publish the full text of the administrative judgments entirely for discretionary reasons.

Of the intermediate people's courts, one court never published any administrative judgment, and 19 courts disclosed the full text of all the published administrative judgments. Among the remaining 29 courts, five courts never cited discretionary reasons for the nondisclosure of the full text of the administrative judgments, accounting for 17.24%. Three courts had discretionary reasons for not publishing the complete text of the judgments, the proportion of which was not less than 60% (inclusive), accounting for 10.34%; 21 courts had discretionary grounds for not publishing the complete text of the judgments, the proportion of which was over 60%, accounting for 72.41%. Thirteen courts did not publish the full text of the administrative judgments entirely for discretionary reasons.

Five of the specialized people's courts did not make any administrative judgment public, and five disclosed the full text of all the published administrative judgments. Two courts that did not disclose the full text of the administrative judgments cited discretionary grounds.

Eight of the primary people's courts never published any administrative judgment. The administrative judgments published by 60 courts were disclosed in the full text. Of the remaining 56 courts, nine did not cite discretionary reasons for the nondisclosure of the full text, accounting for 16.07%. Four courts had discretionary

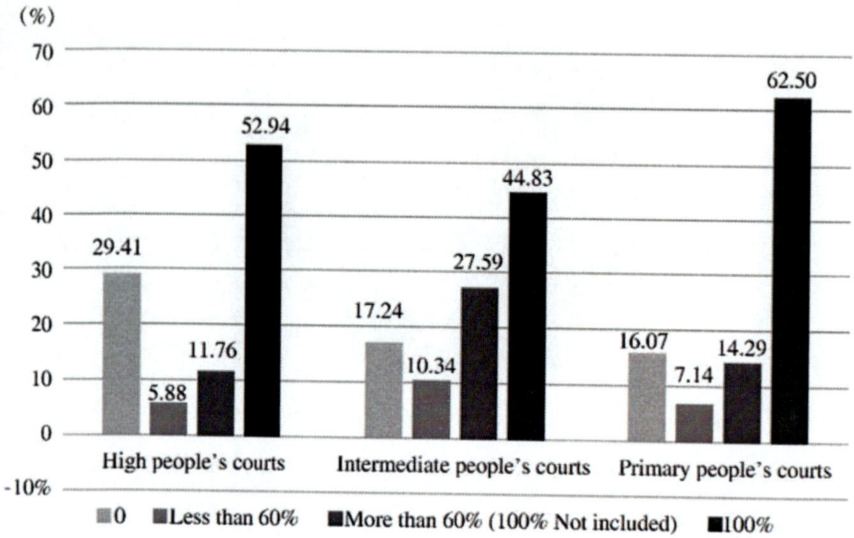

Fig. 42 Application of discretionary reasons by courts of various types in the nondisclosure of the full text of administrative judgments

reasons for not publishing the complete text of the judgments, the proportion of which was less than 60% (inclusive), accounting for 7.14%; 43 courts had discretionary grounds for not publishing the complete text of the judgments, the proportion of which was over 60%, accounting for 76.79%. Thirty-five courts did not publish the full text of the administrative judgments entirely for discretionary reasons (see Fig. 42).

In conclusion, almost 70% of all the assessed courts withheld the full text of the administrative judgments for discretionary grounds, the proportion of which was over 60%, although the full text of administrative judgments was much more disclosed than that of civil and criminal judgments. The majority of the assessed courts did not release the full text of the administrative judgments for discretionary reasons. Failure for discretionary grounds to disclose the full text of the administrative judgments by courts at all levels was commonly seen. From the perspective that discretionary grounds were applied in the nondisclosure of the full text of all the published judgments, the primary people's courts assumed a leading position, followed by the high people's courts and the intermediate people's courts. Further analysis and study are in need to figure out any problem arising in handling administrative cases.

6.4.4 Application of Discretionary Reasons in Enforcement Cases

The assessed courts did not disclose the full text of the judgments primarily for discretionary reasons in enforcement cases. Of the selected 709,196 judgments, 112,041 were not made public in the full text. Among them, the full text of 101,691 was not

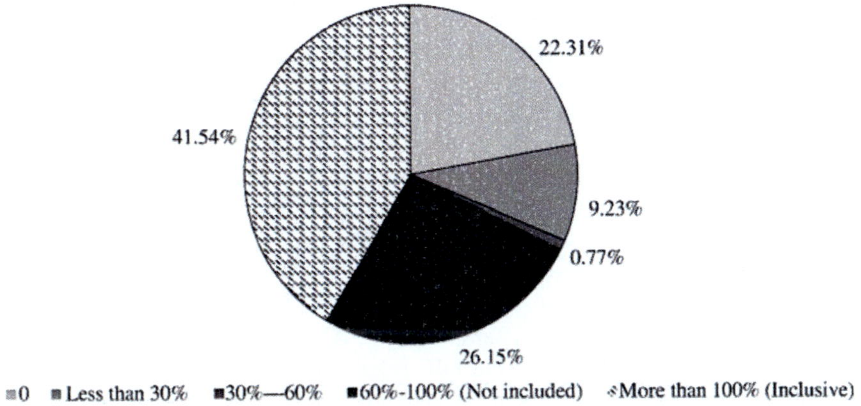

Fig. 43 The proportion of courts that did not disclose the enforcement judgments in the full text for discretionary reasons

released for discretionary reasons, accounting for 90.76%, higher than that of civil and criminal judgments.

Nine courts did not publish any enforcement judgment. Seventy-nine courts disclosed the enforcement judgments in the full text. Among the remaining 130 courts, 29 never cited discretionary reasons for not releasing the full text of the judgments, accounting for 22.31%. Twelve courts cited discretionary reasons for not publishing the complete text of the judgments, the proportion of which was less than 30% (inclusive), accounting for 9.23%. One court had such reasons for not publishing the complete text of the judgments, the proportion of which was 30–60%, accounting for 0.77%; 88 courts had discretionary reasons for not publishing the complete text of the judgments, the proportion of which was over 60%, accounting for 67.69% (see Fig. 43). Fifty-four courts did not publish the full text of the judgments entirely for discretionary reasons, accounting for 41.54%.

Of the high people's courts, one court did not make enforcement judgments public, and 21 courts published the enforcement judgments in the full text. One court cited discretionary reasons for not publishing the complete text of the judgments, the proportion of which was 36.36%, and one court cited such grounds for not publishing the complete text of the judgments, the proportion of which was 75%. The remaining eight courts did not publish the full text of the judgments entirely for discretionary reasons, accounting for 80% of the courts that had enforcement judgments published.

Of the assessed intermediate people's courts, nineteen courts disclosed the full text of enforcement judgments. Of the other 30 courts that did not disclose the full text of some enforcement judgments, four did not cite discretionary reasons for not disclosing the complete text, accounting for 13.33%. One court cited discretionary reasons for not publishing the complete text of the judgments, the proportion of which was less than 30%, accounting for 3.33%; 25 courts cited such reasons for not publishing the complete text of the judgments, the proportion of which was over 60%, accounting for 83.33%. Fifteen courts did not publish the full text of the judgments entirely for discretionary reasons.

Of the specialized courts, fourteen courts disclosed the enforcement judgments, all in the full text. Of the remaining eight courts, four did not cite discretionary reasons for not disclosing the complete text, accounting for 50% of the courts that had enforcement judgments published. One court cited discretionary grounds for not publishing the complete text of the judgments, the proportion of which was 74.78%, accounting for 12.50%; three courts did not publish the full text of the judgments entirely for such grounds, accounting for 37.5%.

Of the primary people's courts, four courts never made any enforcement judgment public, and 34 courts disclosed the enforcement judgments in the full text. Of the remaining 86 courts that did not publish the full text of the enforcement judgments, 25 did not cite discretionary reasons, accounting for 29.07%. Eleven courts cited discretionary reasons for not publishing the complete text of the judgments, the proportion of which was less than 30%, accounting for 12.79%; 50 courts cited such reasons for not publishing the complete text of the judgments, the proportion of which was over 60%, accounting for 58.14%. Twenty-eight courts did not publish the full text of the judgments entirely due to discretionary grounds (see Fig. 44).

A comprehensive analysis of the above data shows that many courts had discretionary grounds for not disclosing the full text of the enforcement judgments, the proportion of which was over 60%. The number of such courts significantly exceeded 60%. In other words, most courts did not publish the full text of the enforcement judgments due to discretionary reasons. This phenomenon is evident in the courts at all levels. From the perspective of the court level, 90.00% of the high people's courts,

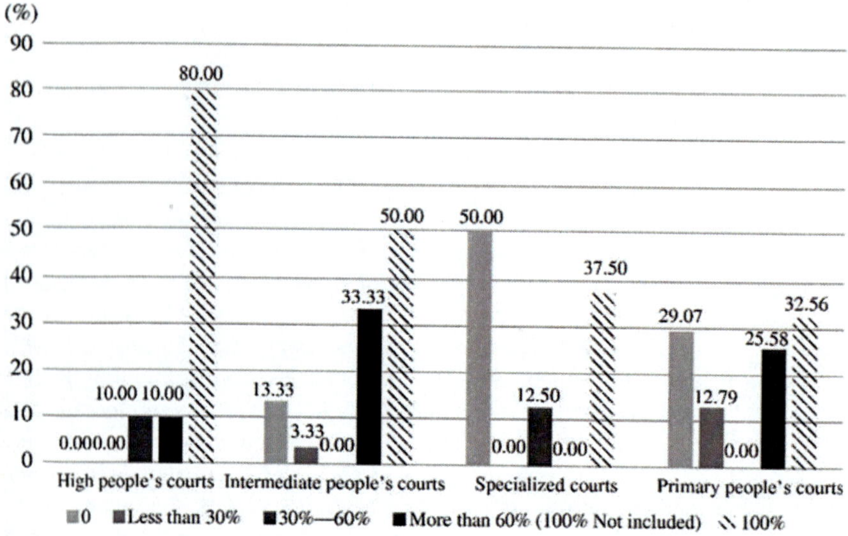

Fig. 44 Application of discretionary reasons by courts of various types in the nondisclosure of the full text of judgments in enforcement cases

83.33% of the intermediate people's courts, 50.00% of the specialized courts, and 58.14% of the primary people's courts cited discretionary grounds for not disclosing the full text of the enforcement judgments accounting for over 60% of those judgments the full text of which was not published. It is the power granted by judicial interpretations to courts at all levels to withhold the full text of enforcement judgments for discretionary reasons. It also aims at preventing the statutory causes for nondisclosure from being incomplete. However, in consideration of promoting the disclosure of information on enforcement cases and standardizing the publication of judgments on the Internet, discretionary reasons applied so frequently in enforcement judgments deserve great concern.

6.4.5 Summary

In the beginning, courts at all levels were required to upload judgments that could be made public to China Judgements Online. China has made remarkable achievements in judgment disclosure by requiring courts to upload information items on a judgment, including its case number, the trial court, the date of judgment, and the reasons for nondisclosure, even if it is inappropriate to disclose the judgment in the full text. By doing so, China has better attained the goal of taking disclosure as a rule and nondisclosure as an exception. Based on judicial practice and disclosure of judgments, judicial interpretations enumerated statutory reasons for not publishing the full text of judgments and authorized courts to decide on discretionary reasons. It is supposed that such provisions would be feasible. In practice, the application of discretionary reasons in judicial openness is a matter of concern. According to the judgment data of the assessed courts in 2020, many courts cited discretionary reasons for not disclosing the full text of a lot of published judgments but only making public information items. Between January and September 2020, 51.22% of the judgments delivered by 218 assessed courts that were not published in the full text were not disclosed in the full text due to discretionary reasons, that is, "other circumstances for which people's courts deem it inappropriate to publish the full text of judgments on the Internet".

Specifically, discretionary reasons were prominently applied in the nondisclosure of the full text of administrative and enforcement judgments. According to our statistics, judgments that were not published in the full text totaled 41.54% of the civil judgments, 67.99% of the criminal judgments, 93.61% of the administrative judgments, and 90.76% of the enforcement judgments (see Fig. 45). Criminal cases are more sensitive, administrative cases are more tricky, and civil cases trigger more concerns among the parties. Then it is interesting to figure out why discretionary reasons were applied so highly in enforcement judgments.

Except for the number of judgments, a large proportion of courts that did not disclose the full text of the judgments primarily applied discretionary reasons. In the civil cases, 13.94% of the courts cited discretionary grounds for not disclosing the full text of the judgments, which was over 60%, in the criminal cases, 59.55%,

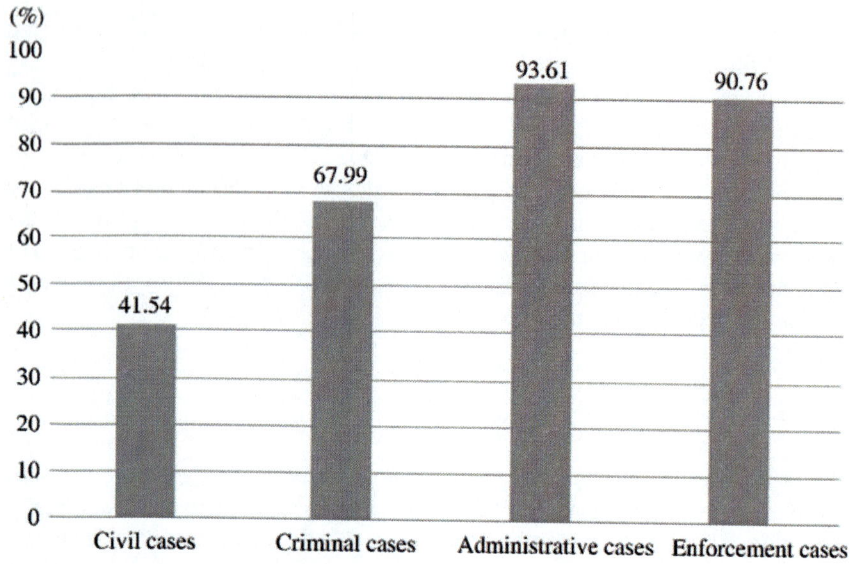

Fig. 45 The proportion of the judgments not disclosed in the full text for discretionary reasons in four types of cases

in the administrative cases, 74.29%, and in the enforcement cases, 67.69%. Discretionary reasons were more often applied in administrative and enforcement cases (see Fig. 46).

Moreover, some courts did not publish the judgments in the full text entirely for discretionary reasons. Of the 208 courts that had some civil judgments not published in the full text, ten courts relied on discretionary grounds for the nondisclosure of the complete text of the civil judgments, accounting for 4.81%. Of the 178 courts that had some criminal judgments not published in the full text, 27 courts relied on discretionary grounds, accounting for 15.17%. Of the 105 courts with some administrative judgments not published in the complete text, 59 courts drew support from discretionary grounds, accounting for 56.19%. Of the 130 courts with some enforcement judgments not published in the full text, 54 courts cited discretionary grounds, accounting for 41.54% (see Fig. 47). Similarly, discretionary reasons were more often applied in administrative and enforcement judgments than civil ones, which deserves more attention.

According to the previous survey, there is the possibility that discretionary reasons of "other circumstances for which people's courts deem it inappropriate to publish the full text of judgments on the Internet" have been abused. The Zhejiang Court judicial transparency index assessment of 2013–2015, the Beijing court judicial transparency index assessment of 2014–2015, and the 2018 third party assessment of national judicial openness carried out by the project team have presented many instances of

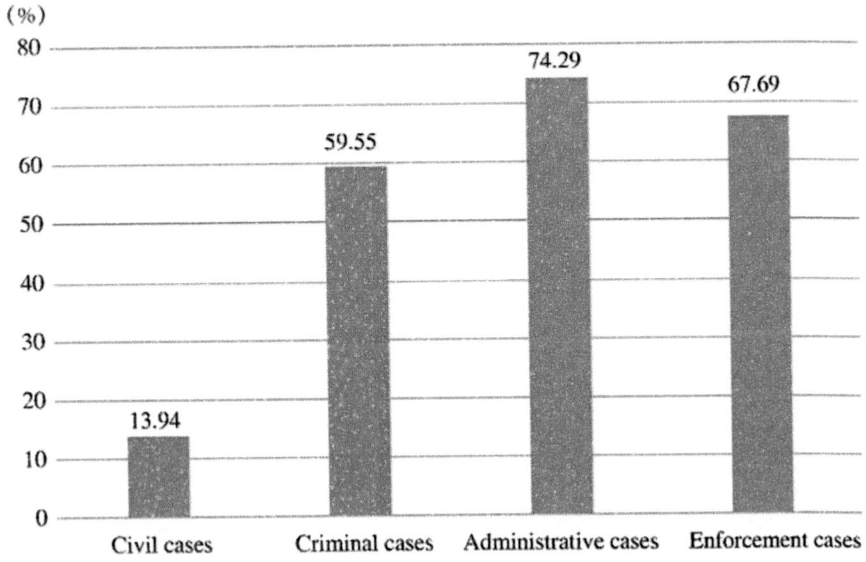

Fig. 46 The proportion of the courts with 60% of the judgments not published in the full text for discretionary reasons

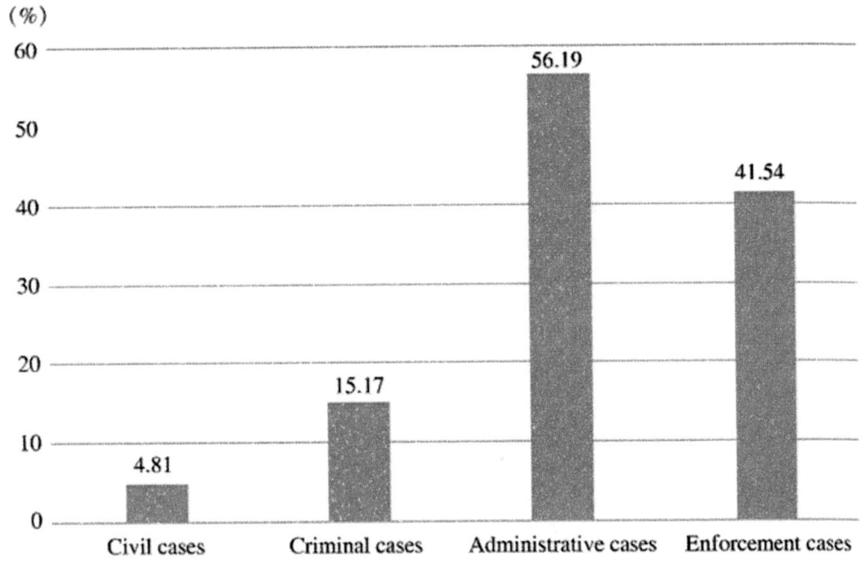

Fig. 47 The proportion of the courts with some judgments not published in the full text entirely for discretionary reasons

irregularities in the application of the discretionary reasons.[8] The results of the 2020 Assessment further show the seriousness that discretionary reasons were misused or inappropriately applied in the process of publishing judgments on the Internet. However, suppose there are some reasons for not disclosing the full text of a judgment. In that case, it is necessary to reflect on whether the judicial interpretations issued by the Supreme People's Court on the disclosure of judgments cover all of the possible circumstances for not disclosing the full text of judgments and whether we should add new causes in light of actual circumstances to meet the needs of judicial practice and prevent potential mistakes in the flexible application by the courts.

6.5 The Time When Judgments Are Published Online

According to the *Provisions of the Supreme People's Court on the Publication of Judgments on the Internet by People's Courts*, an effective judgment shall be published on the Internet within seven working days when it comes into force. Where an appeal is filed against the judgment or ruling of first instance according to the law, the judgment of second instance shall be published on the Internet within seven working days as of the date when it comes into force. It must be admitted that it may take a long time to publish the judgment online after it is made since it is hard to determine when the judgment will come into force. The data on the judgments of the assessed courts between January and September of 2020 reveals that the time interval differed vastly from court to court.

This book briefly analyzes the efficiency of uploading judgments online according to the average time interval between making a judgment and its release on China Judgements Online. The average time interval refers to the quotient that the time interval between the time when judgments were uploaded by the court and the time when judgments were made is divided by the total number of judgments uploaded online in that period. This average value is affected by factors such as a court's internal management, informatization level, and the types of cases and the types of judgments made in the same period. Therefore, this average value may not accurately reflect the efficiency of disclosing judgments by a particular court and may not even reflect the court's internal management regarding judgment disclosure. Nevertheless, the average value and its distribution are significant in our survey of the overall efficiency of disclosing judgments.

According to the 2020 Assessment, the shortest average time interval was 21 days, and the longest was 766 days (see Table 2). Among the 218 courts, 30 courts had an average time interval of fewer than 50 (not included) days, accounting for 13.76%; 61 courts had an average time interval of 50–99 days, accounting for 27.98%. Sixty courts had an average time interval of 100–149 days, accounting for 27.52%; 28

[8] See Tian and Lv [6], Innovation Project Team for Index of Rule of Law of the Institute of Law of CASS [8], Center for National Index of Rule of Law of CASS & Innovation Project Team for Index of Rule of Law of the Institute of Law of CASS [7].

courts had an average time interval of 150–199 days, accounting for 12.84%; 39 courts had an average time interval of more than 200 (inclusive) days, accounting for 17.89% (see Fig. 48).

According to the 2018 *third party assessment report on judicial openness*, of the 160 assessed courts, eight courts had an average time interval of fewer than 50 (not included) days, accounting for 5%. Forty-three courts had an average time interval of 50–99 days, accounting for 26.88%; 53 courts had an average time interval of 100–149 days, accounting for 33.13%. Thirty-six courts had an average time interval of 150–199 days, accounting for 22.5%; 20 courts had an average time interval of more than 200 (inclusive) days, accounting for 12.5%.[9] By comparison, excluding those courts with an average time interval of more than 200 days, the proportion of the courts with an average time interval of fewer than 200 days in 2020 was not higher than that in 2018 or even slightly lower (see Fig. 49).

In addition, all courts uploaded some judgments in a short period after they were made. According to the statistics, 62 courts uploaded some judgments to China Judgements Online on the same day they were made, accounting for 28.44%. One hundred and two courts uploaded some judgments on the second day after making them, accounting for 46.79%, 29 courts on the third day, accounting for 13.30%, eight on the fourth day, accounting for 3.67%, five on the fifth day, accounting for 2.29%, one on the sixth day, accounting for 0.46%, two on the seventh day, accounting for 0.92%, two on the eighth day, accounting for 0.92%, three on the tenth day, accounting for 1.38%, three on the eleventh day, accounting for 1.38%, one on the fourteenth day, accounting for 0.46% (see Fig. 50). In the 2018 Assessment, of the 160 assessed courts, 41 courts uploaded some judgments to China Judgements Online on the same day they were made, accounting for 25.63%. Sixty-seven courts uploaded some judgments the second day after making them, accounting for 41.88%. By comparison, the uploading efficiency slightly increased.

In addition, all the assessed courts uploaded some judgments quite long after they were made. According to the collected judgments, the minimum time interval was 305 days, and the maximum time interval was 6,475 days (17 years). More specifically, 12 courts uploaded some judgments within 730 days after they were made, accounting for 5.50%. Twenty-eight courts had a time interval of 731–1,095 days, accounting for 12.84%; 25 courts had a time interval of 1,096–1,460 days, accounting for 11.47%; 40 courts had a time interval of 1,461–1,825 days, accounting for 18.35%. Thirty-four courts had a time interval of 1826–2190 days, accounting for 15.60%; 33 courts had a time interval of 2191–2555 days, accounting for 15.14%; 13 courts had a time interval of 2556–2920 days, accounting for 5.96%; and 33 courts had a time interval of more than 2,921 days, accounting for 15.14% (see Fig. 51). Since the judgments we selected were not those precisely concluded in a specific period but the judgments published online between January and September of 2020, some of the selected judgments were likely made many years ago. Due to the lack of the backend's effective management of these judgments, it is impossible to determine

[9] Center for National Index of Rule of Law of CASS & Innovation Project Team for Index of Rule of Law of the Institute of Law of CASS [7].

Table 2 The time interval between making judgments and publishing them online

Type of court	Court	The average time interval (Days)	The minimum time interval (Days)	The maximum Time interval (Days)
The Supreme People's Court	The Supreme People's Court	115	2	1720
High people's courts	The High People's Court of Beijing Municipality	26	1	1899
	The High People's Court of Tianjin Municipality	99	1	1769
	The High People's Court of Hebei Province	102	1	898
	The High People's Court of Shanxi Province	189	1	1522
	The High People's Court of Inner Mongolia Autonomous Region	156	2	3591
	The High People's Court of Liaoning Province	131	1	1725
	The High People's Court of Jilin Province	67	2	645
	The High People's Court of Heilongjiang Province	155	1	2389
	The High People's Court of Shanghai Municipality	172	2	3202
	The High People's Court of Jiangsu Province	129	1	3725
	The High People's Court of Zhejiang Province	96	4	4365
	The High People's Court of Anhui Province	73	2	1294

(continued)

Table 2 (continued)

Type of court	Court	The average time interval (Days)	The minimum time interval (Days)	The maximum Time interval (Days)
	The High People's Court of Fujian Province	234	2	1857
	The High People's Court of Jiangxi Province	168	0	3920
	The High People's Court of Shandong Province	197	1	1892
	The High People's Court of Henan Province	149	2	1534
	The High People's Court of Hubei Province	129	2	2838
	The High People's Court of Hunan Province	90	1	1022
	The High People's Court of Guangdong Province	141	0	2208
	The High People's Court of Guangxi Zhuang Autonomous Region	241	3	2998
	The High People's Court of Hainan Province	46	1	1465
	The High People's Court of Chongqing Municipality	143	9	2194
	The High People's Court of Sichuan Province	80	2	884
	The High People's Court of Guizhou Province	178	2	1530

(continued)

Table 2 (continued)

Type of court	Court	The average time interval (Days)	The minimum time interval (Days)	The maximum Time interval (Days)
	The High People's Court of Yunnan Province	160	1	1562
	The High People's Court of Xizang Autonomous Region	160	13	1024
	The High People's Court of Shaanxi Province	126	0	1686
	The High People's Court of Gansu Province	96	2	770
	The High People's Court of Qinghai Province	41	2	1788
	The High People's Court of Ningxia Hui Autonomous Region	122	3	1369
	The High People's Court of Xinjiang Uygur Autonomous Region	22	0	1198
	The Production and Construction Corps Branch of the High People's Court of Xinjiang Uygur Autonomous Region	121	9	448
Specialized courts	The Primary People's Court of Zhuhai Hengqin New Area of Guangdong Province	270	1	1349
	Beijing Intellectual Property Court	110	1	1083
	Guangzhou Intellectual Property Court	178	0	1748

(continued)

Table 2 (continued)

Type of court	Court	The average time interval (Days)	The minimum time interval (Days)	The maximum Time interval (Days)
	The Primary People's Court of Shenzhen Qianhai Cooperation Zone of Guangdong Province	200	1	1867
	Shanghai Intellectual Property Court	325	1	1958
	The Primary People's Court of Guangdong Free Trade Zone (Nansha) of Guangdong Province	125	1	774
	Hangzhou Internet Court	217	5	916
	Shanghai Financial Court	111	2	757
	Beijing Internet Court	47	1	588
	The Primary People's Court of Sichuan Pilot Free Trade Zone	70	1	595
	Guangzhou Internet Court	219	1	673
	The Primary People's Court of Chongqing Pilot Free Trade Zone	145	0	3797
Intermediate people's courts	The Intermediate People's Court of Shijiazhuang City of Hebei Province	111	1	3512
	The Intermediate People's Court of Tangshan City of Hebei Province	159	1	3214

(continued)

Table 2 (continued)

Type of court	Court	The average time interval (Days)	The minimum time interval (Days)	The maximum Time interval (Days)
	The Intermediate People's Court of Handan City of Hebei Province	221	2	1848
	The Intermediate People's Court of Taiyuan City of Shanxi Province	94	4	5713
	The Intermediate People's Court of Datong City of Shanxi Province	148	3	2107
	The Intermediate People's Court of Hohhot City of Inner Mongolia Autonomous Region	122	1	3472
	The Intermediate People's Court of Baotou City of Inner Mongolia Autonomous Region	175	6	5169
	The Intermediate People's Court of Shenyang City of Liaoning Province	71	0	2275
	The Intermediate People's Court of Dalian City of Liaoning Province	43	0	1343
	The Intermediate People's Court of Anshan City of Liaoning Province	38	0	966
	The Intermediate People's Court of Fushun City of Liaoning Province	36	0	835

(continued)

Table 2 (continued)

Type of court	Court	The average time interval (Days)	The minimum time interval (Days)	The maximum Time interval (Days)
	The Intermediate People's Court of Benxi City of Liaoning Province	62	0	1685
	The Intermediate People's Court of Changchun City of Jilin Province	64	1	1481
	The Intermediate People's Court of Jilin City of Jilin Province	35	0	1256
	The Intermediate People's Court of Harbin City of Heilongjiang Province	122	0	2539
	The Intermediate People's Court of Qiqihar City of Heilongjiang Province	169	1	1190
	The Intermediate People's Court of Nanjing City of Jiangsu Province	108	0	1172
	The Intermediate People's Court of Xuzhou City of Jiangsu Province	76	0	2426
	The Intermediate People's Court of Wuxi City of Jiangsu Province	102	0	3089
	The Intermediate People's Court of Suzhou City of Jiangsu Province	227	0	6475
	The Intermediate People's Court of Hangzhou City of Zhejiang Province	106	1	1454

(continued)

Table 2 (continued)

Type of court	Court	The average time interval (Days)	The minimum time interval (Days)	The maximum Time interval (Days)
	The Intermediate People's Court of Ningbo City of Zhejiang Province	148	2	2344
	The Intermediate People's Court of Hefei City of Anhui Province	89	0	2612
	The Intermediate People's Court of Huainan City of Anhui Province	38	1	1260
	The Intermediate People's Court of Fuzhou City of Fujian Province	160	2	3170
	The Intermediate People's Court of Xiamen City of Fujian Province	124	2	1171
	The Intermediate People's Court of Nanchang City of Jiangxi Province	77	0	3035
	The Intermediate People's Court of Jinan City of Shandong Province	119	0	1972
	The Intermediate People's Court of Qingdao City of Shandong Province	52	0	1271
	The Intermediate People's Court of Zibo City of Shandong Province	48	1	988
	The Intermediate People's Court of Zhengzhou City of Henan Province	42	0	1901

(continued)

Table 2 (continued)

Type of court	Court	The average time interval (Days)	The minimum time interval (Days)	The maximum Time interval (Days)
	The Intermediate People's Court of Luoyang City of Henan Province	130	1	2593
	The Intermediate People's Court of Wuhan City of Hubei Province	53	1	1805
	The Intermediate People's Court of Changsha City of Hunan Province	59	0	2191
	The Intermediate People's Court of Guangzhou City of Guangdong Province	59	1	2472
	The Intermediate People's Court of Shenzhen City of Guangdong Province	107	0	2236
	The Intermediate People's Court of Zhuhai City of Guangdong Province	125	1	1885
	The Intermediate People's Court of Shantou City of Guangdong Province	214	1	1751
	The Intermediate People's Court of Nanning City of Guangxi Zhuang Autonomous Region	254	6	1878
	The Intermediate People's Court of Haikou City of Hainan Province	100	1	1582

(continued)

Table 2 (continued)

Type of court	Court	The average time interval (Days)	The minimum time interval (Days)	The maximum Time interval (Days)
	The Intermediate People's Court of Chengdu City of Sichuan Province	122	2	1499
	The Intermediate People's Court of Guiyang City of Guizhou Province	131	1	1780
	The Intermediate People's Court of Kunming City of Yunnan Province	211	1	2487
	The Intermediate People's Court of Lhasa City of Xizang Autonomous Region	118	4	1583
	The Intermediate People's Court of Xi'an City of Shaanxi Province	93	0	2416
	The Intermediate People's Court of Lanzhou City of Gansu Province	59	4	840
	The Intermediate People's Court of Xining City of Qinghai Province	256	1	1832
	The Intermediate People's Court of Yinchuan City of Ningxia Hui Autonomous Region	109	7	1191
	The Intermediate People's Court of Urumqi City of Xinjiang Uygur Autonomous Region	21	1	1476

(continued)

Table 2 (continued)

Type of court	Court	The average time interval (Days)	The minimum time interval (Days)	The maximum Time interval (Days)
Primary people's courts	The Primary People's Court of Haidian District of Beijing Municipality	72	0	2317
	The Primary People's Court of Xicheng District of Beijing Municipality	86	1	2016
	The Primary People's Court of Fengtai District of Beijing Municipality	65	0	4204
	The Primary People's Court of Chaoyang District of Beijing Municipality	75	1	1791
	The Primary People's Court of Nankai District of Tianjin Municipality	53	0	1368
	The Primary People's Court of Wuqing District of Tianjin Municipality	81	0	1777
	The Primary People's Court of Hexi District of Tianjin Municipality	117	0	5081
	The Primary People's Court of Binhai New Area of Tianjin Municipality	109	0	1205

(continued)

Table 2 (continued)

Type of court	Court	The average time interval (Days)	The minimum time interval (Days)	The maximum Time interval (Days)
	The Primary People's Court of Chang'an District of Shijiazhuang City, Hebei Province	175	1	2872
	The Primary People's Court of Weichang Manchu and Mongolia Autonomous County of Hebei Province	87	1	1545
	The Primary People's Court of Haigang District of Qinhuangdao City, Hebei Province	297	1	2110
	The Primary People's Court of Sanhe City of Hebei Province	281	1	3152
	The Primary People's Court of Xiaodian District of Taiyuan City, Shanxi Province	146	1	2652
	The Primary People's Court of Yanhu District of Yuncheng City, Shanxi Province	161	10	1733
	The Primary People's Court of Hejin City of Shanxi Province	103	0	1551
	The Primary People's Court of Linyi County of Shanxi Province	130	0	1916

(continued)

Table 2 (continued)

Type of court	Court	The average time interval (Days)	The minimum time interval (Days)	The maximum Time interval (Days)
	The Primary People's Court of Saihan District of Hohhot City, Inner Mongolia Autonomous Region	148	3	1667
	The Primary People's Court of Ulanhot City of Inner Mongolia Autonomous Region	73	0	2125
	The Primary People's Court of Songshan District of Chifeng City, Inner Mongolia Autonomous Region	392	7	2353
	The Primary People's Court of Ar Horqin Banner of Inner Mongolia Autonomous Region	146	1	1025
	The Primary People's Court of Shenhe District of Shenyang City, Liaoning Province	71	0	2306
	The Primary People's Court of Heping District of Shenyang City, Liaoning Province	96	0	3042
	The Primary People's Court of Haicheng City of Liaoning Province	56	1	2611

(continued)

Table 2 (continued)

Type of court	Court	The average time interval (Days)	The minimum time interval (Days)	The maximum Time interval (Days)
	The Primary People's Court of Suizhong County of Liaoning Province	44	1	445
	The Primary People's Court of Chaoyang District of Changchun City, Jilin Province	31	0	488
	The Primary People's Court of Ningjiang District of Songyuan City, Jilin Province	88	0	860
	The Primary People's Court of Qian Gorlos Mongolia Autonomous County of Jilin Province	49	0	2735
	The Primary People's Court of Yanji City of Jilin Province	48	0	1039
	The Primary People's Court of Daoli District of Harbin City, Heilongjiang Province	254	1	2303
	The Primary People's Court of Nangang District of Harbin City, Heilongjiang Province	200	1	2259
	The Primary People's Court of Binxian County of Heilongjiang Province	89	1	1077

(continued)

Table 2 (continued)

Type of court	Court	The average time interval (Days)	The minimum time interval (Days)	The maximum Time interval (Days)
	The Primary People's Court of Nehe City of Heilongjiang Province	119	0	1633
	The Primary People's Court of Minhang District of Shanghai Municipality	369	0	5772
	The Primary People's Court of Pudong New Area of Shanghai Municipality	341	0	2742
	The Primary People's Court of Jing'an District of Shanghai Municipality	174	0	3430
	The Primary People's Court of Hongkou District of Shanghai Municipality	257	1	2391
	The Primary People's Court of Shuyang County of Jiangsu Province	187	0	2224
	The Primary People's Court of Jiangyin City of Jiangsu Province	162	0	2018
	The Primary People's Court of Wujiang District of Suzhou City, Jiangsu Province	99	0	2135
	The Primary People's Court of Kunshan City of Jiangsu Province	163	4	2911

(continued)

Table 2 (continued)

Type of court	Court	The average time interval (Days)	The minimum time interval (Days)	The maximum Time interval (Days)
	The Primary People's Court of Yuhang District of Hangzhou City, Zhejiang Province	100	1	1766
	The Primary People's Court of Cangnan County of Zhejiang Province	118	2	1381
	The Primary People's Court of Zhuji City of Zhejiang Province	85	1	948
	The Primary People's Court of Yiwu City of Zhejiang Province	162	1	1313
	The Primary People's Court of Yaohai District of Hefei City, Anhui Province	179	1	3610
	The Primary People's Court of Baohe District of Hefei City, Anhui Province	160	1	1711
	The Primary People's Court of Taihe County of Anhui Province	114	1	2567
	The Primary People's Court of Chaohu City of Anhui Province	97	1	1573
	The Primary People's Court of Siming District of Xiamen City, Fujian Province	118	2	3440

(continued)

Table 2 (continued)

Type of court	Court	The average time interval (Days)	The minimum time interval (Days)	The maximum Time interval (Days)
	The Primary People's Court of Huli District of Xiamen City, Fujian Province	163	1	3162
	The Primary People's Court of Jinjiang City of Fujian Province	200	1	3250
	The Primary People's Court of Huian County of Fujian Province	120	2	1014
	The Primary People's Court of Donghu District of Nanchang City, Jiangxi Province	118	1	2066
	The Primary People's Court of Xihu District of Nanchang City, Jiangxi Province	124	1	2406
	The Primary People's Court of Nanchang County of Jiangxi Province	58	1	1980
	The Primary People's Court of Gao'an City of Jiangxi Province	27	1	1546
	The Primary People's Court of Huangdao District of Qingdao City, Shandong Province	776	0	2414
	The Primary People's Court of Jiaozhou City of Shandong Province	88	1	4166

(continued)

Table 2 (continued)

Type of court	Court	The average time interval (Days)	The minimum time interval (Days)	The maximum Time interval (Days)
	The Primary People's Court of Lanshan District of Linyi City, Shandong Province	170	2	2473
	The Primary People's Court of Feixian County of Shandong Province	102	1	1532
	The Primary People's Court of Jinshui District of Zhengzhou City, Henan Province	88	1	2316
	The Primary People's Court of Xinzheng City of Henan Province	46	1	1360
	The Primary People's Court of Zhengzhou High-Tech Industrial Development Zone of Henan Province	27	0	1911
	The Primary People's Court of Huaxian County of Henan Province	52	1	2089
	The Primary People's Court of Jiang'an District of Wuhan City, Hubei Province	55	1	1246
	The Primary People's Court of Wuchang District of Wuhan City, Hubei Province	143	1	3885
	The Primary People's Court of Yangxin County of Hubei Province	66	1	2538

(continued)

Table 2 (continued)

Type of court	Court	The average time interval (Days)	The minimum time interval (Days)	The maximum Time interval (Days)
	The Primary People's Court of Enshi City of Hubei Province	50	1	1357
	The Primary People's Court of Yuelu District of Changsha City, Hunan Province	41	1	2014
	The Primary People's Court of Furong District of Changsha City, Hunan Province	29	0	2239
	The Primary People's Court of Liuyang City of Hunan Province	31	0	1551
	The Primary People's Court of Youxian County of Hunan Province	40	1	1167
	The Primary People's Court of Yuexiu District of Guangzhou City, Guangdong Province	341	1	3520
	The Primary People's Court of Futian District of Shenzhen City, Guangdong Province	253	0	3053
	The Primary People's Court of Huidong County of Guangdong Province	339	0	2629
	The Primary People's Court of Yingde City of Guangdong Province	223	1	3413

(continued)

Table 2 (continued)

Type of court	Court	The average time interval (Days)	The minimum time interval (Days)	The maximum Time interval (Days)
	The Primary People's Court of Qingxiu District of Nanning City, Guangxi Zhuang Autonomous Region	453	1	3324
	The Primary People's Court of Xixiangtang District of Nanning City, Guangxi Zhuang Autonomous Region	347	2	1956
	The Primary People's Court of Binyang County of Guangxi Zhuang Autonomous Region	377	2	2755
	The Primary People's Court of Guiping City of Guangxi Zhuang Autonomous Region	326	3	3180
	The Primary People's Court of Longhua District of Haikou City, Hainan Province	276	1	2144
	The Primary People's Court of Meilan District of Haikou City, Hainan Province	205	1	1461
	The Primary People's Court of Chengmai County of Hainan Province	130	1	798

(continued)

Table 2 (continued)

Type of court	Court	The average time interval (Days)	The minimum time interval (Days)	The maximum Time interval (Days)
	The Primary People's Court of Danzhou City of Hainan Province	147	1	889
	The Primary People's Court of Jiangbei District of Chongqing Municipality	78	0	1674
	The Primary People's Court of Yubei District of Chongqing Municipality	75	1	1059
	The Primary People's Court of Yunyang County of Chongqing Municipality	51	0	1037
	The Primary People's Court of Yuzhong District of Chongqing Municipality	82	1	1615
	The Primary People's Court of Qingyang District of Chengdu City, Sichuan Province	84	2	2317
	The Primary People's Court of Pidu District of Chengdu City, Sichuan Province	84	1	1144
	The Primary People's Court of Chengdu High-Tech Industrial Development Zone of Sichuan Province	111	1	1839

(continued)

Table 2 (continued)

Type of court	Court	The average time interval (Days)	The minimum time interval (Days)	The maximum Time interval (Days)
	The Primary People's Court of Langzhong City of Sichuan Province	86	2	1898
	The Primary People's Court of Yunyan District of Guiyang City, Guizhou Province	161	1	1476
	The Primary People's Court of Nanming District of Guiyang City, Guizhou Province	99	1	1998
	The Primary People's Court of Xishui County of Guizhou Province	334	1	1956
	The Primary People's Court of Xingyi City of Guizhou Province	106	0	1412
	The Primary People's Court of Wuhua District of Kunming City, Yunnan Province	179	1	2114
	The Primary People's Court of Xishan District of Kunming City, Yunnan Province	81	1	2215
	The Primary People's Court of Xuanwei City of Yunnan Province	345	0	2259
	The Primary People's Court of Zhenxiong County of Yunnan Province	116	0	2203

(continued)

Table 2 (continued)

Type of court	Court	The average time interval (Days)	The minimum time interval (Days)	The maximum Time interval (Days)
	The Primary People's Court of Chengguan District of Lhasa City, Xizang Autonomous Region	104	3	1413
	The Primary People's Court of Lhünzhub County of Xizang Autonomous Region	86	10	663
	The Primary People's Court of Doilungdêqên County of Xizang Autonomous Region	216	2	996
	The Primary People's Court of Gar County of Xizang Autonomous Region	111	9	516
	The Primary People's Court of Weiyang District of Xi'an City, Shaanxi Province	66	0	1474
	The Primary People's Court of Yanta District of Xi'an City, Shaanxi Province	76	1	1774
	The Primary People's Court of Dingbian County of Shaanxi Province	35	0	624
	The Primary People's Court of Shenmu City of Shaanxi Province	177	0	2374

(continued)

Table 2 (continued)

Type of court	Court	The average time interval (Days)	The minimum time interval (Days)	The maximum Time interval (Days)
	The Primary People's Court of Chengguan District of Lanzhou City, Gansu Province	69	3	943
	The Primary People's Court of Yumen City of Gansu Province	248	10	2636
	The Primary People's Court of Ganzhou District of Zhangye City, Gansu Province	85	1	1951
	The Primary People's Court of Longxi County of Gansu Province	47	1	705
	The Primary People's Court of Chengdong District of Xining City, Qinghai Province	224	1	1858
	The Primary People's Court of Chengbei District of Xining City, Qinghai Province	84	1	2110
	The Primary People's Court of Huangzhong District of Xining City, Qinghai Province	30	1	917
	The Primary People's Court of Golmud City of Qinghai Province	322	0	2442

(continued)

Table 2 (continued)

Type of court	Court	The average time interval (Days)	The minimum time interval (Days)	The maximum Time interval (Days)
	The Primary People's Court of Xingqing District of Yinchuan City, Ningxia Hui Autonomous Region	71	1	2201
	The Primary People's Court of Jinfeng District of Yinchuan City, Ningxia Hui Autonomous Region	148	2	2226
	The Primary People's Court of Lingwu City of Ningxia Hui Autonomous Region	109	3	1565
	The Primary People's Court of Helan County of Ningxia Hui Autonomous Region	117	1	2120
	The Primary People's Court of Sayibak District of Urumqi City, Xinjiang Uygur Autonomous Region	53	1	1436
	The Primary People's Court of Xinshi District of Urumqi City, Xinjiang Uygur Autonomous Region	44	2	1064
	The Primary People's Court of Kuqa City of Aksu Prefecture, Xinjiang Uygur Autonomous Region	23	1	305

(continued)

Table 2 (continued)

Type of court	Court	The average time interval (Days)	The minimum time interval (Days)	The maximum Time interval (Days)
	The Primary People's Court of Changji City of Changji Hui Autonomous Prefecture, Xinjiang Uygur Autonomous Region	40	1	813

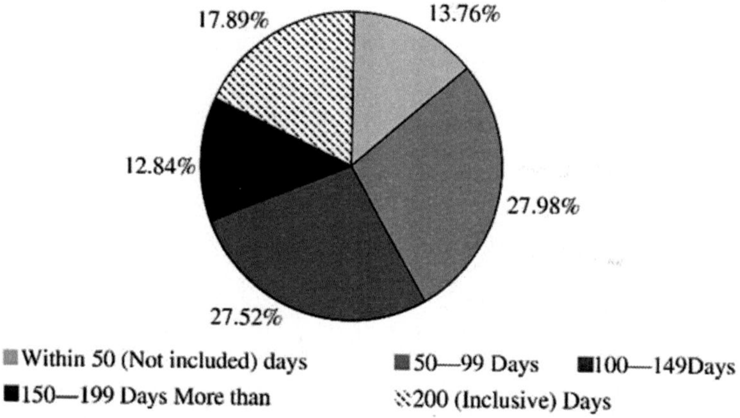

Fig. 48 Distribution of courts regarding the average time interval between making judgments and publishing them online

whether these judgments took effect between the end of 2019 and September 2020, had already been in force but were slow to be disclosed, or had been re-uploaded for other reasons.

7 Disclosure of Enforcement Information

Enforcement is a critical part of realizing judicial judgments. Disclosing enforcement information can satisfy the need of the parties to know the progress and that of society to supervise law enforcement. Also, it helps build the social consensus and fulfill the comprehensive enforcement management. The assessment shows many striking measures some courts took in disclosing enforcement information, such as setting

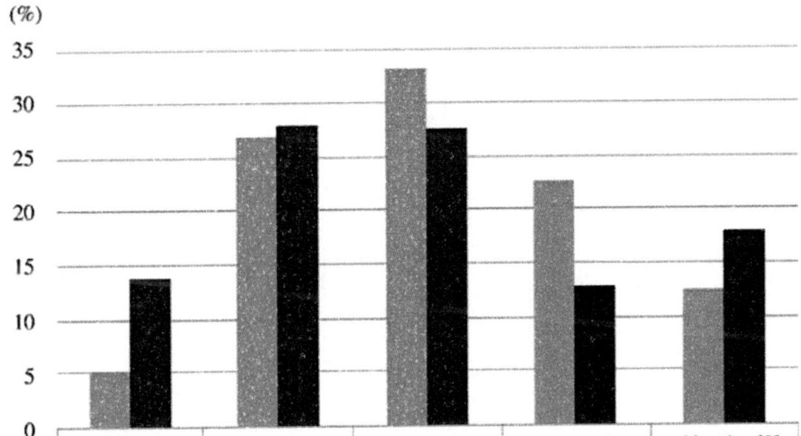

	Within 50 (Not included) Days	50—99 Days	100—149 Days	150—199 Days	More than 200 (Inclusive) Days
2018Year	5.00%	26.88%	33.13%	22.50%	12.50%
2020Year	13.76%	27.98%	27.52%	12.84%	17.89%

Fig. 49 A comparison of the average time interval between 2018 and 2020

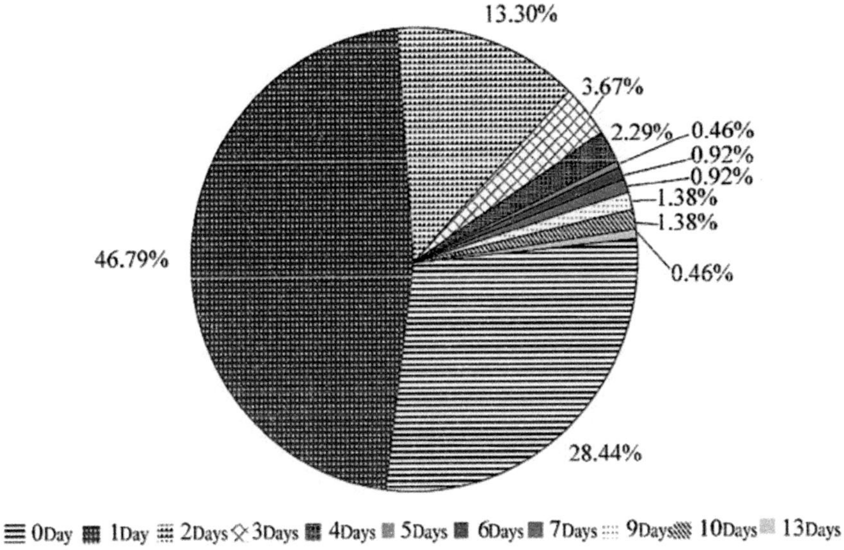

Fig. 50 Distribution of courts in terms of the minimum time interval

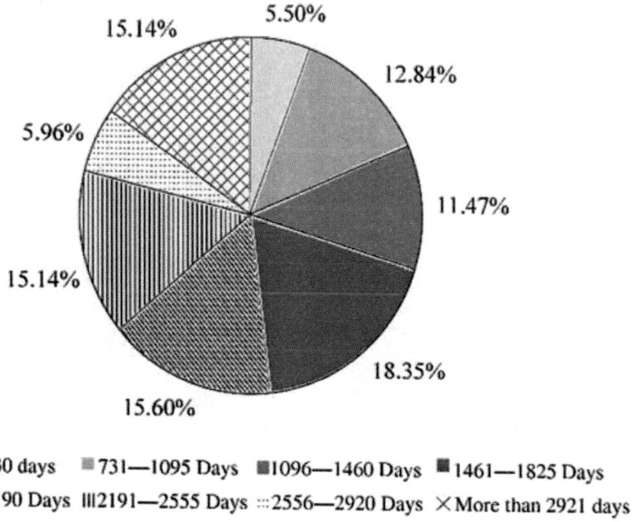

Fig. 51 Distribution of courts in terms of the maximum time interval

up columns and sub-columns on the court website to disclose enforcement information by category to facilitate inquiries. For example, the Intermediate People's Court of Qingdao City of Shandong Province had a precise classification and relatively complete disclosure of enforcement information. The Intermediate People's Court of Shantou City of Guangdong Province classified the punishments for refusing to pay a judgment or ruling into fines, detention, and a crime for refusing to fulfill a judgment or ruling. However, overall, the enforcement information disclosure was not good enough. Only one high people's court and five intermediate people's courts disclosed information on fines on their website, accounting for 3.13% and 10.20%, respectively. Only one high people's court, three intermediate people's courts, and one primary people's court disclosed information on detention, accounting for 3.13%, 6.12%, and 0.84%, respectively. Only five high people's courts, four intermediate people's courts, and two primary people's courts disclosed information on exit restrictions, accounting for 15.63%, 8.16%, and 1.68%, respectively. Only one intermediate people's court disclosed information on those cases involving refusal to fulfill a judgment or ruling, accounting for 2.04%. Nine high people's courts, 21 intermediate people's courts, four specialized Courts, and 51 primary people's courts disclosed the information on dishonest judgment debtors, accounting for 28.13%, 42.86%, 30.33%, and 42.86%, respectively. Four high people's courts, 12 intermediate people's courts, three specialized courts, and ten primary people's courts disclosed information on dishonest special judgment debtors, accounting for 12.50%, 24.49%, 25.00%, and 8.40%, respectively. Only two high people's courts, six intermediate people's courts, two specialized courts, and four primary people's courts disclosed and kept updating the cases in which enforcement proceedings were terminated, accounting for 6.25%, 12.24%, 16.67%, and 3.36%, respectively. Only two high people's courts, one intermediate people's court, one specialized court, and one primary people's court disclosed the rulings on those cases in which enforcement proceedings were terminated in the past three months on the court website, accounting for 6.25%, 2.04%, 8.33%, and 0.84%, respectively.

Generally, the disclosure of enforcement information by the courts of the four types was far from satisfactory. Some courts failed to timely update the enforcement-related information. Although many courts had set up relevant columns and disclosed some data, there was no updated content for a long time, with the latest data published in 2018. Most of the courts assessed in 2020 set up an enforcement information disclosure column on the website. However, some courts did not disclose any relevant information; some courts did not timely update information; some courts did not disclose information regularly. For example, some courts set up a column on enforcement disclosure on the homepage and several sub-columns, but no information was found. Some courts did not disclose auction announcements on the court website, and the latest information on the website of Litigation Assets of People's Courts was posted in 2018.

8 Disclosure of Judicial Reform Information

The judicial system reform is an integral part of comprehensively promoting the reform. Making public relevant policies, measures, and reform progress and allowing all walks of life to participate in the reform helps guarantee the scientific nature of reform measures. In March 2015, at the 21st Collective Study Session of the Political Bureau of the CPC Central Committee, General Secretary Xi Jinping emphasized that to further the reform of the judicial system, we need to have views from the people. We also need to thoroughly study the actual judicial situation and understand what the people expect. We need to have the number of problems solved and the people's satisfaction with the solutions as the criteria for judging the effects of the reform.[10] Therefore, it is essential to disclose judicial reform information to the public. One can participate in and appraise and supervise the reform when they are well-informed. According to the Opinions of the Supreme People's Court on Furthering Judicial Openness (Fa Fa [2018] No. 20), people's courts should take the initiative in disclosing judicial reform documents, the progress of major judicial reform tasks, typical cases regarding the judicial reform, and other information that should be known by society.

However, the assessment shows that although the number of courts of the original three types that disclosed judicial reform information slightly increased compared with that in the 2019 Assessment, the overall situation of judicial reform information disclosure was still poor. Only 15 high people's courts, 18 intermediate people's

[10] Xi Jinping emphasized at the 21st Collective Study Session of the Political Bureau of the CPC Central Committee: firmly further the reform of the judicial system with the improvement of judicial credibility as the fundamental standard. *People's Daily*, March 26, 2015, at the front page.

courts, six specialized courts, and 17 primary people's courts set up a column on judicial reform on the court website, accounting for 46.88%, 36.73%, 50.00%, and 14.29%, respectively.

Eight high people's courts, ten intermediate people's courts, one specialized court, and five primary people's courts disclosed the overall plan for judicial reform, accounting for 25.00%, 20.41%, 8.33%, and 4.20%, respectively. Two high people's courts, seven intermediate people's courts, and five primary people's courts disclosed the plan for selecting quota judges, accounting for 6.25%, 12.24%, and 4.20%, respectively. One high people's court, seven intermediate people's courts, and four primary people's courts disclosed the plan for removing quota judges, accounting for 3.13%, 14.29%, and 3.36%, respectively. One high people's court, seven intermediate people's courts, and four primary people's courts disclosed the plan for job security, accounting for 3.13%, 14.29%, and 3.36%, respectively.

Twelve high people's courts, 18 intermediate people's courts, two specialized courts, and 27 primary people's courts disclosed the reform progress, accounting for 37.50%, 36.73%, 16.67%, and 22.69%, respectively.

Three intermediate people's courts and one primary people's court disclosed the number of cases handled by every quota judge, accounting for 6.12% and 0.84%, respectively. Two high people's courts, four intermediate people's courts, one specialized court, and two primary people's courts disclosed the aggregate data on handling cases by quota judges, accounting for 6.25%, 8.16%, 8.33%, and 1.68%, respectively. Two high people's courts, four intermediate people's courts, and one primary people's court disclosed the number of cases handled by every court president and chief judge, accounting for 6.25%, 8.16%, and 0.84%, respectively. Three high people's courts, six intermediate people's courts, two specialized courts, and one primary people's court disclosed the aggregate data on the handling of cases by court presidents and chief judges, accounting for 9.38%, 12.24%, 16.67%, and 0.84%, respectively.

Twenty-six high people's courts, 35 intermediate people's courts, seven specialized courts, and 27 primary people's courts disclosed a support system for case filing registration, accounting for 81.25%, 71.43%, 58.33%, and 21.69%, respectively. One high people's court and nine intermediate people's courts disclosed the dynamic data on case filing registration, accounting for 3.13% and 18.37%, respectively.

Regarding the reform of a novel trial supervision mechanism, one high people's court, six intermediate people's courts, and four primary people's courts disclosed the list of powers and responsibilities, accounting for 3.13%, 12.24%, and 3.36%, respectively. One high people's court, eight intermediate people's courts, one specialized court, and four primary people's courts disclosed the support regulations on trial management and supervision powers, accounting for 3.13%, 16.33%, 8.33%, and 3.36%, respectively.

As far as indicators for the protection of lawyers' rights and interests were concerned, six high people's courts, seven intermediate people's courts, one specialized court, and five primary people's courts disclosed the implementation mechanism, accounting for 18.75%, 14.29%, 8.33%, and 4.20%, respectively. Four high people's courts, seven intermediate people's courts, and two primary people's courts disclosed the feedback channels, accounting for 12.50%, 14.29%, and 1.68%, respectively.

One high people's court, five intermediate people's courts, and one specialized court disclosed a record of the intervention by non-parties, accounting for 3.13%, 10.20%, and 8.33%, respectively.

It can be concluded from the above data that the judicial reform information disclosure did not receive due attention from courts at all levels, and the overall situation was severe. Moreover, the data shows that the lower a court was, the poorer its disclosure was. Indeed, the lower courts are the judicial reform's main objects and implementers. However, despite the demands for disclosure from the Supreme People's Court, the courts at all levels still performed poorly, which suffices to show that the implementation of relevant policies was highly unsatisfactory.

9 Disclosure of Judicial Data

Strengthening the collection and utilization of judicial data is the basis for refining the court's internal management. Disclosing relevant data helps the public understand the court's work, supervise it, and enhance their trust. It is also helpful for the government to use appropriate data to guide the public to view the court's work objectively and impartially. The assessment shows that some courts set up a judicial statistics (data disclosure) column on the website and divided it into multiple sub-columns, such as financial data, litigation fee collection and refund, case collection and settlement, and analysis reports. For example, the Intermediate People's Court of Qingdao City of Shandong Province designed a data disclosure column in which relevant business data, financial information, litigation fee collection and refund, and other information were disclosed in a comprehensive and specific manner. The Intermediate People's Court of Shantou City of Guangdong Province and the High People's Court of Guangdong Province set up a judicial statistics column to disclose relevant information on the website. The Intermediate People's Court of Ningbo City disclosed the dynamic data of cases accepted and settled in real time daily, and its records could be inquired. The Court's work reports were also disclosed from 2001 to 2020 (2004 not included). Overall, in 2020, the courts performed the best in disclosing financial data. The disclosure of case handling data and data analysis reports was slightly poor. The disclosure of the data on the property involved and on collection and refund of litigation fees was the least satisfactory.

Information on the fiscal budget and final account is an essential part of the information on the administrative affairs of a court. Disclosing the sources and uses of budgetary funds is the duty of public authorities at all levels and the essential requirement for them to perform their duties by law. It is also an effective way to accept public supervision and fight corruption and a key measure to further the reform and promote transparency in finance. Over the years, the state has been sparing no effort to promote the disclosure of financial information of various departments. The more standardized and detailed disclosure by governments at all levels of their fiscal budget and final account and their use of "Three Official" expenses[11] has promoted the disclosure of financial information by courts and other authorities. According to the 2020 Assessment results, among the high people's courts, 32 disclosed the current year's budget (three publishing it on the government website), 30 disclosed the previous year's final account (four publishing it on the government website), and 30 disclosed the final account of the "Three Official" expenses (four publishing it on the government website), accounting for 100.00%, 93.75%, and 93.75%, respectively. Among the intermediate people's courts, 47 disclosed the current year's budget (three publishing it on the government website), 41 disclosed the previous year's final account, and 42 disclosed the final account of the "Three Official" expenses, accounting for 95.92%, 83.67%, and 85.71%, respectively. Among the specialized courts, ten disclosed the current year's budget, seven disclosed the previous year's final account, and eight disclosed the final account of the "Three Official" expenses, accounting for 83.33%, 58.33%, and 66.67%, respectively. Among the primary people's courts, 83 disclosed the current year's budget (15 publishing it on the government website), 65 disclosed the previous year's final account (nine publishing it on the government website), and 65 disclosed the final account of the "Three Official" expenses (nine publishing on the government website), accounting for 69.75%, 54.62%, and 54.62%, respectively (see Fig. 52). In general, the disclosure of the fiscal budget was better than that of the final account of "Three Official" expenses and better than that of the final account. Besides, the courts at the higher level performed better in disclosing financial data. The performance by the primary people's courts in financial data disclosure was much poorer.

A people's court should report its work to the people's congress at the same level. The content of its work report should be reviewed by members of the people's congress and be disclosed to the public so that the public can understand its accomplishments, future working plans, and other things. According to the 2020 Assessment results, among the high people's courts, 16 disclosed the work report on the website, one disclosed its report on the government website, three disclosed the report on platforms such as the WeChat official account, and five disclosed the report through other media, accounting for 50.00%, 3.13%, 9.38%, and 15.63% respectively. Among the intermediate people's courts, 23 disclosed the work report on the website, no court disclosed the report on the government website, seven disclosed the report on platforms such as the WeChat official account, and six disclosed the report through other media, accounting for 46.94%, 0.00%, 14.29%, and 12.24%, respectively. One specialized court disclosed its work report on its website, and two disclosed the report through other media, accounting for 8.33% and 16.67%, respectively. Among the primary people's courts, 18 disclosed the work report on the website, four disclosed the report on the government website, 14 disclosed the report on platforms such as the WeChat official account, and nine disclosed the report through other media, accounting for 15.13%, 3.36%, 11.76%, and 7.89%, respectively (see Fig. 53). Although a specialized court does not need to report its work to

[11] "Three Official" expenses: the spending on official overseas visits, official vehicles, and official hospitality.

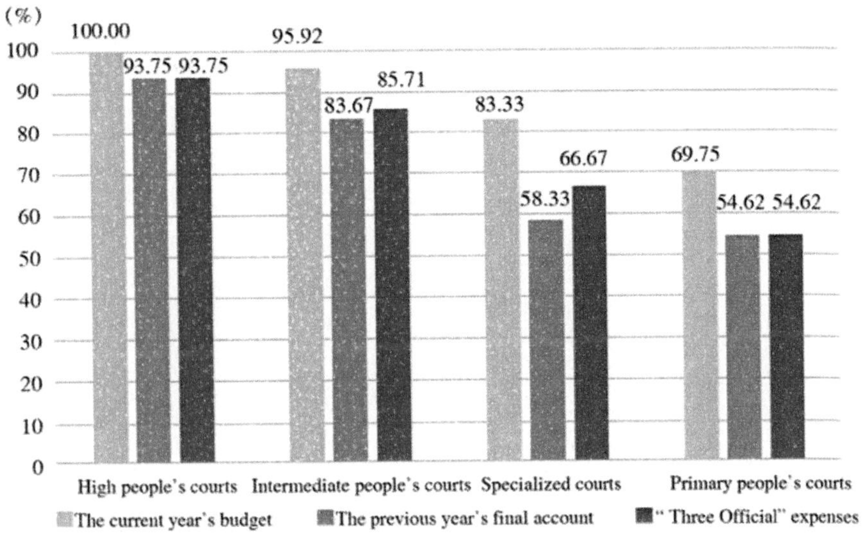

Fig. 52 Financial data disclosure by courts of all types

the people's congress, it does need to report its previous year's work to the society. The assessment results reveal the unsatisfactory disclosure. The above data presents the disclosure of work reports by the courts through various channels. Generally, a relatively high proportion of the primary people's courts did not release a work report. Seventy-four primary people's courts did not disclose the work report of the previous year, with a proportion of 62.18%.

Information on trials by people's courts serves as a barometer of national economic development, social work, and life. The Information Center of the Supreme People's Court has completed 850 research projects based on information about cases and judgments gathered from various platforms. More than 40 reports have been released to the public, covering divorce disputes, criminal cases caused by conflicts between bus drivers and passengers, cybercrimes, and other hot issues concerning the Party, the government, and the public. These analysis reports on judicial data play a significant role in assisting the central government's decision-making, helping the modernization management of the court, and enhancing the public's awareness of the rule of law.

Disclosing all kinds of statistics is helpful for a court to objectively show the situation and effect of its adjudication and enforcement. It also serves the public. In particular, disclosing the analysis of some judicial data promotes education in the general knowledge of the law and guides public behaviors. The 2020 Assessment shows that the disclosure of judicial data by the courts was not satisfactory. Six high people's courts, ten intermediate people's courts, one specialized court, and five primary people's courts disclosed judicial data monthly, accounting for 18.75%, 20.41%, 8.33%, and 4.20%, respectively. Only one high people's court, ten intermediate people's courts, one specialized court, and one primary people's court

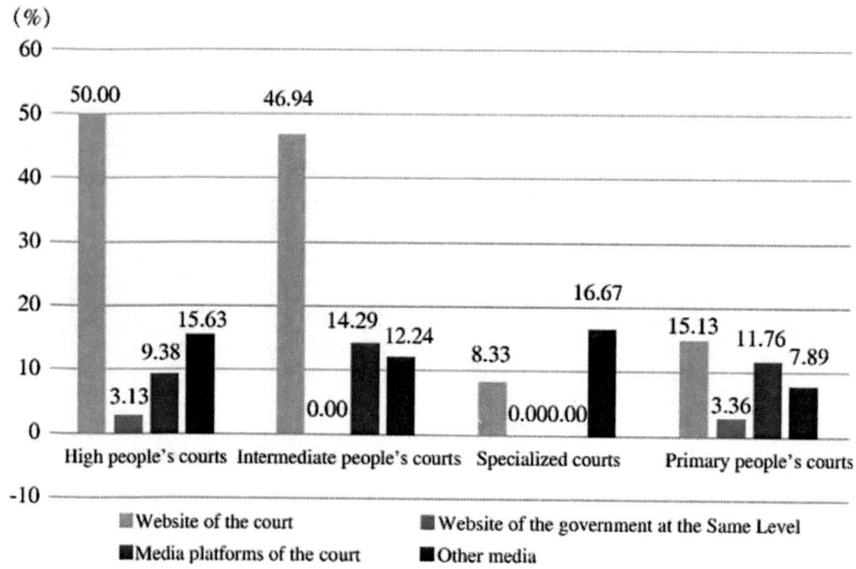

Fig. 53 Work report disclosure by courts of all types

disclosed the big data analysis report, accounting for 3.13%, 20.41%, 8.33%, and 0.84%, respectively. One high people's court, 12 intermediate people's courts, one specialized court, and nine primary people's courts disclosed the analysis report on judicial research, accounting for 3.13%, 24.49%, 8.33%, and 7.56%, respectively.

Only one high people's court and three intermediate people's courts disclosed the data on the property involved in a case and on collection and refund of litigation fees, accounting for 3.13% and 6.12%, respectively. It indicates that the courts have not generally recognized the disclosure of such relatively sensitive data.

In general, the lower a court was, the less satisfactory its judicial data disclosure was. In particular, most primary people's courts were generally weak in disclosing judicial data and related data analysis reports.

Besides, the contents of the disclosed judicial data differed from court to court. For judicial data on cases accepted and settled, some people's courts disclosed only the general data. However, they did not disclose the data on cases handled by every judge and when the data was collected. For example, the Intermediate People's Court of Changchun City disclosed the general data but failed to disclose when the data was collected. Many courts disclosed only the general data on cases accepted and settled.

In addition, the disclosure methods and channels differed. For example, fiscal budgets, final accounts, and other information were disclosed through channels such as the court website, the government website, and the WeChat official account, which was not convenient for the public to inquire about relevant information. For data on cases accepted and settled, some courts disclosed it on the website of a higher court; some courts disclosed it on their own website. Moreover, some courts did not set up a column on judicial data disclosure, causing difficulty in searching for data. For example, the fiscal budget and final account reports were scattered in different columns on the court website. Some courts had the court work report, the budget report, and the final account report mixed with other news on the website, making it difficult to inquire for relevant information.

10 Construction of Openness Platforms

Like disclosure of government affairs, judicial openness could rely on various methods, such as traditional news media, bulletin boards, and printed materials. However, websites and media platforms are undoubtedly the channels of the most significant value for judicial openness in the information age. The effect of the court's judicial openness is primarily judged by its portal's construction and its media platforms' operation. To this end, as provided in the Opinions of the Supreme People's Court on Furthering Judicial Openness, we should strengthen the construction and management of the websites of people's courts by actively adapting to the development of information technology and the innovation of dissemination methods. We should enhance the capacity of the websites of people's courts to serve judicial openness, respond to public concerns, and advocate the spirit of the rule of law. We should strive to build the websites of people's courts into timely, accurate, standardized, and efficient judicial openness platforms, interaction and communication platforms, and public service platforms. We should strengthen the content construction and standardized management of the websites by enhancing the release and updating of information and timely consolidating and removing those columns and sections in which the updating of contents cannot be guaranteed so as to avoid negative impacts on judicial disclosure arising out of untimely updating of contents, release of inaccurate information, and failure to respond to opinions and suggestions. In addition, we should strengthen the overall planning of the construction of court websites nationwide and formulate and improve guidelines on the development of court websites nationwide to specify the functional orientations and content construction requirements of court websites and set up unified technical standards.

The project team verified the retrieval function of court websites in the 2020 Assessment. According to the results, the assessed 32 high people's courts had the website equipped with an effective retrieval function. Among the 49 intermediate people's courts in larger cities, 41 had the website equipped with such function, accounting for 83.67%. Nine of the 12 specialized courts had the website equipped with the effective retrieval function, accounting for 75%. Among the 119 primary people's courts, 99 had the website equipped with the effective retrieval function, accounting for 83.19%. The websites of the specialized courts had a relatively poorer retrieval function, which did not conform to their status.

Regarding media platforms' construction and operation, the 2020 Assessment focused on information disclosure by courts of all kinds and at all levels on WeChat and Weibo. Among the 32 high people's courts, 28 disclosed the entrance to their

WeChat platform on the website, two did not disclose this information, and one did not have a WeChat account, accounting for 87.5%, 6.25%, and 3.13%, respectively. Among the 49 intermediate people's courts in larger cities, 42 disclosed the entrance to the Wechat platform on the portal, and seven failed to do so, accounting for 85.71% and 14.29%, respectively. Among the specialized courts, nine disclosed the entrance to the WeChat platform on the website, and three failed, accounting for 75% and 25%, respectively. Among the 119 primary people's courts, 69 disclosed the entrance on the website, 46 did not disclose such information, and four did not have a WeChat account, accounting for 57.98%, 38.66%, and 3.36%, respectively. In terms of the update of the WeChat platform, among the high people's courts, 31 updated it every week. Among the intermediate people's courts, 47 updated it weekly, and two updated it more than a week apart, accounting for 95.92% and 4.08%, respectively. Among the specialized courts, ten updated it weekly, one had an update interval of more than a week, and one had not updated it for a long time, accounting for 83.33%, 8.33%, and 8.33%, respectively. Among the 119 primary people's courts, 98 updated it weekly, 17 updated it more than a week apart, and four did not have a WeChat account, accounting for 82.35%, 14.29%, and 3.36%, respectively. Generally, the courts at the higher lever performed more actively in disclosing information through media platforms. Seemingly, a court at the higher level should have had more content to release on its WeChat platform. A primary people's court has more contact with the public, so the public is more eager for the information that may be disclosed through media platforms, such as information on the court work and its case handling. However, the actual situation was not satisfactory.

The Assessment also shows that some courts' WeChat and Weibo accounts were missing or wrong. After scanning the WeChat QR code and Weibo QR code of the Primary People's Court of Furong District of Changsha City, we entered the WeChat and Weibo pages of the Primary People's Court of Zhenyuan Yi, Hani, and Lahu Autonomous County under the jurisdiction of Pu'er City of Yunnan Province. The Weibo account of the Primary People's Court of Sichuan Pilot Free Trade Zone was linked to the official Weibo page of the Primary People's Court of Morin Dawa Daur Autonomous Banner of Hulunbeier City of Inner Mongolia Autonomous Region. The WeChat official account of the Primary People's Court of Pidu District of Chengdu City of Sichuan Province was found to have been moved. However, the new QR code was not disclosed on its website. The WeChat official account of Guangzhou Intellectual Property Court had a low update frequency, and no information was updated after July 20, 2017.

Judicial openness should also meet the needs of different groups of people, which entails consideration for non-Chinese-speaking people and those who have difficulty browsing the Internet. First, as the opening-up goes wider, more and more people overseas need to make contact with Chinese courts and obtain relevant information on them through court websites. The assessment reveals that very few courts provided multilingual versions of the website. Only one high people's court, three intermediate people's courts, and eight specialized courts provided multilingual versions of the website, namely the High People's Court of Shanghai Municipality, the Intermediate People's Court of Guangzhou City, the Intermediate People's Court of Haikou City, the Intermediate People's Court of Xiamen City, Beijing Internet Court, Shanghai Intellectual Property Court, the Primary People's Court of Shenzhen Qianhai Cooperation Zone of Guangdong Province, the Primary People's Court of Guangdong Free Trade Zone (Nansha) of Guangdong Province, the Primary People's Court of Zhuhai Hengqin New Area, the Primary People's Court of Sichuan Pilot Free Trade Zone, Shanghai Financial Court, and the Primary People's Court of Chongqing Pilot Free Trade Zone. The specialized courts, such as the people's courts of free trade zones, performed far better than other courts in providing multilingual versions of the website. For example, the Primary People's Court of Zhuhai Hengqin New Area provided three linguistic versions of its website: Chinese, English, and Portuguese.

Strengthening the accessibility construction of websites is a meaningful way to bridge the "digital divide", embody "information equality", and facilitate the access of the disabled and other special groups to information and public cultural services. It helps benefit people through the Internet, encourages special groups to participate in social life and share society's material and cultural achievements, and builds an inclusive society. It is also a sign of social civilization and progress. According to the Guidelines on Strengthening the Construction of Accessibility Service of Websites jointly issued by the China Disabled Persons' Federation and the Office of the Central Cyberspace Affairs Commission, we should continuously improve information accessibility to meet the requirements of the disabled, senior citizens, and other special groups for information on the Internet. This Assessment shows that only one high people's court, three intermediate people's courts, and one primary people's court had the website equipped with the accessibility function, proving that information accessibility has not received enough attention in judicial openness and website construction.

In addition, some courts disclosed on the website less information on the court work but more irrelevant information. For example, many columns on the websites of the Primary People's Court of Youxian County of Hunan Province and the Primary People's Court of Chaohu City of Anhui Province had too much redundant information irrelevant to their work, such as Chaohu Culture, Chaohu Landscape, and Chaohu Specialties.

In fact, in addition to the retrieval function, multilingual versions, information accessibility, and media platforms that this Assessment focused on, it can also be found from the previous analysis of relevant information disclosure that the website construction of courts nationwide was generally poor. For instance, multiple platforms for judicial disclosure were running simultaneously, and similar information was disclosed on different platforms with inconsistent content. The layout of website columns was not scientific or rigorous, and sometimes the litigation guide was placed under the column on law popularization. The information disclosed was not well displayed for convenience, resulting in much information stacked in one column. The absence of sub-columns and the effective retrieval function made it inconvenient for the public to search for information, thus damaging the disclosure effect.

References

1. Zhou, Y., & Xie, Z. (2004). Civil Litigation Risks and Their Prevention and Control. *The People's Judicature*: (11).
2. Center for National Index of Rule of Law of CASS. (2016). *A Third Party Assessment Report on the Informatization of Chinese Courts.* China Social Sciences Press, pp. 56–57.
3. Li, L., & Tian, H. (2017). *Blue Book of Rule of Law: Annual Report on the Informatization of Chinese Courts No. 1 (2017).* Social Sciences Academic Press (China), pp. 18–19.
4. Chen, S., & Tian, H. (2019). *Blue Book of Rule of Law: Annual Report on the Informatization of Chinese Courts No. 3 (2019).* Social Sciences Academic Press (China), p. 18.
5. China Judgements Online: The Bright "Billion" Landscape of China Under the Rule of Law. *People's Court Daily*, September 5, 2020 (1).
6. Tian, H., & Lv, Y. (2017). *Judicial Openness: From Dimness to Transparency—A Third Party Assessment of Zhejiang Court Judicial Transparency.* China Social Sciences Press, pp. 140–141.
7. Center for National Index of Rule of Law of CASS & Innovation Project Team for Index of Rule of Law of the Institute of Law of CASS. (2019). *A Third Party Assessment Report on National Judicial Openness.* China Social Sciences Press, pp. 53–57.
8. Innovation Project Team for Index of Rule of Law of the Institute of Law of CASS. *Beijing Court Judicial Transparency Index Report (2015).* In Li, L., & Tian, H. (2016). *Blue Book of Rule of Law: Annual Report on Rule of Law in China No. 14 (2016).* Social Sciences Academic Press (China), pp. 303–304.

Chapter 7
Promoting More Transparent Justice

1 Analysis of the Reasons for the Problems in Judicial Openness

The analysis of the assessment results reveals many problems in judicial openness despite the achievements made, such as incomplete disclosure, unsatisfactory continuity, restricted contents to be disclosed, lack of uniformity in disclosure standards, and relatively lagging judicial openness in primary people's courts. In general, the reasons for the above problems are multifaceted.

1.1 Insufficient Attention to Judicial Openness

Many courts have paid insufficient attention to judicial openness, which can be found in their non-standardized disclosure, no improvement, and even retrogression in this regard. Even in underdeveloped areas, judicial openness would have been standardized if its significance had been realized and importance attached. On the contrary, economically developed regions may accomplish nothing in this aspect. Therefore, against the backdrop of comprehensively furthering the reform of the judicial system and promoting judicial credibility, it is still necessary for courts at all levels to pay more attention to judicial openness.

1.2 Gap in Understanding Judicial Openness

Some courts are leader-oriented rather than user-oriented. Therefore, a court's leaders will decide the content and location of disclosure. Some courts misunderstand their responsibility for disclosure, believing that the disclosure task is completed once the information has been posted on the platforms of higher courts or other organs.

Y. Wang and H. Tian, *Judicial Transparency in China*,
https://doi.org/10.1007/978-981-19-7822-7_7

They ignore that their own websites are the primary platforms for judicial openness, thus causing inconvenience to the public during information inquiry. In addition, we should treat seriously and clarify some opinions and understandings concerning judicial openness. For instance, court hearings and judgments should not be disclosed to irrelevant people because civil cases mainly involve private rights between the plaintiff and the defendant. In some cases, the party who was ever involved in a lawsuit and thus inappropriately treated in employment and other aspects might censure the court for disclosing the information about his case. A court might be blamed for excessive and improper disclosure once a published judgment has aroused public sentiments. Undoubtedly, such views may obstruct judicial openness, which is originally short of impetus.

1.3 Lack of a Regular Mechanism for Judicial Openness

The core value of information disclosure lies in its timeliness. Timely, comprehensive, accurate, and adequate disclosure of judicial information is the inevitable requirement for constantly improving judicial transparency as well as the key to enhancing judicial credibility. Many courts have seen a high fluctuation in their judicial openness assessment results, which is affected by multiple factors such as the degree of leaders' attention, institutional setting, personnel allocation, and fund support. In general, the effect of openness will dramatically increase if leaders attach importance; otherwise, judicial openness will stagnate or even plummet. It proves that, over the years, judicial openness has been affected by individuals instead of running on an institutionalized track, causing poor institutionalization and standardization to be improved. Much information that should have been disclosed has not been disclosed or has not been disclosed promptly. There is no synchronous disclosure of some information but lots of abrupt disclosures.

1.4 Low Ranking of Scattered Provisions Governing Judicial Openness

In the first place, judicial openness bears a relatively low ranking in the legal system with insufficient authority. At present, the provisions on judicial openness are mainly from judicial interpretations and other judicial documents issued by the Supreme People's Court. Only several fundamental principles can be found in Civil, Criminal, and Administrative Procedure Laws. There is no specific legal basis for the principles to be followed in judicial openness, the scope of application, openness means, and accountability and supervision. In the second place, the provisions on judicial openness are somewhat scattered. Although the Supreme People's Court has promulgated some documents on judicial openness and some judicial interpretations concerning disclosure of judgments and judicial process information, the relevant provisions are scattered and lack coherence and coordination. Some judicial interpretations are subject to the duty and authority of the drafting department and lack overall planning for judicial openness. Furthermore, the scattered provisions on judicial openness in various judicial documents are detrimental to their implementation.

1.5 *Low Standardization of Judicial Openness*

Although multiple judicial interpretations have been issued by the Supreme People's Court to standardize judicial openness in all fields, the assessment results show a lack of general standards. By and large, all assessment indicators are those required by relevant judicial interpretations. However, these provisions are less specific. There is no rule for contents, disclosure frequency, and the platform and its column. A typical case is a guide to litigation. The litigation services provided by more than 3,000 courts throughout the country for the public and litigants are those litigation practices classified under Civil, Criminal, and Administrative Procedure Laws. The main differences among the four levels of courts lie in their judicial hierarchy, jurisdiction, and location. Compared with the services offered by governments at all levels, a court's litigation guide is concise and explicit. However, few courts have complete and accurate litigation guides, which confirms the low standardization of judicial openness.

1.6 *Lack of Strict Requirements for Judicial Openness*

Judicial openness in all fields by people's courts is governed by relevant laws and judicial interpretations, especially the provisions in the documents issued by the Supreme People's Court. However, there is no requirement for strict implementation of the above stipulations by lower courts, leading to a lot of cases of non-implementation despite institutional provisions in many fields and no accountability mechanism or means taken by upper courts.

1.7 *Insufficient Pressure in and Outside of the Courts*

Reviewing the progress made in judicial openness by people's courts around China since the beginning of the 21st century, we find that such progress is mainly the result of the courts' standardizing the operation of judicial and enforcement powers, safeguarding judicial justice, and enhancing judicial credibility internally. However, there is no sufficient supervision, guidance, appraisal, or accountability from upper courts. Externally, there is no effective intervention mechanism similar to that for government information disclosure. Therefore, the courts rely on conscientiousness and interest to promote judicial openness. When it comes to tasks of more importance, judicial openness, which tends to bring more difficulties, will inevitably be put aside.

1.8 Inadequate Informatization of the Courts

Judicial openness in modern times must rely on the ever-developing informatization of courts. Many courts have backward construction of websites, unreasonable website columns, and inconvenient access. More seriously, a large amount of information has been manually uploaded, which increases the workload and the probability of erroneous information data. The same information on different platforms has different sources and contents, thus reducing the effect of judicial openness.

2 Ways to Further Judicial Openness

According to the Decision of the CPC Central Committee on Some Major Issues Concerning How to Uphold and Improve the System of Socialism with Chinese Characteristics and Advance the Modernization of China's System and Capacity for Governance, we should adhere to the transparency of power and accountability, promote the open exercise of power, make affairs of the Party, governments, the judiciary, and relevant areas more transparent, and establish a feedback mechanism through which the exercise of powers can be inquired about and traced. At the 2020 Central Conference on the Work of Comprehensive Law-based Country Governance, General Secretary Xi Jinping stressed that we should carry forward the strict, standardized, fair, and civilized law enforcement to raise judicial credibility, promote the comprehensive reform supporting the judicial accountability system, and strengthen the oversight of judicial power.[1] Judicial openness, beneficial to standardizing the operation of judicial power and safeguarding judicial justice, is an indispensable system for comprehensively advancing law-based governance. In light of the problems revealed in the 2019 Assessment and especially the 2020 Assessment, efforts should be made to build a system for and improve the standards of judicial openness in the future to ensure steady progress herein. Implementing justice for the people, standardizing the operation of judicial power, and enhancing judicial credibility require us to improve judicial openness. Such improvement is additionally a significant way of modernizing the national governance system and capacity. In the future, we should advance judicial openness in the following aspects.

---

[1] The Decision of the CPC Central Committee on Some Major Issues Concerning How to Uphold and Improve the System of Socialism with Chinese Characteristics and Advance the Modernization of China's System and Capacity for Governance, *People's Publishing House,* 2019.

2.1 Unifying Various Understandings of Judicial Openness

We should further unify various understandings of judicial openness in academia and practice through publicity and discussion. Disclosure of judicial process information to the parties is an essential reflection of the protection of their litigation rights. The more detailed and timely disclosure is, the more helpful it is to protect their exercise of the right of action and enhance their recognition of trial and enforcement. Disclosure of court trial information and information on judgments is an effective way to implement the public trial principle stated in the Constitution, strengthen the supervision over and restriction on people's courts, and ensure that they perform judicial functions as per the law. The state provides arbitration, mediation, and other alternative dispute resolutions. Where a judicial means has been chosen to settle the dispute in a case, national judicial resources will be used to support the resolution thereof. The case itself no longer merely involves private rights but has entered the public domain. The resulting information hence gains public attributes. As a result, information of all kinds at all stages in a trial should be disclosed, except for cases involving state secrets, trade secrets, individual privacy, marriage and family, and minors. For court officers, their exercise of judicial and enforcement powers in accordance with the law should be subject to supervision. Besides, disclosure of their actions, procedures, and results is the best protection for them, although seemingly they are restricted and allotted excessive workload. Only when the whole society embraces a unified understanding of judicial openness can we ensure that judicial openness always moves forward without doubts or detours.

2.2 Detailing the Standards for Judicial Openness

Based on existing documents on judicial openness, the Opinions of the Supreme People's Court on Furthering Judicial Openness issued in November 2018 systematically stated the items that should be disclosed. Standards for disclosure of various information should be further detailed on such a basis. For example, we should define to what extent the information about judicial personnel such as court leaders, judges, and administrative personnel should be disclosed. We should draw experience from grassroots governments regarding their standardized disclosure of government affairs and promote the top-down compilation of standard catalogue templates for judicial openness in various fields. We should coordinate case handling, internal management, and public service and link the case-handling system with the office system, thus forming an integrated mechanism from case handling, office work, and service to disclosure to the public. In addition, we should make a judicial openness list by referring to the management model regarding a list on disclosure of government affairs, in which disclosure elements, ways, subjects, and time limits should be specified. As for litigation guides and other information, higher courts should compile unified templates to avoid the differences in content and style caused by the compilation by courts at different levels.

2.3 *Attaching Importance to the Supply-Side Reform of Judicial Openness*

Judicial openness should be user-oriented. What and how to disclose must be decided from the perspective of the general public and the parties to the case to satisfy their needs for access to judicial information. In addition to doing the "prescribed actions" regarding judicial openness to disclose the information as required by laws, judicial interpretations, and judicial documents, courts at all levels shall make a thorough investigation into users' demands to timely expand disclosure contents and optimize disclosure means.

2.4 *Establishing a Regular Mechanism for Judicial Openness*

A regular mechanism for judicial openness should be established. The latest, most accurate, and most authoritative information should be shown to society through judicial openness. Judicial openness is neither a hasty task to be completed nor a mere response to inspection and evaluation. With the rapid advancement of smart courts, the information that can be disclosed should be uploaded to the Internet immediately for the general public and the parties involved. Only by establishing a regular mechanism can we meet the need of the public and the parties for information and timely respond to social concerns about the work of the people's courts.

2.5 *Strengthening the Assessment of and Supervision Over Judicial Openness*

The practice has proven that if we only issue documents and make requirements, but we never track the implementation hereof, and there is no accountability system, they will sooner or later be put aside and ignored. Higher courts should conduct a stricter assessment of and supervision over judicial openness by assessing courts at all levels and of all kinds about their achievements and problems in respect of judicial openness in all fields to find out problems and urge timely rectification. Besides, higher courts should create internal and external pressure and motivation by disclosing assessment results externally and strengthening accountability and recognition internally. Courts should combine incentives and accountability to implement various requirements further and ensure that judicial openness will move steadily and not be affected by court leaders' focus.

2.6 *Promoting the Construction of Judicial Openness Platforms*

A court website remains the primary site for judicial openness in this information era. Even if unified disclosure platforms in various fields are established, a court website is still the preferred channel for the public to inquire about information. Thus, all courts should own well-established websites. Only with court websites as the main channel and other websites and various new media platforms as auxiliary means can an all-around judicial openness model be formed to meet the public's need for information. Judicial openness in the information era must rely on the Internet to build websites and new media platforms. A court should ensure that its unified website can undertake disclosure function and service provision function, and it should improve and standardize the website column setting and function configuration. The Supreme People's Court should refer to A Guide to the Development of Government Websites issued by the State Council and then set a standard for or a guide to the construction of court websites. The Court should define titles and configuration requirements of primary columns, advance the intelligent retrieval function of court websites, and set multi-language and free access functions. For example, all court websites should set a column dealing with enforcement information. Such a column should contain case inquiry, enforcement and punishment, enforcement exposure, cases with their enforcement proceedings temporarily terminated, judicial auctions, and enforcement reporting. Its sub-columns should further publish rulings for cases with their enforcement proceedings temporarily terminated and channels for reporting. As for media platform construction, a court should refer to the management regulations of new media on government affairs, advance its content management and function configuration, and improve its content updating and real-time link with the information released on the court portal.

2.7 *Enhancing Informatization to Promote Judicial Openness*

To build a smart court, we should enhance the intelligence of case handling and office work within the court. We also should promote the construction of the court portal and various application systems in connection with judicial openness and data transmission, thus presenting to the public and the parties involved the achievements of the smart court building through judicial openness platforms. Meanwhile, we should strengthen supervision over judicial openness via information technology to promote precise management of judicial openness with the aid of the achievements of smart court construction.

2.8 Promoting Legislation on Judicial Openness

We should write judicial openness into law by learning from many years of experience and lessons in this regard. Given that the provisions on judicial openness rank lower and are scattering and lack rigidity, it is suggested that we should promote legislation on judicial openness step by step. Such domains as government affairs disclosure and procuratorate affairs disclosure can unite in formulating a unified law on government affairs disclosure. When establishing general principles and requirements concerning judicial openness, we should define subjects, contents, scope, time limit, ways, the parties' and the public's rights and obligations, and the supervision and accountability mechanism. Separate legislation can also be adopted in the context of a specialized law on government information disclosure by formulating a separate law on judicial openness to unify the requirements in various fields.

Afterword

Since 2006, we have been focusing on the national situation of the rule of law in response to the call of the Chinese Academy of Social Sciences. In 2009, we started to develop an indicator system to assess the rule of law index. After launching the government transparency index, we developed the judicial transparency index to assess the courts' judicial openness. Adhering to the principle of setting assessment indicators by law, relying on objective data to conduct the assessment, reflecting the current situation, and guiding the development, we have been engaged in assessing the rule of law index for over a decade. In the areas of open government, open justice, and even rule of law construction, we promote the construction of rule of law with academic research results.

In the past, it seemed a bit out of reach for academic researchers to evaluate the work of authorities exercising public power from the public's perspective. However, we made it, and it is the result of more than a decade of research. At the beginning of the assessment results release, there were doubts about "Who you are" and "How you can evaluate us". More questions were "How you have evaluated us", "What our shortcomings are", and "Where we should improve". Isn't that a manifestation of China's progress in the rule of law? Moreover, more and more courts are willing to commission us to conduct the assessment. From 2013 to 2015, courts in Zhejiang province gave us full access to internal data for the judicial transparency assessment. Then, the Supreme People's Court removed obstacles for us to assess courts' judicial openness and results of "basically solving difficulties in enforcement" around China. In 2020, we retrieved a large amount of data on judgment disclosure for the judicial transparency assessment with the support of the Supreme People's Court. Such help allowed us to assess courts from external and internal perspectives, making the results more objective, accurate, and comprehensive.

In recent years, judicial openness has made rapid progress. Significant achievements have been made in establishing openness platforms for judicial process information disclosure, judgment disclosure, enforcement information disclosure, and court trial disclosure. Constantly updating judicial openness has promoted the construction of China's judicial system. Nevertheless, there are many difficulties and problems in judicial openness. We should take seriously how to further adapt to the

Y. Wang and H. Tian, *Judicial Transparency in China*,
https://doi.org/10.1007/978-981-19-7822-7

new requirements of the judicial system reform in the new era and meet the people's growing demand for judicial openness. We hope through this book to draw further attention to the necessity of moving forward with judicial openness and the ways to break through in the fight against obstacles in judicial openness by analyzing the assessment results of 2019 and 2020 to show the progress and problems in various aspects of judicial openness in detail. This book attempts to study the previous and current situation of judicial openness from historical and realistic perspectives and provides suggestions for the future trend of judicial openness.

There is nothing more necessary than collaboration for assessment and empirical research. Like the other rule of law index assessments, judicial transparency assessment has been one of the collective projects of the Research Office of National Situation of Rule of Law of the Institute of Law since the very beginning. Over the years, research fellow Lv Yanbin, associate research fellow Wang Xiaomei, associate research fellow Li Yanjie, assistant research fellow Hu Changming, assistant research fellow Wang Yiming, and assistant research fellow Liu Yanpeng have participated to varying degrees in the judicial transparency assessment, local courts' judicial transparency index assessment, the third-party assessment of judicial openness of the Supreme People's Court and other assessments. Since 2019, assistant research fellow Wang Yiming has taken over the judicial transparency index assessment.

Carrying out the assessment is the most energy-draining. Each data needs to be retrieved and confirmed on the court website, and analyzing each set of data requires repeated verification. In the 2019 and 2020 Assessments, some postgraduate students of 2019 and 2020 majoring in law at the University of Chinese Academy of Social Sciences assisted us with a lot of basic work. They are Chen Wen, Gu Chenhan, Guo Chuying, Hou Suzhi, Lai Yana, Li Shiju, Liang Jie, Liang Yufei, Liu Zhiqun, Lu Qiyuan, Niu Wanyun, Qi Yi, Shi Qingping, Tang Ling, Tao Fenpeng, Wang Yafeng, Xiao Liping, Yuan Pengfei, Yuan Zihan, Zhang Lei (The names are listed in alphabetical order).

This book would not have been possible without strong support from Zhao Jianying, President of China Social Sciences Press, Wang Yin, Director of Major Project Publishing Center and Deputy Editor-in-chief of China Social Sciences Press, and editor Li Mo.

We extend our deepest gratitude to whoever has supported this study. We sincerely hope people from all walks of life will continue paying attention to and supporting our rule of law assessment research.

Tian He

April 2021 in Beijing